VO

TOP DOG
RECESSION-BUSTING
SALES SECRETS

50 EXPERTS SHOW YOU PROVEN WAYS TO SELL
MORE IN TOUGH TIMES

Compiled & Edited by Michael Dalton Johnson

Presented by SalesDog.com

Published by
PENNY UNION CORPORATION

CARLSBAD, CALIFORNIA

Published by
Penny Union Corporation
2701 Loker Avenue West, Suite 148, Carlsbad, California 92010
www.salesdog.com

ISBN: 978-1-934346-15-0

Printed in the United States of America
Publisher's Cataloging-In-Publication Data
(Prepared by The Donohue Group, Inc.)

Top dog recession-busting sales secrets : 50 experts show you proven
ways to sell more in tough times / edited by Michael Dalton Johnson.

p. ; cm. — ([Top dog sales secrets] ; v.2)
"Presented by SalesDog.com."

ISBN: 978-1-934346-15-0

1. Selling. 2. Sales personnel—Training of. 3. Sales management. I.
Johnson, Michael Dalton.

HF5438.25 .T68 2010
658.85

This publication is designed to provide accurate and authoritative
information with regard to the subject matter covered. It is sold with
the understanding that the publisher is not engaged in rendering
legal, accounting, or other professional advice. If legal advice or
other expert assistance is required, the services of a competent professional person should be sought.

This book is available at quantity discounts.
For information, call 760-476-3700.

CONTENTS

ACKNOWLEDGMENTS

I want to acknowledge the inspiration and support of my friends, colleagues, and readers who encouraged me to bring out this special volume. These wonderful sales professionals are the foundation of our economy and will drive its recovery.

I would like to thank Tina Lo Sasso for her work with the authors and her ability to juggle scores of tasks and bring everything together with humor and professionalism.

Special acknowledgment is due Susan Daffron, of Logical Expressions, for her superlative work in editing this book.

Thanks to graphic designer Dave Tucker for his work on the cover.

Heartfelt appreciation goes to the fifty sales experts who made this book possible.

Lastly, I want to thank my incredible wife Kathryn, the Goddess Who Walks the Earth, for her support, patience and encouragement. Thanks, honey. ∎

INTRODUCTION

Selling during a recession can be daunting. Money is tight. Companies are scrambling to cut costs and price objections abound.

To win sales in this environment, you need to be prepared. You have to know how to engage buyers, emphasize value, show benefits, and most importantly, overcome objections. It's not easy.

Faced with these uncomfortable facts, many people in sales commit to working harder. But hard work alone is rarely enough.

The rules have changed. In this environment, you need to take a fresh look at ways you can work smarter and more effectively. The difference between success and failure is knowing the new rules and applying them. And this doesn't happen simply by working longer and harder.

You have to work smarter.

Top Dog Recession-Busting Sales Secrets gives you the knowledge you need today. In this book, you'll find proven recession-busting advice from fifty of the world's leading sales experts. These guys and gals know how to accelerate sales, even in the toughest of times.

As the founder of SalesDog.com, I have had the good fortune and privilege of publishing this book and presenting advice from this stellar group of people. These experts have a real passion for excellence in sales and have shown great generosity in sharing their knowledge with the sales community about how you can beat the downturn.

Read on and you'll thank them.

— *Michael Dalton Johnson*

Editor's Note: Jill Konrath was destined to be a sales trainer. A top performer at Xerox, she helped her colleagues with their sales problems for no additional money, title or perks. When she realized this was her favorite thing to do, she launched her consulting firm, Selling to Big Companies. Jill's clients include big names like General Mills, IBM, and Microsoft. She explains how to inoculate yourself against difficult times.

Immunize Yourself against Tough Economic Times
by Jill Konrath

Selling in today's economy is tough, and it's likely going to get a lot tougher. That's not what we want to hear, but it is the reality we face, so it makes sense to address it head on.

Let me ask this: What are you doing about it?

I can tell you right now that I'm taking action. Tough times call for different sales approaches, new offerings, and stronger business cases. It's not enough to just make more calls or have more meetings. We have to be better than we've ever been—in every aspect.

Hope is Not a Strategy

But let's talk about you right now. Are you hoping you can hang in there? Hoping that you'll still have customers? Hoping that you'll make your numbers? As Rick Page says, "Hope is not a strategy." As far as I'm concerned, there's only *one* thing that makes sense right now. It's time to take charge of your own career. You can't count on your employer to take care of you. That's a brutal statement, but it's true.

Whether you work for a big organization or an upstart firm, you could lose your job tomorrow. Even if your boss really cares about you. Even if your company is still doing okay. Of course, you realize that it's not personal. It's just a business decision. But it *is* personal. It's your life, your career, and your family that's at risk. I don't mean to be an alarmist. I just want you to wake up and take responsibility for your future *now* so you can minimize the effects of the economic downturn.

Average Won't Cut It

Too many salespeople I know are complacent, coasting, doing what's expected of them but not a whole lot more. If they continue doing so, it will be their downfall. When companies hit tough times, mediocre sellers are the first to go. Doing an "okay" job or being "average" is no longer an acceptable contribution.

If you're mediocre, you're also disposable to your customers. Being knowledgeable about your product or service is no longer enough. Your customers can find all that information online, so you don't bring any value. When that happens, they replace you with a lower cost solution.

Customers want to work with experts who understand their business and can help them achieve their objectives. To do that well, you need to be a problem-solving, critical-thinking person who can synthesize lots of information and turn it into invaluable, take-action ideas.

In tough times, you have to sharpen your sales skills and bring expertise to your customers. Doing just one is not sufficient. Whew! That's asking a lot. You just have to keep getting smarter and better in order to stay in the game. If that's not your focus, you're vulnerable to the ravages of tough times.

Don't let it happen to you. Give yourself a booster shot. It's time to invest in your own professional development program. Don't wait for your company to send you to training programs to upgrade your knowledge and skills. You're not number one on their priority list, but you are number one on your own priority list. Wake up. Get going. Your livelihood depends on it.

Booster Shot 1: Open Your Mind to New Thinking

When was the last time you read a book that offered fresh perspectives on how you can be a valuable resource or a top sales professional? Honestly? What are you waiting for? Get reading. Blogs are also a great place to get fresh perspectives. I regularly read blogs about sales, marketing, business development, creativity, writing and more.

Booster Shot 2: Increase Your Personal Productivity

Virtually every salesperson I know could get much more done in less time if they leveraged technology better. Not only that, but you'd be a whole lot savvier when you're with your customers which should directly correlate to increased sales success.

There's no excuse any more for not using these resources. In fact, if you don't know about them or can't use them, it's time to get educated. Here's what I recommend for:

- Finding contacts: Jigsaw, Netprospex, LinkedIn
- Triggering event updates: InsideView, Google and BizJournals Alerts
- Account research: Hoovers, D&B, ZoomInfo
- Industry intelligence: First Research
- Email intelligence: Genius
- Sales productivity: Landslide
- Online Meetings: GoToMeeting, Webex

All of these resources are affordable to everyone. If your company doesn't pay for these services, use your own money. The value that you get from them far outweighs the expense. You'll save so much time, plus learn critical insights that can be leveraged for business success.

Booster Shot 3: Get Connected and Stay Connected

The worst time to build your personal network is when you're desperate. No matter how hard you try to sound normal, every contact oozes with your neediness. Start by creating or updating your LinkedIn profile. From a business perspective, it's the place to be. If you're not sure what to do, check out my profile. Once yours is ready for prime time, you can:

- Ask your boss, co-workers and clients to recommend you. Do it now, not when you need it.
- Invite your customers to connect with you online. That way, if anyone changes jobs, you can keep in touch.
- Look up former colleagues, classmates, and friends and invite them to connect.

Get out from your self-imposed isolation too! I know you're busy, but it's important to talk or meet with people from outside your own company. Arrange breakfast meetings. Attend industry events. Take a former colleague to lunch. My favorite? Meet for coffee over the phone. It saves so much time while giving you a dedicated time to talk.

Finally, remember that networking is not a one-way street. You'll find people much more willing to help you out if you're a *giver* first. You can share insights, refer potential customers, make connections, or offer genuine assistance in any area. As a bonus, giving makes you feel good inside too!

Immunity for Tough Times

While these booster shots can't protect you against everything, they will give you the best immunity possible during tough times. Plus, when you make them a part of your life, your success is truly guaranteed—in tough times and in good times!

Everything is within your control. That's why it should be your focus right now. Because it is what you can do. Because it will make you a better seller. Because it changes your life and your career. ■

Jill Konrath is Chief Sales Officer of Selling to Big Companies. For biographical and business information, see page 268.

Editor's Note: It was more than 20 years ago, but Mike Brooks remembers the day he committed to becoming a top producer like it was yesterday. He was at his company's monthly bonus lunch. He watched as his top-producing colleagues marched up to receive their bonus checks and thought, "If they can do it, I can do it better." At that moment, he resolved to learn everything he could to close sales over the phone. He began by studying sales training tapes. In 60 days, he went from being one of the lowest producers in the office to one of the top three closers. 30 days later, he was number one. By the end of the year, he was the number one closer out of the company's five Southern California offices. Today Mike is known as Mr. Inside Sales. He's trained thousands of sales professionals in his methods. He shares some timely tips for overcoming the recession objection.

Three Ways To Handle the Recession Objection
by Mike Brooks

Your last three closes in a row blew you off with "We're just not doing anything right now," or "We need to hold off on anything new until things get better," or some variation of this recession objection. If you're like most sales reps, you recognize when things slow down and you're getting this objection a lot. What to do?

Here are three ways to handle the "recession objection":

1. **Eliminate it in the beginning.** The best time to handle possible objections is during the qualification stage, and that includes any recession-related ones as well. If you're going through a presentation and get one of the objections above, you need to work in a solid qualifying question when you first speak with your prospect.

    Use something like:

    "Bob, I'll email you a (brochure, proposal, etc.) and then I'll get back with you to go over how this would work out for you. Now given what's happening in the economy, if you think this would be a fit for you, what are the parameters your company is working within to allow a purchase like this?"

Then write this answer down word for word.

You'll need it later.

2. **Question before answering the objection.** If the recession objection still comes up at the end, question it before you deal with it. Use:

> "I can certainly understand that, and let's say your company were to approve (your service or product), do you personally feel that this solution would be the one you would go with today?"

> If they still stall, then this isn't the real objection and answering it will get you nowhere. You will have to ask questions to find out the real one. If they say yes, then:

3. **Script out a close based on the information you got while qualifying.** You asked what procedures their company used to approve your specific service or product in the beginning. Go back to that and script out your response.

> Customize something like this:

> "I'm glad you think this service will work for you, and I know you'll be happy using it. When we first spoke, you mentioned that all approvals go through the (repeat what they told you). I'd be happy to present this to them – what should I do to help you get this approved?"

As you can see, this objection can be handled if you are prepared for it in advance (like all objections).

Print these scripts out, adapt them to your product or service, and get in the habit of using them. Believe me, they'll work if you use them! ∎

Mike Brooks is principal and owner of Mr. Inside Sales. For biographical and business information, see page 262.

Editor's Note: Kendra Lee's road to sales success had an inauspicious beginning. Her only previous business experience was in accounting. She failed IBM's entry sales rep exam. She was given a sales territory that had never bought anything before. Despite these obstacles, Kendra placed in the top 1 percent of sales professionals in each IT company for which she sold. The founder of KLA Group, Kendra specializes in new business generation. She shows you how to create opportunities in a downturn.

Create Opportunities in a Tough Economy
by Kendra Lee

When times are tough, I hear it everywhere: prospects won't take calls; budgets are on hold. Yet, I remain optimistic, seeing opportunity all around. While many clients will halt spending, others get creative and look at their businesses from new perspectives. They seek ways to leverage difficult times and evolve their own companies. They refuse to let a difficult economy stall their growth.

One client I was speaking with recently said I must be an eternal optimist, refusing to face reality. Maybe. But that same day I had four new contacts call me.

Another client told me that all budgets were frozen for the year so they wouldn't be able to proceed with the project we had envisioned. We tabled the project. Yet, when we got off the phone, we had another appointment set to discuss two top priorities that just can't wait for the budget.

What happened? Am I so different than you are? No! Creating opportunities is all about keeping your name in front of potential customers, listening hard during sales calls, and thinking deeply to make creative suggestions. You can do it, too. Here's how.

Get Close

While prospecting during a downturn can be discouraging, it's also the time to stay in front of your prospects as if they're your best friends. Where it usually takes nine calls to get a call back, it'll take many more in a bad economy. Instead of giving up, plan an attraction campaign. In my opinion, the most effective strategy today is a combination of phone calls, emails, and simple events to catch prospects' attention. Focus on hot topics that are relevant to their very highest priorities for the changing market. Stay close so you'll be there when your prospects recognize a new need they can't put off investing in. They'll call you first.

Keep the Conversation Going

Listen for opportunities in novel areas. Your clients may be holding back from purchasing your typical offerings, but in dire need of one of your lesser-known solutions. When they tell you all spending has been curtailed, don't stop the conversation. Keep questioning and conversing. Identify their top priorities for succeeding in this new market. As they talk, listen for unusual ways you can assist them. Don't thumb your nose at minor projects. Nothing is too small to get your foot in the door and show the financial return you provide. My philosophy is that small projects add up to big numbers, and I appreciate every one!

Wake Up Your Brain

In boom times, life can be pretty good for us sales professionals. We don't have to work too hard to uncover our prospects' needs. They budget; we spec; they buy. Maybe there is a bit more work than that, but for the most part, it's easy compared to a downturn. In difficult times, you need to wake up your brain and show your clients how you can help them save more, make more, and still grow their businesses. Get creative. Think outside your normal solution box.

I've had my fair share of losses just like you've probably experienced. But I'm not letting them get me down. Rather, I'm using economic troubles as an opportunity to get creative.

Here's a great example of creativity from a sales professional I work with. He was desperately trying to close the sale of a new phone system. His customer couldn't justify the investment. However, during the conversation the customer mentioned his desire to reduce the extraordinary amount of money they were spending on marketing. The salesperson knew the phone system could help track the effectiveness of marketing campaigns, allowing his customer to halt poor performing programs quickly. Once the customer understood that the savings far outweighed the cost of the new phone system, he looked at the seller, said, "This is a no-brainer" and bought.

You can't control the economy, but if you are staying in front of prospects, listening hard and presenting creative ideas, you'll win regardless and you'll win big when the economy rebounds. ■

Kendra Lee is president and founder of KLA Group. For biographical and business information, see page 268.

Editor's Note: Brian Jeffrey got into sales by accident when, as young electronics technician, he was left in charge of the sales department. He quickly became a student of selling. He did so well, his company put him in charge permanently. Years later, he used what he learned to train other sales professionals. Today, he runs his own sales assessment company to help managers select the best salesperson for the job. He explains how to respond to a common objection.

"I'm Happy With My Current Supplier"
by Brian Jeffrey

You're sure to come across this "objection" if you're the type of salesperson who does cold-call prospecting. Standard variations are, "I'm happy with who I buy from now," or "I already buy from ABC Company," and "We're happy with who we use now."

The good news about getting this response is you know the prospect uses the type of stuff you sell. He's just not buying it from you. Now all we have to do is get him to switch to you or wait until his current supplier bungles a job so you can have a chance to strut your stuff.

By the way, this "objection" is not really an objection but rather a rejection or a statement of fact. The phrase, "I'm happy with my current supplier," is most likely to be a statement of fact and he doesn't want to go through the hassle of changing suppliers, at least not without some very good reasons. Keep in mind, if the prospect was unhappy with his current supplier, he'd probably be calling you, and you wouldn't have to call him.

It is possible, however, that your opening statement didn't include any information about how your product or service would benefit the prospect, and he is simply using the phrase, "I'm happy with my current supplier," to reject you. Remember, an effective opening must have something of benefit or real value for the prospect or he won't give you the time of day.

Whether the phrase is a rejection or a statement of fact doesn't really matter. You need to be prepared to deal with it.

I'm not suggesting that you prepare a canned response for it, but you need to have a planned response. In other words, remember the Boy Scout motto and be prepared with a memorized response that you can modify on the fly whenever your prospect says, "I'm happy with my current supplier."

Here are some ideas that may help. The key is to keep the prospect talking, so you need to continue your approach in a non-threatening manner. In every case you should acknowledge the "objection" and whatever you do, avoid using the words "why" or "but" because this can put him on the defensive. For example, asking the prospect, "Why do you buy from them?" can be perceived as challenging his decision to buy from a competitor and cause him to defend his decision rather than respond to you with an open mind.

Examples:

Prospect: "I'm happy with my current supplier."

SalesPro: "I understand. Every supplier appreciates that kind of loyalty (acknowledgment). What (type, brand, size, etc.) are you buying from them now?"

Or:

Prospect: "I already buy from ABC Company."

SalesPro: "I understand. Probably 95% of the people I talk to are satisfied with their current suppliers (acknowledgment). How long have you been dealing with them?"

Or:

Prospect: "I'm happy with who I buy from now."

SalesPro: "I understand (acknowledgment). What prompted your decision to go with them?"

Or:

Prospect: "I'm happy with my current supplier."

SalesPro: "Most people are and I appreciate that (acknowledgment). What prompted the decision to go with them?"

Or:

Prospect: "We're happy with who we use now."

SalesPro: "That sounds reasonable (acknowledgment). Who are you buying from now?"

Notice that all these responses are intended to keep the prospect talking. Some additional questions you might use are:

- "What have they been doing to earn your business?"
- "When you chose to go with them you probably switched from someone else. What caused the change?"
- "What would you like to get that you don't have now?"
- "What would you change in your present situation?"
- "Who do you use as a backup supplier?"
- "How can I get on your list of alternate suppliers?"
- "If there was one area you would like to see improved, what would it be?"

If you're getting reasonable responses, you can use one of the following techniques to get your foot in the door:

Prospect: "I already buy from ABC Company."

SalesPro: "I understand. Probably 95% of the people I talk to are satisfied with their current suppliers (acknowledgment). How long have you been dealing with them?"

Prospect: "Oh, about four or five years now."

SalesPro: "Obviously you're happy with their services if you've been dealing with them for that long. Here's an idea for you. Why not let me quote on your next requirement? If nothing else, it will confirm that you're getting the best price from ABC. How does that sound?"

Or:

Prospect: "I already buy from ABC Company."

SalesPro: "I understand. Probably 95% of the people I talk to are satisfied with their current suppliers (acknowledgment). How long have you been dealing with them?"

Prospect: "Oh, about four or five years now."

SalesPro: "Mr. Williams, I'm not asking you to stop buying from ABC. I'm just asking you to consider us as another source for some of the items we can save you money on. That way you'll have the best of both worlds. Does that make sense?

These approaches often make sense to the prospect. He has nothing to lose and it allows you to get your foot in the door. Remember, people aren't going to switch suppliers just because you showed up on their doorsteps. Be patient, be persistent, and be there when the primary supplier stumbles and the prospect gives you a chance to perform. ■

Brian Jeffrey is president of Salesforce Assessments Ltd. For biographical and business information, see page 266.

Editor's Note: John Costigan started his training company on a bet from his brother who doubted John would succeed by using real live sales scenarios in his training programs. John's brother was wrong and John's been training sales professionals in companies like Hewlett Packard, Experian, and SAS Software this way ever since. He shows you how to succeed in shortening your sales cycle. Priceless information in tough times!

Three Tips to Shorten Your Sales Cycle
by John Costigan

Over my many years as a sales trainer to the Fortune 500, I've found there's one issue in particular that plagues virtually every salesperson's career. I've heard countless tales, from veterans and rookies alike, of the deal that "got stuck." If you're an entrepreneur handling your own sales, you've probably also suffered at the hands of those indecisive customers who jeopardize your bottom line by stretching the selling cycle to unbearable lengths.

Wait a minute! Did I just hear you blame a sales obstacle on a customer? Repeat after me: There is no such thing as a bad customer. There are only bad salespeople. Before you can really apply any of the tips I am about to describe you must embrace the fact that, to get to the next level in your career, you have to focus on the one thing you can always change—your own behavior.

That said, here's the very first step you must take to improve your productivity and close more deals, faster:

Get to Power!

There is nothing that will shorten the selling cycle more effectively than getting to the right level early on in the sales cycle. I find it mind boggling how much time sales pros spend courting lower-level people who are not the real decision-makers and who waste their time with requests that almost never lead to a sale.

The main reason salespeople start at a lower level is a lack of self-confidence. One of the best ways to overcome your insecurity is to make sure the first call you make is to an A-level executive's office. Here's why: By reaching, say, the CEO's office, you will have an opportunity to find out exactly who's responsible for what in that organization. Specifically, you'll learn who is directly responsible for fixing the problem that your solution addresses.

At that point, you can ask to be transferred to the appropriate contact and actually claim you were referred by the CEO's office. Not only will you have saved yourself a great deal of time you might have otherwise spent jumping through hoops for lower-level people, but now you also hold the referral trump card. Moreover, if the deal gets stuck, you can always contact a higher-ranking person than the one you were dealing with because the sales cycle started at power!

The second step you must take in order to boost your productivity and shorten the sales cycle is:

Uncover the Customer's Pain

One of the most important lessons that I try to impart to my students is that people buy emotionally and justify logically. Therefore, one of the most important parts of our jobs as salespeople is to find out exactly what is at stake for the customer if he does not do something about the problem that your solution can fix. Find out how much the issue is costing him, personally.

As sales pros, we have a tendency to get on the phone and skip straight to questions like: "Have you had a chance to look over my proposal? How does my deal work?" You had better believe me when I tell you that will not help you close the deal. Instead, try: "Mr. Customer, let me ask you a question. I was driving into work this morning and was wondering why you want to do the deal with us? You mentioned you wanted to fix this issue in Q1. What happens if you don't?" By asking these questions, you are essentially setting the stage for him to sell you more than you're selling him.

How so? By making the customer very aware of the consequences that dragging out a decision will have, not only on his company, but also on his career and his day-to-day work life. How much more paperwork will he have to deal with if the problem persists? How many more meetings will take place that fail to solve the issue? Once you have forged a connection between the customer and your solution, then you will be ready to help him sell it logically.

The third step you must take in order to boost your productivity and shorten the sales cycle is:

Find out Exactly How Much Your Time is Worth

To some, this may seem obvious but you would not believe how many hours salespeople spend on the job doing things that have absolutely nothing to do with selling. Recent studies have indicated that the average sales rep gets a measly four to six hours per week of face time with customers. If you don't believe me, try asking yourself how many hours you spent filing expense reports, creating spreadsheets and tracking the pipeline in the past week. If that number is enough to make you gasp, try dividing a year's income by 1,780. (That's roughly how many working hours there are in a year.) Now you have a good idea of how much it costs you, personally, not to turn more time into opportunity.

Having been a sales rep myself, I am aware that busy work comes with the territory. As much as you wish you didn't have to deal with it, there's a spreadsheet waiting for you at the end of every day. To fix this problem, you must do two things:

- **Learn to work smarter.** You must constantly improve your processes so that tasks will not take longer to complete than necessary.
- **Stop working for free.** You must ensure that the face time you manage to secure with your customer is quality time and that you are not jumping through a lot of hoops for nothing. Always make sure the next step is in sight before you get cracking on that proposal. Try: "Mr. Customer, my biggest fear is that you're asking me to do all this work for you and then I'll get back to you and nothing else will happen." Express to the customer that you would love having his business but, first and foremost, he must commit to getting his problem fixed. You may find it difficult to say this to a client, but once you convey that you're trying to make the best use of not only your time but also his, most will appreciate, rather than resent you.

Good luck and good selling! ■

John Costigan is president and founder of John Costigan Companies. For biographical and business information, see page 263.

Editor's Note: Tim Wackel's sales and sales management experience ranges from being the number one salesperson in a 10,000 person sales organization to running a $50 million team for a Fortune 500 company. Today Tim runs his own training firm where his clients include big names like Cisco, Hewlett Packard, PricewaterhouseCoopers, and Raytheon. He shows you what you need to do to keep selling despite the downturn.

Stop Blaming the Economy!
by Tim Wackel

The experts say recession, and you can almost hear the collapse of sales funnels everywhere. Account managers are complaining about how difficult it is to close business in this slowing economy. This doesn't come as a big surprise.

Less than half of today's business-to-business sales professionals have ever weathered a true economic downturn. Most folks learned how to sell in the nifty '90s, which was one of the longest business expansions in U.S. history. Hey, it's not that hard to hit quota with double-digit market returns and huge growth in the number of new jobs. But what do you do when the economy starts to tap the brakes?

Don't Blame the Economy

Companies still have to buy goods and services no matter what the economy is doing. They may buy differently, they may buy less, but they still have to buy. If you can't convince prospects that what you're offering is a solid investment with meaningful return, then maybe the problem lies closer to home.

Let's look at this a different way. The major objection most reps face during slow times is, "I have no money." How is that possible? If your customer has no money then he's out of business. What he's really saying to you is, "Your ideas stink."

What can you do to close more business in a slowing economy? Start by answering these three questions that will put you back on the path to success.

How Much Energy Are You Wasting on Insignificant Activities?

You've probably been told that business will improve if you just make more appointments, increase the number of demos, give more presentations and ramp up your number of cold calls. Don't get me wrong, there's nothing wrong with increasing these selling activities, especially if you sell low-value products to one-time customers.

Experience tells me that chasing everything that looks like an opportunity keeps you busy but makes you very ineffective. You'll be working hard, but you won't be working smart. Eventually you'll burn out your prospects and yourself.

Start today by re-qualifying every prospect and work on cleaning out your funnel. Focus on your best-selling opportunities, and put your energy there. You'll create more success by investing the right resources into 10 solid opportunities than you will by chasing 25 half-baked leads.

Are You Making Every Conversation Count?

Clients and prospects should be impressed with your preparation for every sales call. When you demonstrate that you've done your homework, it becomes easier for them to have an open and honest dialogue with you. When the economy slows down, people get nervous. They don't want to waste time meeting with sales reps unless they see some potential value.

The "smile-n-dial" mentality of simply pounding on more doors with the same pitch may produce extra appointments. But it also creates the fear that you're going to sell them something that they don't need.

Open your next client conversation with this simple phrase, "In preparing for this meeting I took some time to… ." Then simply highlight the two or three critical things that you did to prepare and watch what happens to the atmosphere of the call. You'll blow away the last rep who opened his meeting by announcing that he was just "checking in" to see if anything new was going on.

The goal is to stop "educating" your customers. They don't care unless they are engaged. Talking about your company, your products and your reputation will not engage customers. Talk about them, ask about them, provide ideas for them and communicate in terms of them.

Who are you talking about—you or them?

Do You Have Any Questions?

Knowledge is a key ingredient to sales success, especially in a slowing economy. The more you demonstrate knowledge, the more prospects will take time to listen. The best way to establish expertise is not by pitching features, it's by asking questions that differentiate the value you bring to every call.

Many reps fall into the common trap of asking questions that are self-serving. "What does your purchasing process look like?" is a mind-numbing, self-serving question that doesn't create new insights. Your customer hears these types of questions every day and they bring zero value to the dialogue.

Instead ask questions that get customers to stop and think. Ask questions they haven't been asked before. Ask questions that get the customer to pause and say, "That's a really good question." Here are some examples:

> "Prior to this meeting I spent some time doing research about your company. What do you believe are the most important things we need to focus on so that I can serve you properly?"

> "What would have to happen in order for you to feel like this project was a success?"

> "What do you believe are the top three reasons you're exploring new ideas right now?"

Creating high impact questions takes extra time. But it's worth every minute. Start investing 60% of your time doing research, and 40% of your time making calls. I know this contradicts traditional wisdom, but this isn't a traditional selling environment.

Don't pick up the phone or walk into the lobby until you're absolutely ready to engage in a meaningful dialogue. You're not going to get a second chance in a slowing economy, so make sure every one counts! ∎

Tim Wackel is the president of The Wackel Group. For biographical and business information, see page 274.

Editor's Note: Susan C. Daffron is a business owner with more than 15 years' experience in publishing. She is the author of 11 books and hundreds of articles that have appeared in national magazines and newspapers. As publishing consultant, she has watched many aspiring writers perfect the art of procrastination and hand wringing, neither of which are effective long-term business strategies, as she explains here.

Three Absurdly Simple Ways to Recession-Proof Yourself
by Susan C. Daffron

Depending on which politician you'd like to believe, the economy is in the tank, heading for a recession, deep in a recession, having just a bit of a slow down, or on the upswing. I'm no economist, but given the ever-increasing price of food and gas, I've noticed a lot more people pinching pennies these days.

During down times you need to resist the temptation to freak out. When the economy goes downhill, doom and gloom news is everywhere, so it's natural to look for quick fixes or the "next big thing." The reality is that some businesses actually make more money during a recession because they focus on the basics and don't curtail their marketing when everyone else does.

Over the years in our business, we have weathered a number of down cycles, so here are a few absurdly simple ways you can ensure your business thrives, even when the economy does not.

When in Doubt, Do Something

A lot of people do nothing and then wonder why nothing happens. What did they expect? After all, nothing begets nothing.

Emotional hand wringing seems to have reached a new level since the economy went into the dumpster. People now have a new excuse for their level of inactivity: "It's not my fault; the economy stinks!"

A related complaint comes from those people who blame everything on "overwhelm." First I'd like to point out that overwhelm is a verb. You can overwhelm something or you can be overwhelmed yourself, but this word seems to have morphed into a wide range of uses, many of which don't make any sense. You cannot "avoid overwhelm." You can avoid becoming overwhelmed by something, however.

In any case, in addition to the increased misuse of the word, I take issue with the complaint in general. You may be busy, but using the term "overwhelm" implies that you can't do anything about your situation. An earthquake or a hurricane is overwhelming. Having too much to do is not.

If you have too much to do, obviously you aren't delegating well (or enough) or you are avoiding doing work for some reason. Many people have astounding procrastination skills. If you put off doing work, you might end up feeling overwhelmed because now deadlines loom and you have a lot of stuff to do. Again, doing nothing is at the root of the problem.

Focus on One Thing at a Time

Many people say they are overwhelmed because they have too many "to do" items. Trying to do everything at once is not the answer to this problem.

People seem to think that "multi-tasking" is a fantastic thing, but in reality it just means that you do a bunch of things poorly and never finish any of them. The rise in computing technology makes multitasking seem more feasible. Unfortunately, multi-tasking mostly leads to a lot of extra stress.

If you try to do everything at once, you end up actually accomplishing nothing. Have you ever looked back upon the expanse of a day and wondered what happened? You may have been busy, but you weren't actually productive.

Think about it. If you are getting beeps from incoming email from six email accounts, checking your Blackberry every 30 seconds, and posting to Twitter 16 times a day, you probably aren't getting any actual productive work done.

Here's a new productivity mantra for you to ponder: pick one thing. Then work on just that one thing. Do it well, get it done, and take it off the list. Too many people let themselves become distracted by every technological widget out there. Turn off the cell phone, turn off your email, and get something done.

Do What You Say You're Going to Do

If more people just did what they say, everyone would be a lot happier. Sadly, common courtesy is becoming less common, particularly online. If you actually do what you say you're going to do when you say you're going to do it, you will stand out. It's the Golden Rule at work. Treat people as you would like to be treated.

Maybe it's because I've been in business for a while, but over the years, I've noticed a trend among people who start to "believe their own PR" a little too much. After this happens, they start treating their customers and business partners like peons. They don't show up for meetings, blow off conference calls, or spend time talking on a cell phone, rather than focusing on the human being right in front of them.

These examples aren't exactly malicious, but do you really want to give your business partners and customers this type of experience?

Certainly mistakes happen, but when they do, admit them, apologize, and try and make the person feel like he or she actually matters to you and your business. Everyone wants to feel important. The Golden Rule is a magical thing. If people believe you care, you will go far in business.

Instead of freaking out and spinning your wheels, during this down cycle, consider what you do and don't do on a daily basis. Caring about your clients, being productive, and focusing on profit-generating activities yield results in both good times and bad. ■

Susan C. Daffron is the president of Logical Expressions, Inc. For biographical and business information, see page 263.

Editor's Note: John Carroll is a professional speaker, author and business consultant with first-hand experience in manufacturing, distribution, and services industries. John is a recognized expert in consulting to emerging growth companies. His focus is on helping sales leaders win in the game of business as well as the game of life. He explains how a lesson from the game of golf relates to winning sales presentations.

Heads Up!
by John Carroll

One of the first pieces of golf advice I received was, "Keep your head down and your eyes on the ball." I learned quickly and often that it's difficult to do one without the other. Pull your head away from the ball too early and your eyes naturally follow. Likewise, try to behold the beautiful flight of your drive and invariably you lift your head up, causing lost golf balls and other calamities. A similar paradox is often seen in sales only it's "heads up and eyes down."

Focus on the Buyer

In selling, it's quite easy to put your head down and your mouth in high gear to fly through a sales presentation. You're focused on what you're saying. After all, you want to be sure you provide a thorough, fact-filled and persuasive presentation. You've worked hard to understand your product. You've listened hard for insights into your buyer's needs. Now it's time to show what you've learned, right?

Here's where that good advice comes in: Heads up! Keeping your head up in selling is simply checking to see where your prospect or customer is in relation to you and your objective in the sales process. Taking all available airtime by talking for the duration of your sales presentation prevents you from reading the three relative positions and planning your next move accordingly. Constant talking can also remove you from the buyer's consideration for both this sale and additional opportunities. When you verbally leave your buyer in the dust, you risk losing him permanently.

In fact, your likelihood of getting the sale moves in direct proportion to the amount of airtime you give your prospect during the discussion. The more time your prospect is speaking, the greater the chances that you'll get the business.

How do you use this to your advantage in selling? Plan your presentation, complete with the necessary product knowledge and the relevant benefits to your buyer, in the form of questions that force the buyer's participation. This accomplishes two things: First, you give yourself the advantage of being able to take a breath and regroup, even if only for a moment. Second, and more importantly, you make sure that you and your buyer are on the same page. A single answer to a key question or concern from the buyer, which you can answer on the spot, provides the opportunity to continue toward the sale. Conversely, a single question on the buyer's mind that remains unasked and unanswered can kill the sale.

Here's an example: Let's say you sell a service that employs digital technology. You could say, "Of course our service is completely digital, and that means you can be sure your information is completely secure." Or, you could say, "How important is it for your own peace of mind to know that the information you're sending is only seen by you and your intended recipient?" If your prospect responds that security is critically important, you can go into greater detail, providing some peace of mind on that particular issue. If, on the other hand, you get a noncommittal nod in response, you know you can move on to other benefits.

Use Trial Closes

If adding questions to your sales presentation seems difficult or awkward, simply plan to stop at several spots and ask, "Does this make sense to you so far? What questions or concerns do you have at this time?" These questions are called trial closes and are intended to help you gauge your progress in the sales discussion.

Sales presentation skills are overrated. The practice of asking relevant questions and listening closely for the answers, then incorporating those answers into the discussion as appropriate, is a much more critical skill. To be sure, the sales process requires both. The point here is simply that the focus needs to be on the buyer and the buyer's concerns, not on your product, your service, or your presentation.

Pick your head up when you sell. Check to see where your buyer is and plan accordingly. The sale never happens without the participation and agreement of the buyer. Plan for both and you'll see the improvement in your results. ■

John Carroll is president of Unlimited Performance, Inc. For biographical and business information, see page 263.

Editor's Note: Linda Richardson is a recognized leader in the sales training industry. Widely credited with the move to consultative selling, Linda has over 28 years' experience in sales consulting and training. She's authored ten books on selling and sales management, and teaches sales and management courses at the Wharton Graduate School of the University of Pennsylvania, and the Wharton Executive Development Center. Her insights will have you rethinking how you begin your sales calls.

Rethink How You Open
by Linda Richardson

Most salespeople take the way they open sales calls for granted. Many hardly think about it at all.

But your opening is an ideal place to differentiate yourself and get your calls, especially first calls, off to a great start. Although it takes only a small amount of time, you set the tone for the entire call with your opening.

Time and planning are required to create a great opening. Let me share with you the five elements to a first-rate opening. Master them and you'll enjoy a distinct competitive advantage.

- **Remember to build rapport.** Prepare for rapport. In addition to your prepared opening, look for rapport cues. Be sensitive to customer signals, but do not bypass rapport. People buy from people they like when all else is fairly equal, and sometimes even when it's not.
- **Rethink your purpose.** Instead of saying, "I'm here to tell you about us and what we do in …" say, "I'm here to learn more about your objectives and share with you what we do in …" (for a first meeting) or "Before I discuss what I've prepared, I'd like to learn about …"
- **Leverage your preparation.** You probably are well prepared, so leverage your preparation. Say, "In preparation for the meeting, I have … (example: discussed X with our specialists, researched …)." This will help you gain credibility and more time with your prospect.
- **Flash your credentials.** Establish your credentials with a prospect by giving a 30- to 60-second overview of what your company does. Tailor this to your prospect. Check to see if he has any questions.

- **Launch into needs.** Segue from the opening into the prospect's needs rather than into your presentation. When you are ready to wrap up the opening, ask a question that sets the expectation that you will be asking several needs-related questions. This will help you gain the cooperation of the client. Remember, you have already let the client know you prepared for the meeting, so this will help the client give you information. For example, say, "So that I can focus on what the priorities are for you, may I ask a few questions about … before I share with you what I have prepared?" Then you are in the "need dialogue" where you can question, listen, and drill down. You'll gather critical information to help you be persuasive when you present.

These opening steps may seem like small points. In fact, many, if not most, salespeople miss several of them.

When you open the call effectively, you open the dialogue and the rest of the call will be much more productive. ∎

Linda Richardson is president and founder of Richardson. For biographical and business information, see page 271.

Editor's Note: During tough times, buyer trust is money in the bank. Charles Green is a leading authority on building trusted relationships in business. A noted speaker, author, and consultant, he has over 25 years' experience with the professional services industry. He explains how to turn the sometimes tedious task of proposal writing into a relationship building activity.

Write Your Next Proposal Sitting Next to the Client
by Charles H. Green

We all know we should write proposals that are less about us and more about the client. We know we should spend less space on credentials and methodology; we know we should focus more on results, benefits, and adding value in the proposal.

But we nearly always miss the biggest proposal opportunity of all—building the relationship with the prospect.

Round Up the Usual Suspects

You know the drill; it varies in detail and only differs slightly with the complexity of your business. It probably sounds pretty much like this:

> "Great meeting, Joe. We got a lot better feel for things today face-to-face than we could have done with more phone calls. Thanks for making the time. We'll have the proposal to you as a PDF file by end of the week, and FedEx a hard copy with full graphics to you at the same time.

> "It'll include all the specs we discussed to date: capabilities, costing, time estimates, benefits, payback and ROI calculations—everything we talked about.

> "After that, we'll look forward to hearing back from you, and, of course, I hope you'll feel completely free to call us with any questions. OK, then, see you. We'll get this to you by Friday. Thanks a lot."

Here are four things that can be predicted from this dialogue:
- The proposal will start from an existing proposal as a template
- The proposal will take about the average amount of time and cost the average amount
- The likelihood of acceptance is your usual hit rate
- No matter how much you stress "feel free to call with questions," you will not hear back from the client with any questions. None.

You had a great meeting. If you get the job, you'll have an even better relationship after the contract is signed. But right now, you're in the twilight zone of what I call PIRL or "proposal-induced relationship limbo."

What if you could keep the relationship momentum going? What if you could break out of PIRL and do something to really accelerate the value, and the likelihood of doing something great for the client? And cinch the job as a result?

You can. All you have to do is change one major feature of the proposal. Don't write it by yourself.

Why Proposals Exist

The socially acceptable presumption is that crafting a proposal means writing something at arms' length, so that the clients can objectively study the various options facing them.

Most of the consequences of this evolved social behavior are disastrous for the seller and buyer alike. It draws an awkward halt to a developing relationship. It forces the seller to revert to the kinds of things he did at the beginning of the relationship, re-hashing credentials and third-party testimonials. It forces the buyer to take a step back, to be rational and unconnected. It forces both parties to put benefits into cold, unemotional, factual terms, which means it forces them to translate relationships into clinical terms.

It makes some sense if your objective is to guard against irrational things like trust, relationships, and collaboration. If you think the essence of the commercial transaction, however, lies at least as much in people interactions as it does in blinded reverse online auctions, then the proposal process is pretty much a big splash of cold water to the face.

Yet, there's one very valuable thing that happens when you say, "I'll send you the proposal." You give the client an emotionally acceptable way of saying "no" to you. This may be the biggest reason of all that proposals exist. No one wants to reject you to your face, and frankly, you don't want to be rejected in person either.

So breaking out of proposal induced relationship limbo will require an answer to the burning question: "How will I say 'no' if I have to?"

The Joint Proposal

What if, instead of the usual "send it to you Friday" line, you were to say:

> "Great meeting, Joe. We got a lot better feel for things today face-to-face than we could have done with more phone calls. Let me suggest we keep up that progress, rather than shutting it down.

> "Let me suggest you book this conference room again for next Tuesday, and we write your proposal together.

> "Together, we'll address all the specs we've discussed: capabilities, costing, time estimates, benefits, payback and ROI calculations—everything we talked about. We'll put in the stuff you need, and leave out whatever boilerplate you don't need.

> "I'll bring everything I need from our side—pricing sheets, work design outlines—and I'll be quite open about it. You come with the audience you need this to speak to, and the critical issues the proposal must address. As issues of interpretation arise, we'll address them together. As issues of understanding arise, we'll address them together.

> "Together, we'll write the best proposal that can possibly be written for both our companies. Will it be the best possible proposal for you? Maybe, maybe not. But we'll both know that we got the best we had to offer for you out on the table.

"Joe, I know this approach is no guarantee we'll get the job. In fact, it may become very clear to both of us as we write the proposal that we are particularly well qualified, or poorly qualified, to do this work for you. But that means we're reducing the likelihood of misunderstanding and surprise, which is good for both of us."

Now, what is Joe going to say, and think, and feel? He may say yes, or he may say no. Here are some possible responses from Joe:

- He may think and feel that you are clever, creative and trustworthy, or at least enough so to try your idea. If that's the case, you have achieved PIRL escape velocity and you'll both benefit.
- He may think it's just a little too risky and avant garde for him to try and sell it upstairs, yet still feel like it was a good idea and you are to be commended for being willing to be that open and constructive. But at least you've offered some value, an interesting new idea, and gained some relationship credibility in the process, even if you still do the conventional proposal.
- Or, he may think you are a very devious, manipulative person, and feel that you're putting him into an emotionally stressful and embarrassing position, say no, and even be suspicious of you.

If your client is suspicious of your offer, then you are probably dealing with a particular personality type, one for whom proposals provide emotional protection and insurance against relationships. In such cases, gently acknowledge that you understand many people prefer the traditional proposal process, and you will be happy to comply.

Then go back to your office, downgrade the probability of winning that proposal, and consider cutting your investment in time in writing it. Because the joint proposal is also a test of whether the client can handle a relationship. If the answer is no, wouldn't you rather find out sooner than later? ■

Charles H. Green is CEO and founder of Trusted Advisor Associates. For biographical and business information, see page 265.

Editor's Note: Known as The Sales Hunter, Mark Hunter is a popular speaker and sales consultant. His training is based on consultative selling principles. If you're faced with having to raise prices—tough at any times, but extremely difficult in a downturn—you'll appreciate Mark's advice on how to handle telling your customers.

Communicating a Price Increase
by Mark Hunter

Even the most sales savvy among us have had to fight back the nerves that arise when we're about to tell a customer about a price increase. It never makes for an easy conversation but it's one that's happening more and more during this economic downturn.

When relaying a price increase in a business-to-business environment, remember that your customers have probably had the same discussion with their own customers. A company exists only as long as it earns a profit, and it can only do that if it delivers a quality product or service at the right price. The key to any conversation about raising prices is emphasizing that the increase will ensure product quality.

To prepare your strategy for announcing a price increase, ask yourself the following questions:

- **Does the customer take your product or service and add a standard percentage increase in price when selling to his customers?** If so, you can point out that your customer will make more money by taking a standard percentage of a higher amount.
- **What percentage of the customer's business is your product/service?** If the percentage is small, tell him that the amount of increase is only a small percentage of his total business. If the percentage is great, then emphasize that the price increase is necessary to maintain the level of product quality required for him to serve his customers.
- **Has the customer faced any price increases from other vendors?** If so, try to identify the percentage range of the increases. If yours falls into the low end, you can point out that your increase is small compared to the others. If your increase falls in the high end, you can either explain how this is the only increase you expect to make, or

suggest that you wouldn't be surprised to see other vendors initiating another round of increases.

- **How does the customer view you and the products/services you sell?** If you have a quality reputation and record, then you can emphasize that the increase has been carefully considered and it is only being taken to ensure continued quality. If you have a spotty record with the customer, you should stress how the price increase will allow you to begin addressing some of the issues in question. You'll now be able to improve the overall quality of service the customer has been receiving. Of course, these statements must be backed up by a firm commitment.

- **Will the customer raise an issue with the price increase?** Be prepared to show documentation of how your costs have escalated and how other companies are experiencing the same increases. For example, when the cost of oil rises many companies that use petroleum in the manufacture or transportation of goods increase prices. When having this discussion, be sure to show empathy for the customer, but remain firm in what you're saying. If the customer senses any hesitation on your part, he will likely try to exploit it in the form of a price concession from you. Be prepared to outline the steps your company has taken in an attempt to avoid a price increase. This can include ways you've already cut costs or how the price increase is the only way to maintain the quality and service the customer expects. A final point to emphasize is the time lag between this price increase and the previous increase. Having information available concerning the rate of inflation during that specific time period may also help diffuse the issue.

- **Why does the customer buy from you?** Use these reasons as reinforcements when talking about the price increase. Also, you should have ready at least two key needs of the customer that your product or service satisfies. Be sure all of your strategic information about the customer is up-to-date before the price increase is announced.

- **How much business is at risk with this customer?** Sometimes, we can get carried away thinking that if we raise prices, we'll lose the customer, even though this is rarely the case. Think through what steps the customer would have to take to move to another vendor. Many times the work involved in switching is not worth the effort, and the business is less at risk than you may think.

Here are some best practices to employ when executing a price increase:

- **Give the customer lead time.** Give the customer enough notice to allow him to make adjustments in his information systems and to place at least one more order at the existing price.

- **Avoid showing favorites.** Pricing integrity is always essential, but especially so during a price change. Do not treat particular customers more favorably than others. Different pricing levels are fine as long as they can be logically defended so that a customer who is not receiving the price break can understand and accept the price change.

- **Communicate up front.** Do not allow your customer to find out about a price increase from your invoice. Notification of a price change must come from the account executive or a person of high position within the company. This information should only appear on an invoice after every account involved has been personally notified. Plan to allow enough time for at least one invoice to contain a note of the pending increase in price.

- **Keep customer service informed.** Make sure that each customer service representative and anyone else who comes in contact with the customer is fully aware of when the price increase will be communicated. Don't allow the customer to hear conflicting information from different departments. Everyone in customer service needs to be fully aware of the price increase, the reasoning behind it, and the logistics for implementation. They should also be provided with a FAQ guide to ensure that when customers do ask them about elements of the pricing increase, they are able to share accurate information.

- **Believe in the price increase.** In order to be paid what you're worth, you must charge what you're worth. Although this is not something that can be explicitly communicated to the customer, this general sense is what sets best practice companies and high-performing sales professionals above the rest.

- **Instill an open-phone/open-door policy.** Whenever a price increase occurs, senior executives must be willing to answer phone calls from customers or make phone calls to key accounts. Nothing sends a stronger signal to a sales organization than seeing its senior executives on the front line dealing with a price increase.
- **Be observant.** Monitor the sales patterns of your individual customers before and after the price increase so you can quickly catch any changes that may occur as a result.

You can't avoid dealing with price increases; they are an inevitable part of business. Instead, you should use them strategically to increase your selling potential, even in a recession. ■

Mark Hunter is known as the "The Sales Hunter." For biographical and business information, see page 266.

Editor's Note: Although no one ever admits to watching them, infomercials bring in millions every year, even in sluggish economic times. Effective salesmanship is a key aspect of selling in any economy. Those TV hucksters have salesmanship nailed. Stating a problem and then offering a solution are part of a fundamental sales formula that never goes out of style.

Isn't That Amazing!
by Michael Dalton Johnson

You can't help seeing them on television. I'm talking about those fast-talking hucksters selling cheesy products that nobody needs, but millions buy. In good times or in tough times, these guys know how to sell.

Who can forget the Inside the Eggshell Scrambler? How about the Snuggie? The Bedazzler? The Pocket Fisherman? GLH (which stands for Great Looking Hair) a pigment in a can to spray on your bald spot and, of course, let's not leave out the Clapper!

How do these cartoonish characters convince millions of people to pull out a credit card, call an 800 number and place an order for a product they don't need?

In a word, salesmanship.

Without exception, these TV pitches are delivered by people who are wildly enthusiastic and breathlessly excited about the product they are hawking. Excitement, apparently even phony over-the-top excitement, grabs buyer's attention and rouses curiosity.

They then state a problem, "The problem with blankets is that they always slip off." The fact that people really don't have much trouble managing a blanket is immaterial. The need for their product, no matter if the need is non-existent, is put forth with great conviction.

A lengthy, fast-moving and repetitious recital of the benefits of ownership, complete with product demonstrations, is then put forth. "You will slice a tomato perfectly every time with one simple motion, and clean up is a snap!" "You'll save time and have perfectly uniform slices for salads and sandwiches!" they add.

Employing a paid studio audience to ooh and ahh and applaud wildly in response to the product demonstrations is often used to establish credibility. Short customer testimonials are sometimes filmed and interspersed throughout the pitch for the same purpose. Statements like, "If you have a car, boat or RV, you'd be crazy not to own one of these!" are typical.

But wait, there's more! "Act now and we'll include a second one free of charge...all you pay is shipping and handling." This offer to double the order appears to be adding value for the buyer but in reality it's an up-sell. The shipping and handling charges more than cover the total cost of adding another unit and generate additional profit.

A sense of urgency is created: "You must act now to get this special offer." "Have your credit card ready and call within the next ten minutes and we'll include Jill's recipes at absolutely no extra cost to you." Some even show a ticking clock counting down the time left to buy.

No matter how silly and shifty these TV pitches are, when you scrape away the hucksterism, you see they follow a legitimate and proven sales formula that includes creating excitement and curiosity, identifying a problem, offering a solution, reciting the benefits of ownership, establishing credibility, adding value, up-selling and ending it all with a strong call to action.

You'd do well to use these fundamentals in your sales pitch but please don't try to sell me a water powered can opener! ■

Michael Dalton Johnson is founder and president of SalesDog.com. For biographical and business information, see page 267.

Editor's Note: The Wall Street Journal calls Andrea Nierenberg a "networking success story." Her mastery of personal marketing and networking techniques has made her an internationally renowned expert in the field. The author of two books on the subject, Andrea also teaches a course on self-marketing at New York University. She shows you how to network on your contact's schedule.

Networking with Patience Makes all the Difference
by Andrea Nierenberg

When we network, we have to learn to respect others' timetables. Of course, sometimes new contacts do not respond in a timely fashion. They may be busy with their own deadlines and projects and have a lot of responsibilities, and therefore cannot immediately respond to us. So how can we move the networking process forward without "pushing" other people too hard?

If your contacts don't call back as soon as you would like, it's critical that you don't badger them with demanding follow-up calls. These are the types of calls that try to disguise the real issue: "I think it's time that my efforts to get some business out of you happened soon," or, "What's taking you so long to respond to me?" If you want to build rapport with other people, you're doing more harm than good when you call them and are impersonal or speak harshly. Instead, ask productive questions and offer to help them in some way. These types of calls can also be avoided by asking questions in earlier conversations.

Another stumbling block in networking happens when we rush communications. This occurs when we hurry off the phone or send correspondence that's not carefully written. It tells the new contact that you're trying to get through the process in a cold and mechanical way. Even when we have long lists of people to contact, it can take very little effort to develop a personalized approach. Here are three ways to do it:

- Ask the contact how he wants the issue to be handled. Some people prefer to have everything in writing, while others would rather receive a quick follow-up phone call or email about new opportunities that can benefit them.

- Check on new contacts regularly. In the workplace, many people are told to quickly deal with people without having a long-term follow-up plan in place. Often the long-term follow-up is more important. Mark your calendar for the next significant date on your contacts' calendars. This might come a month before an important meeting or event where you will see them.
- When you call them, say that you hope to connect with them at the event, or let them know that you have useful information that would help them. When you see them, you can mention trade-related developments or news that would specifically help their companies.

Develop a Game Plan

New contacts often do not develop into anything important because there's no long-term plan in place. Keep a list of your contacts and develop a plan that's appropriate for them all. Then decide which contacts will get unique treatment. For instance, you may see that effective follow-up with one contact may be looking for him at an upcoming business function, while another might appreciate a note with an informative newspaper or magazine article. Once you find out what's effective, build on what works and develop the skills you need, such as writing and speaking, to make meaningful connections with those important people.

Think about your strengths. You may discover that you effectively network through written communications or are better at speaking to people at business functions. If you find any areas that need improvement, make sure to get the help you need so that your networking will be fruitful.

Networking is a process, and you must constantly develop, build, and cultivate relationships that can give you results beyond your expectations. ∎

Andrea Nierenberg is president of The Nierenberg Group. For biographical and business information, see page 270.

Editor's Note: Tony Alessandra fought his way out of New York City to success as a graduate professor of marketing, an entrepreneur, business author, and keynote speaker. He earned his MBA from the University of Connecticut, and his PhD in Marketing from Georgia State University. Tony is a widely published author with an unusual streetwise, yet college-smart, perspective on business. Tony knows all about selling in tough times. He shows you how to go beyond the Golden Rule to build rapport, an essential skill for recession-busting sales professionals.

A Rule More Valuable Than Gold!
by Tony Alessandra

An indisputable business fact is that people do business with people they like. It makes sense, therefore, to like and be liked by as many people as possible. The ability to create rapport with a large number of people is a fundamental skill in sales, management, personal relationships, and everyday life.

We have all heard of the Golden Rule—and many people aspire to live by it. The Golden Rule is not a panacea. Think about it: "Do unto others as you would have them do unto you." The Golden Rule implies the basic assumption that other people would like to be treated the way that you would like to be treated. The alternative to the Golden Rule is much more productive. I call it the Platinum Rule: "Treat others the way they want to be treated." Ah hah! What a difference. The Platinum Rule accommodates the feelings of others. The focus of relationships shifts from "this is what I want, so I'll give everyone the same thing" to "let me first understand what they want and then I'll give it to them."

Building rapport with people based on the Platinum Rule is smart—people smart. Applying the Platinum Rule requires some thought and effort, but it is the most insightful, rewarding, and productive way to interact with people. And it is easy to learn.

A Modern Model for Chemistry

Your goal in applying the Platinum Rule is personal chemistry and productive relationships. You do not have to change your personality. You do not have to roll over and submit to others. You simply have to understand what drives people and recognize your options for dealing with them.

To do this, you'll need to understand the four basic behavioral styles: The Director, The Socializer, The Relater, and The Thinker. Everyone possesses the qualities of each style to varying degrees and everyone has a dominant style. For the sake of simplicity, this article will focus only on dominant styles. As you read the descriptions of Directors, Socializers, Relaters, and Thinkers, see which style fits you best. Then think about people around you—at home, in the office—and determine their styles.

Directors

Directors are driven by two governing needs: to control and to achieve. Directors are goal-oriented go-getters who are most comfortable when they are in charge of people and situations. They want to accomplish many things—now—so they focus on no-nonsense approaches to bottom-line results.

Directors seek expedience and are not afraid to bend the rules. They figure it is easier to beg forgiveness than to ask permission. Directors accept challenges, take authority, and plunge headfirst into solving problems. They are fast-paced, task-oriented, and work quickly and impressively by themselves, which means they become annoyed with delays.

Directors are driven and dominating, which can make them stubborn, impatient, and insensitive to others. Directors are so focused that they forget to take the time to smell the roses.

Directors tend to gravitate toward the following positions: the hard-driving journalist, the stockbroker, the CEO, the independent consultant, and the drill sergeant!

Socializers

Socializers are friendly, enthusiastic "party-animals" who like to be where the action is. They thrive on the admiration, acknowledgment, and compliments that come with being in the limelight. Socializers just want to have fun. They are more relationship-oriented than task-oriented. Socializers would rather "schmooze" with clients over lunch than work in the office.

The Socializer's primary strengths are enthusiasm, charm, persuasive-ness, and warmth. They are idea people and dreamers who excel at getting others excited about their visions. They are eternal optimists with an abundance of charisma. These qualities help them influence people and build alliances to accomplish their goals.

As wonderful as Socializers may sound, they do have their weaknesses: impatience, an aversion to being alone, and a short attention span. Socializers are risk-takers who base many of their decisions on intuition, which is not inherently bad. When given only a little data, however, Socializers often exaggerate or make sweeping generalizations. Socializers are not inclined to verify information; they are more likely to assume someone else will do it.

Socializers tend to gravitate toward the following positions: sales (especially non-technical products/services), public relations, advertising, show business, cruise ship social directors, hotel and restaurant personnel and glamorous, high-profile careers.

Thinkers

Thinkers are analytical, persistent, systematic people who enjoy problem solving. Thinkers are detail-oriented, which makes them more concerned with content than style. Thinkers are task-oriented people who enjoy perfecting processes and working toward tangible results. They focus on the trees, whereas Directors and Socializers focus on the forest. Thinkers are always in control of their emotions (note the poker faces of many Jeopardy! contestants) and may become uncomfortable around people who very outgoing, e.g., Socializers.

In the office, Thinkers work at a slow pace, allowing them to double-check their work. They tend to see the serious, complex side of situations, but their intelligence and ability to see different points of view endow them with quick and unique senses of humor.

Thinkers have high expectations of themselves and others, which can make them over-critical. Their tendency toward perfectionism—taken to an extreme—can cause "paralysis by over-analysis." Thinkers are slow and deliberate decision-makers. They do research, make comparisons, determine risks, calculate margins of error, and then take action. Thinkers become irritated by surprises and glitches, hence their cautious decision-making. Thinkers are also skeptical, so they like to see promises in writing.

Thinkers' strengths include an eye for detail and accuracy, dependability, independence, persistence, follow-through, and organization. They are good listeners and ask a lot of questions; however, they run the risk of missing the forest for the trees.

Thinkers tend to gravitate toward the following positions: engineers, statisticians, scientists, doctors, accountants, computer programmers, airline pilots, and tax attorneys.

Relaters

Relaters are warm, supportive, and nurturing individuals. They are the most people-oriented of the four styles. Relaters are excellent listeners, devoted friends, and loyal employees. Their relaxed dispositions makes them approachable and warm. They develop strong networks of people who are willing to be mutually supportive and reliable. Relaters are excellent team players.

Relaters are risk-averse. In fact, Relaters may tolerate unpleasant environments rather than risk change. They like the status quo and become distressed when disruptions are severe. When Relaters are faced with change, they need to think it through, plan, and accept it into their worlds. Relaters—more than the other behavioral types—strive to maintain personal composure, stability, and balance.

In the office, Relaters are courteous, friendly, and willing to share responsibilities. They are good planners, persistent workers, and good with follow-through. Relaters go along with others even when they do not agree because they do not want to rock the boat.

Relaters are slow decision-makers because of: their need for security; their need to avoid risk; their desire to include others in the decision-making process.

Relaters tend to gravitate toward the following positions: nurse, counselor, psychologist, social worker, teacher, minister, and human resource development. Relaters make exceptionally patient and supportive parents.

Do you want to know your style? Go to http://www.platinumrule.com/ assessment and take the free Platinum Rule assessment.

Adapting to Others

What should you do with this knowledge? First, determine your behavioral style. Knowing that, you now have new insights into your preferences: You might prefer relationships to tasks; perhaps you act slowly rather than quickly; or you may like to tell people what you think or feel rather than keep that information to yourself.

The following guidelines will help you get on the same wavelength with the four behavioral styles.

Recognizing and Adapting to Directors

At work, Directors often have large power-desks with lots of projects on them separated into separate piles. Their walls are adorned with diplomas, awards, and perhaps a large planning calendar. The seating arrangement implies a lack of contact; guests' chairs are opposite a big desk and huge leather executive chair. Conversationally, Directors are fast-paced and allow little or no time for small talk.

How should you treat Directors? They're very time-sensitive, so never waste their time. Be organized and get to the point. Give them bottom-line information and options, with probabilities of success, if relevant. Give them written details to read at their leisure.

Directors are goal-oriented, so appeal to their sense of accomplishment. Stroke their egos by supporting their ideas, and acknowledge their power and prestige. Let Directors call the shots. If you disagree, argue with facts, not feelings. In groups, allow them to have their say because they are not the types who will take a back seat to others.

With Directors, in general, be efficient and competent.

Recognizing and Adapting to Socializers

At work, Socializers' offices are inviting to visitors. Their walls are covered with symbols of recognition, including photographs with celebrities or high-profile executives. Their choices of art are upbeat and stimulating. They are outgoing, friendly, and will often come from behind their desks to sit and talk. Conversationally, Socializers focus on themselves. They are enthusiastic and have a penchant for storytelling. It is always obvious that Socializers would rather chat than get down to business.

How should you treat Socializers? Socializers thrive on personal recognition, so pour it on sincerely. Support their ideas, goals, opinions, and dreams. Try not to argue with their pie-in-the-sky visions; get excited about them.

Socializers are social butterflies, so be ready to flutter around with them. A strong presence, stimulating and entertaining conversation, jokes, and liveliness will win them over. They are people-oriented, so give them time to socialize. Avoid rushing into tasks.

With Socializers, in general, be interested in them.

Recognizing and Adapting to Thinkers

Thinkers' desks are structured, organized and neat. Their offices are decorated functionally rather than artistically. Their walls may contain charts, computer printouts, or other exhibits related to their projects. Thinkers keep their desks between themselves and their guests and their office seating implies formality and lack of contact. Conversationally, Thinkers want to know and want to tell virtually every facet of a story. They speak relatively slowly and deliberately, pausing—without self-consciousness—to search for the right word. Thinkers derive joy from speaking precisely and accurately. Ask a Thinker for the time and you will be told exactly. Ask a Director for the time and you will be told the day of the week. Ask a Socializer for the time and you will be told, "Three days until the weekend."

How should you adapt to Thinkers? They are time-disciplined, so be sensitive to their time. They need details, so give them data. They are task-oriented, so don't expect to become their friend before working with them. Friendship may develop later, but—unlike Socializers—it is not a prerequisite.

Support Thinkers in their organized, thoughtful approach to problem solving. Be systematic, logical, well prepared, and exact with them. Give them time to make decisions and work independently. Allow them to talk in detail. In work groups, do not expect Thinkers to be leaders or outspoken contributors, but do rely on them to conduct research, crunch numbers, and perform detailed footwork for the group. If appropriate, set guidelines and exact deadlines. Thinkers like to be complimented on their brainpower, so recognize their contributions accordingly.

With Thinkers, in general, be thorough, well prepared, detail-oriented, businesslike, and patient.

Recognizing and Adapting to Relaters

At work, Relaters' desks often hold family pictures and sentimental items. Their walls are decorated with conservative art, serene pictures, family or group photos, and supportive slogans. Their offices are warm and inviting and they prefer not to have a desk between them and their visitors. Conversationally, Relaters are relaxed, slow-paced, and supportive. As listeners, they are attentive and make good eye contact.

How should you treat Relaters? They are relationship-oriented and want warm and fuzzy relationships, so take things slow, earn their trust, support their feelings, and show sincere interest. Talk in terms of feelings, not facts, which is the opposite of the strategy for Thinkers. Relaters don't want to ruffle feathers. They want to be assured that everyone will approve of them and their decisions. Give them time to solicit co-workers' opinions. Never back a Relater into a corner. It is far more effective to apply warmth to get this chicken out of its egg than to crack the shell with a hammer.

With Relaters, in general, be nonthreatening and sincere.

Understanding the Platinum Rule and how to apply it will serve you well in all your relationships: business, friends, family, spouse, and children. Improved relationships create infinite possibilities. ■

Tony Alessandra is president of AssessmentBusinessCenter.com. For biographical and business information, see page 261.

Editor's Note: A noted author, speaker and trainer, Paul McCord has over 25 years of real-world experience as a salesperson, sales manager, executive and business owner. His clients include such big names as GE, Wells Fargo, Microsoft, New York Life, Siemens, and Merrill Lynch. A leading authority on referral selling, Paul has been featured in Forbes, Fox Business News, Advisor Today, Selling Power and many more. Use his advice to turn referrals into business-generating introductions.

"Referrals" Are a Waste — Introductions are Gold
by Paul McCord

See if this scenario sounds familiar: Rick's client was somewhat uncomfortable with his request for referrals. The sale had gone well enough—everything considered. But this last question about referrals made the client feel a bit uneasy. His client was caught completely off guard. He wasn't at all prepared to give a referral, and he certainly wasn't comfortable giving one. But Rick asked and stood his ground until his client coughed up the name and phone number of one of his vendors that might be able to use Rick's services.

Rick was excited because the referral was to a company he had wanted to get into for quite a while. Better yet, it was a referral to Nadia, the company's COO, just the person he wanted to reach. He quickly thanked his client and headed to his office to call his new prospect.

As soon as he was in his office, he picked up the phone and called Nadia. However, he reached her assistant who refused to put him through, even though Rick insisted that one of the Nadia's clients had asked him to call. Instead, the assistant asked Rick to leave his name and number, saying she would pass the information along to Nadia, who would get back to Rick if she were interested.

Rick tried several more times to reach Nadia. He called and left messages. He took the liberty of emailing her. He sent two letters. Finally, after months of trying, he gave up.

Unfortunately, this scenario is played out thousands of times a day. Salespeople get referrals, thank their clients, rush off to call the prospects, and never have the opportunity to make contact.

Why does this happen?

Because Rick didn't get a referral; he simply got a name and phone number. Most salespeople like Rick think a referral just means getting a name and phone number and the client's permission to use his name as the referring party. In reality, it is nothing but a name and phone number.

By simply getting a name and phone number and running off to make the phone call, Rick committed the most common error salespeople make when they get a referral. He failed to capitalize on the power of the referral, and instead turned it into a warm call.

The power of a referral is its potential to open doors, generate interest, and get an appointment. Seldom can a referral sell for you. That's not the goal of a referral. The goal is to open a door and, hopefully, begin the relationship from a position of strength and trust.

When you receive a referral, you are hoping to build a relationship with the referred prospect based on his trust and respect of your client. If the prospect trusts and respects your client, a portion of the trust and respect he has for your client is transferred to you because someone he trusts referred you.

However, that trust is useless if you fail to set an appointment with the prospect. In many cases, the fact someone he trusts gave you his name and phone number is often not enough to convince him to meet with you. You need something more compelling than just your client's name to open the door.

What you need is a direct introduction from your client to the prospect. A direct introduction is powerful for several reasons:

- **It is unusual.** It isn't often that someone is personally asked by someone he trusts to meet a salesperson. The act itself places you in a different category than other salespeople.
- **It demonstrates trust.** A direct introduction demonstrates a high level of trust. Most people will not go to the trouble of taking the time and effort to give a direct introduction unless they have a high degree of trust and respect for the person they are introducing.
- **It makes it difficult for the prospect to decline a meeting.** There is implied pressure on the prospect to meet with you since he doesn't want to offend the client.

A call using the client's name doesn't have the power of an introduction and it gives the prospect an easy out—he simply doesn't accept your call or declines a meeting. After all, the client wasn't really involved—you simply used the client's name.

On the other hand, a properly executed introduction virtually guarantees a meeting.

In most instances, you have three introduction methods at your disposal:

- **A letter of introduction written by you and signed by your client.** A letter from the client to the prospect is the most basic form of introduction. Rather than asking the client to write the letter, write it for him on his letterhead and have him sign it. Let the prospect know what you accomplished for the client; let him know why the client referred you; give him a specific time and date to expect your call; and have the client ask the prospect to let him know his impression of you and your company after you have met.

  Mail the letter and then a day or two after the prospect should have received it, give him a call. Don't introduce yourself first. Rather, introduce the letter and client first, then ask for the appointment.

- **A phone call from your client to the prospect.** A phone call is stronger than a letter and almost guarantees an appointment because it's very difficult for the prospect to say no to your appointment request while the client is on the line. The call gives the prospect the opportunity to ask your client specific questions and to get detailed information. Do not have your client call unless you are present—you want to know exactly what was said.

- **A lunch meeting with your client, the prospect, and yourself.** A stronger method than either a letter or a call, a lunch meeting allows you to get to know the prospect as a friend before you get to know him as a salesperson. Like a phone call, it virtually guarantees a private meeting. Also, in a lunch meeting, your client becomes your salesperson and you're there as the consultant. Although a very powerful introduction format, most clients will only agree to do one, maybe two at the most, so use this option judiciously.

If you want to turn your client referrals into customers, don't settle for just getting names and phone numbers. Learn how to turn those names and phone numbers into real referrals through a direct introduction to the prospect. Not only will the number of appointments you set go up—your sales will increase, your income will increase, and you'll find selling will be a lot easier. ∎

Paul McCord is president of McCord Training. For biographical and business information, see page 269.

Editor's Note: For over 15 years, Colleen Francis sold in some pretty tough fields: life insurance and technology. She led one of her sales teams to increase its average per sale size by 50 percent. In another instance, she grew her corporate customer base by 300 percent in just over a year. This is an excellent lesson on how to use testimonials to help you sell in hard times.

Harness the Amazing Power of Testimonials
by Colleen Francis

For any sales professional interested in selling more to more people in less time, testimonials are a vital part of the formula for success. If you're not using them in your business right now, you're missing out on one of the most useful sales tools ever!

Consider the story of legendary businessman W. Clement Stone. He built what would one day become a multi-billion dollar empire by selling fire insurance policies door-to-door during the Great Depression.

There's no denying Clem's knack for people skills was a big part of his success. But, he also had a little something extra—a binder overflowing with testimonials from his customers. Legend has it that binder never left his side when he was knocking on all those doors. It was chock full of stories—and not just happy accounts from people who were satisfied. It also told painful stories about how people had lost houses, husbands and wives to misfortune and how relieved they were that, thanks to Clem, they had signed on the dotted line long ago, and now were covered. Frankly, after reading stories out of that binder, it's hard to imagine how anyone could ever say no to him!

That's the amazing power of testimonials. They work because they reaffirm for others what you already know is true.

Show 'em the Steak

When you meet with prospects, it's likely you talk about all the great things you do for your clients. You might also talk about how often you go the extra mile because service matters to you. But let's face it: in sales, no one ever becomes successful and stays that way for long if all they ever do is talk about the sizzle without ever showing the steak.

That's where testimonials come in. They back up what you say with what noted psychologist Robert B. Cialdini calls *social proof*. If we drill down a little deeper into human psychology, we also learn that testimonials have amazing persuasive powers. That's because they touch on both the fact-based and emotion-based motivators that drive people to buy things. They reaffirm that your claims are credible and your services are the real deal. They validate the feelings that a prospect has for you. And they do so with a message that is unmistakably authentic and sincere.

When you combine all those motivators, it helps you make a very convincing case to prospects. You can say, "Don't just take my word for it, have a look at what my customers say... ." It deepens the confidence people will have in your message and it can dramatically reduce the barriers you face in closing the sale.

Let's look at how you can harness the power of testimonials to help you sell.

- **Keep your ears open wide.** When you're talking to your customers, does anyone ever share with you a little story about how he was able to make great use of your product or service? Check your email. Has anyone ever sent you a note just to say "thanks for the great work" on the last job you did for him? Or have you ever received glowing feedback from a client who responded to a survey you sent out? Each of those is a testimonial, just waiting for you to act on it.

- **Ask and you shall receive.** Remember our friend W. Clement Stone? He once famously said, "If there is something to gain and nothing to lose by asking, by all means ask!" When a client says great things about you, about your work or the products you sell, give him the opportunity to turn that praise into a testimonial. Simply ask: "I'd really love it if I could include what you just said in my client testimonials. Would that be OK?" People generally like to be helpful, but they'll never get the opportunity to give you that all-powerful testimonial if you don't ask.

- **Newer customers are passionate.** Get on the phone and call your newest customers. No matter what industry you serve, the most passionate praise you'll find for your work and the service you sell tends to come from customers with whom you have only recently started doing business. Andy Sernovitz, the author of *Word of Mouth Marketing: How Smart Companies Get People Talking*, explains why: They are the ones who are most excited about having found you. Your repeat customers, on the other hand, are already accustomed to the great service you provide.

- **Repeat customers are wise and insightful.** Your repeat customers provide people (and that includes you) with important insight about what makes your product or service worth coming back to—again and again. So make a point of calling up those you have been doing business with for a long time and ask them why it is they call on you. The answers you get will often include a great sentence or two you can add to your testimonial collection. Again, all you have to do is ask.

- **Make it easy for people.** One of the most common comments you'll hear from clients when asking for testimonials is: "Well I'm really not much of a writer, so it's hard for me to put it into words." The real power of testimonials comes from the fact that they're not polished— they're authentic and from the heart. A marketing professional I know quite well recently shared with me his secret about how he addresses this issue in his business. "I borrowed an idea from John Caples—one of the great copywriters of the 20th century. When asking a client for a testimonial, he'd say 'Finish this sentence in 25 words or less: I really like (product/service/person) because... .' This really works because it gets right to the point about the feelings people have for you, for what you do and for what you're selling."

- **Make testimonials part of your strategy for cold calls.** Turn a testimonial into an opening statement you can use when making your cold calls. It's a great way to get the conversation started on the right note because it's one (or more) of your customers talking about all the great things you can do for that prospect at the other end of phone. This strategy can be really compelling when the testimonial is one the person you're calling can relate to specifically in his line of work. Let's say I'm calling a prospect in the tourism industry and

I share with him a sample of the great feedback I received recently from a client who works for that industry's national association; I'm making it clear that I understand the challenges he has to deal with in his work. There's also a deeper message being processed by the person I'm calling: "If Colleen has worked with them, then she understands what we need and if she understands what we need, then she understands me."

- **Do unto others.** Write testimonials for others with whom you do business and whose services have impressed you. It's a good thing to do. It also helps to deepen those all-important reciprocal relationships. Plus testimonials you write about others send an important message to everyone about the high standards you have not only as a supplier but as a buyer, too. The social networking site, LinkedIn is a handy tool for doing this. Not only does it encourage reciprocity, it also helps you become part of a trusted network of professionals.

- **Make testimonials noticeable.** As you build your collection of testimonials, you'll need to find a place where people can read them. Lucky for you, you have a lot more choices than W. Clement Stone did back in the Depression era. Not only can you put them all in a binder to show prospects, you can also include testimonials in other products, and most won't cost you much more than a few minutes of your time. Here are some examples. Create a special Web page devoted to testimonials. Consider ways that you can include sample quotes from that collection and feature them in steady rotation on the main page of your site. Another approach that I've seen is to include a new testimonial on the signature line of every outbound email. The possibilities are endless and the potential benefits to your sales can be quite amazing, even lucrative. ■

Colleen Francis is president of Engage Selling Solutions. For biographical and business information, see page 264.

Editor's Note: Sales guru Dave Kahle has a unique set of qualifications in the sales training industry. He's been highly successful in the real world of sales. In addition, Dave's MA in Education makes him uniquely qualified to teach. Dave shares his advice on the best ways to work with customers who are too busy to meet.

Dealing With Your Customer's Time Constraints
by Dave Kahle

My customers don't have as much time to spend with me as they used to.

That's a comment I'm hearing more frequently in my sales seminars. It's a growing phenomenon. Your customers used to be able to spend more time with you. But lately, it seems like they're on tighter schedules and are harder to see. You just can't spend as much time with them as you'd like, because they're pressuring you to move on.

It's not that your customers don't like you, or that they're not interested in your products and services. It's just that they have too much to do, and they simply don't have as much time to spend with you as you'd like.

Here's how to attack this challenge.

First, remember to respect your customer's time constraints. If you try to overstay your welcome, you'll only succeed in making him more irritated with you. Do unto him as you would have him do unto you, if you were in his place. Protect the relationship.

Then, focus on making the time that you do have with him more productive for both of you. Think of the issue being quality time, not quantity time. Here are three strategies that will work for you.

Focus on Quality of Time

If you're not going to have as much time in front of the customer as you'd like, then you must concentrate on making the time that you do have as valuable and productive as possible. That requires you to spend more time planning and preparing for each sales call.

Gone are the days when you could just "stop in." Rather, make sure that you have at least three things prepared for every sales call:

- a specific objective—what do you want to accomplish in this call?
- an outline of how you're going to accomplish that objective, and
- all the necessary tools you'll need to do it.

That way, the actual time that you spend with your customer will be more productive. Your customer will appreciate your organization and your respect of his time, too.

Set an Agenda

Begin every sales call with an agenda. Tell your customer what you want to cover and how you're going to proceed. Mention the needs and objectives that interest him, and explain how you're going to address them. This will relieve him of the worry that you're going to appropriate his time unnecessarily, and will allow him to focus on you.

For example, at the beginning of your sales call, you could say something like this:

> "John I know you're interested in the cost payback of a possible investment in a new telephone system. I'd like to share with you some of the numbers that others have used to investigate this kind of purchase. After we go through these, I'll address any other questions you may have, and then we'll talk about the next step in this process. Does that sound reasonable?"

Make it Worthwhile

Always have something of value to discuss. This is a longer-range strategy. As you consistently hold to this principle, over time you'll build up a certain expectation in the customer's mind. Don't expect an immediate payback from this strategy, but, nonetheless, stick to it for the long haul.

Think of the time that your customer does spend with you as an investment by the customer. Put yourself in his shoes, and see the situation from his perspective. Is he gaining something of value from you in exchange for his investment of time? You want the answer to that question to be "yes."

To generate that perception in your customer's mind, make sure that every time you see him, you have something of value to share or to discuss with him. That means something in which the customer is interested. If you have nothing that the customer will think is of value, don't take his time. Wait until you do have something then see him.

After a few such calls, your customer will come to respect you and look forward to your calls, knowing that you're not there just to work some agenda of yours, but rather he'll come to expect to gain something from your sales calls.

You'll find it easier to make appointments and get time with your customers when you've instilled in them the expectation that the time spent with you will be well worth the cost of it. ■

Dave Kahle is president of The DaCo Corporation. For biographical and business information, see page 267.

Editor's Note: As president of his own training firm, Kelley Robertson has helped thou-sands of sales professionals improve their sales skills. His clients include Sony of Canada, Samsung, LG Electronics, Preferred Nutrition, and Delta Resorts. He explains the importance of being persistent when following up with prospects.

Persistence Pays Off
by Kelley Robertson

Persistence is a vital skill that every salesperson needs. It's been said that most sales are made after eight contacts with a prospect. However, most people tend to give up after just three or four attempts. Let's explore the behind-the-scene dynamics involved in a typical scenario.

An executive's day is usually booked solid. There are internal meetings, as well as meetings with customers, suppliers and business partners to attend. In addition, an executive is always juggling a number of high-priority tasks. She has several major goals to accomplish over the next year but progress has been slow because there are so many demands on her time.

Fortunately, the executive has an extremely competent executive assistant, a gatekeeper, who knows what projects her boss is working on and who helps her achieve those goals. This executive assistant, who is very profi-cient at managing her boss's time, is also very adept at shielding her from inter-ruptions, such as unwanted telephone calls from salespeople. That means you have to persuade the assistant to let you talk to her boss.

Your first prospecting call to the company goes very well. You explain to the assistant how your solution will save her boss time and money. Your well-developed opening captures her interest; she schedules a telephone meeting for you with her boss and gives you her direct number.

You call the executive at the agreed-upon time. You've done your home-work and the call goes well. By asking the right questions you are able to garner the additional information necessary to present your solution in an even more positive light. The executive asks you to send her an overview of your solution and you agree to email it to her within 24 hours. You also schedule a follow-up call for the next week.

But when you make the call you reach her voice mail, so you leave a message and say you will follow up soon. You call several more times with the same result. Self-doubt takes over and you wonder why she hasn't returned any of your calls even though she has expressed interest in your solution.

During this time, the executive has been trying to deal with some critical issues as well as put out some unexpected fires. Then when she has successfully resolved those problems, the CEO heaps some additional projects on her plate—projects he makes clear are extremely crucial to the company.

The executive puts her other high-priority projects on hold so she can deal with the demands of the CEO. On top of this, the Director of the company, her right-hand person, resigns. Now she's scrambling to put systems and processes into place to help her deal with this unexpected situation. She also needs to begin the recruiting process to hire the Director's replacement. Although she's still interested in your solution, she simply does not yet have the time or the resources to deal with it.

Here's the dilemma: Do you keep calling, or do you leave one final message telling the executive to call you when she's ready to discuss your solution? So far, you have made five contacts with her, which means you will probably have to make three more connections before the sale moves forward.

It is critical to recognize that executives are exceptionally busy. While they may want to discuss your solution, they have other priorities to handle. But if you stop making contact with them, there is a good chance that they will forget about you and your particular solution when they are ready to move forward.

Your goal is to keep your name in the minds of your prospects and develop a "stay-in-touch" campaign. This can include sending email, letters, and cards or leaving a voice mail. Each point of contact should offer something of value and must be brief. Respect the decision-makers' time. Recognize that they are balancing multiple projects at any given time. Like you, they can only work on a certain number of them at once.

Many people close sales long after the initial contact simply because they have been persistent and executed a solid strategy and keep-in-touch plan. While the standard number of contacts is eight, this number is not carved in stone. You can rest assured that if you give up after three or four attempts, a competitor who is more persistent will eventually get the business. Are you willing to give business away or are you prepared to persist until you succeed? ∎

Kelley Robertson is president of The Robertson Training Group. For biographical and business information, see page 272.

*Editor's Note: Steve Marx held just about every type of job in the broadcasting busi-
ness, including general manager and station owner, but the job he liked the best was
selling, where he went "from worst to first" in just five months and was never
knocked off the top spot. He went on to found The Center for Sales Strategy, a
media sales and management consultancy, now in its 26th year. Steve explains why
you shouldn't be so quick to submit your proposal.*

Slow Down the Proposal—Speed up the Yes!
by Steve Marx

Delivering the proposal is a very big step in the sales process. You know
this already, but if you're like most salespeople, you don't fully understand why.

You think the proposal needs to look professional, so that you and your
company will look professional, and that's true. You think the proposal
needs to demonstrate clearly that you understand what the prospect's needs
are, and I agree. You think the proposal needs to show benefits and demonstrate value, and, of course, that's correct, too. You think the proposal needs
to be clear and complete, so it doesn't present any obstacles to the sale, and
you're right again. And you think the proposal needs to be convincing, and
no one will argue with you on that.

But you still haven't put your finger on why delivering the proposal is such
a major event in your work with that prospect. Here's the answer the pros
know. Passing that proposal across the desk (or across the Internet, if you must
deliver it electronically) is your Last Hurrah. It's the final scene in the final
act of the drama we call selling. As soon as you commit everything to paper,
organize it, index it, proofread it, print it in full color, and drop it into that
elegant corporate portfolio—*it replaces you.* The prospect no longer needs *you*
once she has your proposal.

The drama may well continue beyond your delivery of the proposal, but
it won't be selling. At that point, it will be buying. And you won't be there.
The prospect now takes the stage, and her role is to vet the proposal, to
analyze it and scrutinize it and compare it, to confer with her colleagues or
her boss or legal or accounting or all of them. You're off-stage as this drama

continues. She may call you with a question or to seek clarification on something, but usually not.

More typically it's *you* trying to call *her*. You know how much more difficult it is to get the prospect on the phone after you've handed over the proposal than it was before. Been there, done that, right? And now you're starting to understand why. The proposal delivery marks the moment when the monkey moves from your back to the prospect's. In the typical sales cycle, very little of the work of buying happens before the proposal arrives, and little to no selling takes place after that day. So the faster you deliver the proposal, the less time there is for selling, the less opportunity there is to meet all the people who matter, the less chance there is for problem solving, the fewer occasions there are to refine your understanding of the prospect's needs and refine your proposal at the same time.

Farmers know they must "make hay while the sun shines." Sales pros know the sun sets on them the minute they deliver the proposal. You can't stop the rotation of the earth and alter the time of nature's sunset, but you have more control than you think over when the sun sets on your selling.

I know you're eager to get the order (I am, too). And I know your boss is even more eager than you are (that blast of hot air from over your shoulder is the boss breathing down your neck). But lock on to this truth—and show it to your boss, if necessary: Delivering the proposal sooner rarely gets you the answer any sooner… unless you really don't care whether the answer is yes or no! For those of us seeking a yes, the strategy must be to hold the proposal back until the decision is ready… to keep fine-tuning it until the prospect is ready to sign.

But often, trouble begins early and quite innocently. The prospect tells you she's busy and just needs your proposal or your bid. Because you know you should always be focused on the customer's needs, and her professed need right now is for you to turn that bid around and submit it fast, you head back to the office fully focused on the task. She means no harm, and she's probably as clueless as you are that her request to get your proposal ASAP is neither in her best interest nor yours. Once in your cubicle, you set out to prove to the prospect how well you can perform without bugging her, how much you know and can do without consulting her, and how much of the burden you're willing to lift from her shoulders and scratch off her to-do list.

How could that be wrong?

You're building the proposal in the dark. You're in the dark about the prospect's real needs, about how she's handling the problem currently, and about how others in the organization are affected. You're in the dark about what constraints the company may be dealing with, about what other resources it can tap to make your solution even stronger, and about who holds the purse strings. Most especially, you're in the dark about what you're in the dark about!

The faster you build and deliver the proposal, the fewer opportunities you have to interface with all the decision influencers, the fewer occasions you have to solicit feedback about key elements of the solution you're proposing, the fewer chances you have to gain acceptance for each of the pieces and parts of your plan, the fewer openings you have to float a trial balloon about fees and costs. When you work this way, you're putting yourself behind the eight ball, filling your proposal with guesses about what will fly.

The pros I know are just as eager as you are for the orders. But they don't pop the proposal prematurely. They know that a powerful proposal nails the order far more often than a fast one does. They understand that what makes their proposals powerful is that, unlike in the Cracker Jack box, there's no surprise inside. Their prospects have already seen the ingredients and agreed that each ingredient should be in their proposals. Their prospects get exactly the proposals they expect, seek, and desire… so it's "no surprise" that they often buy on the spot.

Even in this era when so much seems to move at warp speed, the tale of the tortoise and the hare make a fine metaphor for how to run the race in sales. Slow down the proposal—and you'll speed up the yes! ∎

Steve Marx is founder of The Center for Sales Strategy. For biographical and business information, see page 269.

Editor's Note: Lee Salz spent 20 years in the sales trenches selling, managing and leading sales organizations. Today he consults, speaks and trains sales teams to increase performance. His clients range from small businesses to Fortune 500 companies. Use his advice to ace a little-known but highly important test.

Will You Pass the Flinch Test?
by Lee B. Salz

After a lengthy buying process, the time has come to submit pricing. You've spent countless hours formulating a glorious proposal that details your comprehensive solution. Proud of your accomplishment, you present the proposal to the buyer. Skipping the sections about your company and your solution, she flips right to the pricing page and says, "Oh my gosh, I didn't think it would be this expensive!"

You've just been given the flinch test. This is the test procurement agents and other professional buyers give to salespeople when they provide pricing. "Wow! You're 25% higher than your competition." These pros are trained to react with surprise so that they can see if you're confident in your price. The flinch test is nothing more than a straightforward negotiation tactic. Often, buyers will overstate the price difference and if you can do some quick math, you'll see that the differential is bogus.

I can recall a time when I was told that we were 50% higher than the competition. When I reviewed the numbers, this meant that the competitor was losing 18% based on the fixed costs that we both had. It was highly unlikely that the competitor was signing up for this kind of an account. When I asked the procurement agent about that figure again, he flinched and we ultimately won the business.

How to Pass the Test

The key to passing the flinch test is to respond with confidence in your price. If you don't believe you're providing a fair, competitive price for the solution, my question is, why are you presenting it? One would hope that you have integrity, so why present something you don't believe in?

Here are some responses that will cause you to fail the flinch test:

- "What price were you looking for?"
- "I'll ask my manager if we can do better."
- "How about if I take 10% off?"

The reason these responses fail is that they create trust issues with the prospect. Were you trying to rip them off with the price you presented? One of two things is true. Either you were trying to rip them off or you believe you provided a fair price. What other option is there? Some will say that they were preparing for a negotiation. That's a fair point; however, it's a terrible negotiation strategy to give the appearance that you'll drop your price the first moment someone balks. That approach gives the impression that you were trying to gouge them.

Most negotiations end at the middle ground. They wanted five; you wanted 10 and settled at 7.5. That seems logical. However, if you lower your price too soon, the middle ground is lower. In the same scenario, if you dropped to eight right off the bat, the middle becomes 6.5. As I mentioned, you have to manage the negotiation such that the middle is not lower than an acceptable price for your company.

Successful salespeople have a planned response for the flinch test. They don't expect a prospect to respond with excitement about a price. They anticipate shock and have a process to handle it. Here are their secrets:

- **Set expectations upfront.** Early in the buying process, set the expectation that you are not the low price provider. "To be clear, our company is rarely the low bidder, does that mean that we won't be working together on this project?" If they say no, you are set for the later phases of the process. If they say yes, at least you haven't invested a ton of time in an account that you won't win. If you're going to lose, lose early.
- **Don't flinch.** Instead, say something like, "I'm not surprised by your reaction; I get that a lot. As I mentioned at the outset, we're rarely the low bidder."
- **Seek to understand.** Seek first to understand. Do so by asking, "When you say that you're shocked by the price, which part is surprising?"
- **Reinforce your position.** Reinforce your position by saying something like, "Since we're rarely the low price provider, what do you

think our 1000 clients see that leads them to pay a little more to work with us?"

Many years ago, I had the opportunity to participate in procurement training. (Think of it as sales training for buyers.) After the session, I had an interesting conversation with the trainer. Here's what he told me:

"For 25 years, salespeople have asked me for coaching on the price of their proposals because I was the head of procurement for my company. I told each one of them the same thing: 'Provide us with the best price that you feel good about giving and either way, you win.' I always got a puzzled expression from that. Then I'd say, 'Let me explain: If we award the business to you at that price, you're happy. If we award the business to someone else at a lower price, you're happy as well because you wouldn't have been happy to support the account at that price point.'"

To share a little secret, I use the flinch test all the time when I buy. It's amazing how quickly salespeople drop their prices. I bet I've saved my family 20% across the board for all our spending just with that test. It's no wonder that professional buyers use this. I often wonder how many commission dollars are lost just because the salespeople flinch. How may commission dollars have you lost because you flinched? ■

Lee B. Salz is president of Sales Architects. For biographical and business information, see page 272.

Editor's Note: Julie Thomas has been using, teaching and coaching ValueSelling techniques for over 15 years. She learned the system as a technology sales rep and subsequently taught it to her company's sales forces. Later she joined ValueSelling Associates as CEO. The company's Fortune 1000 clients include Cisco Systems, Dun & Bradstreet, Google, Oracle and Toshiba. She explains how to reach top decision-makers.

Calling on the Power to Win the Business
by Julie Thomas

If you can't sell to someone who can't buy—why do you keep trying? My company works with salespeople every day. Regardless of the industry our clients operate in, the products or services they represent, or their levels of experience, we see a common challenge: "How do I call higher, and can I win the business without executive involvement?"

Let's break down this dilemma. How do you call higher and when do you know if you're calling on the power who can actually buy?

One of these questions is easier to answer: Can I win the business without executive involvement? Without sounding trite, the answer is "sometimes" and "maybe." Sometimes you can win without having access to the ultimate decision maker. Sometimes, you get lucky and a sponsor or coach can sell internally, on your behalf, and that will be sufficient to gain the business.

However, the reality is that more often than not, you will need to do the selling rather than let someone do your work for you. While you're always happy to be lucky—luck is not a sales strategy!

Selling Straight to the Top

In today's complex business environment, it's more important than ever to identify who can and will ultimately make the decision, who will execute that decision, and then sell directly to those individuals.

In every company, there are various levels of decision makers, each with different perspectives and degrees of influence. Sometimes you'll call on the individuals who use your products and services, other times you'll call on people who specify them but don't necessarily use them. Sometimes you'll call on the people who make the buying decisions, yet ultimately there's someone else who has overriding decision making authority or influence. Those are the individuals you need to identify and gain access to, for your prospect to be fully qualified. Typically, these are the senior executives whose responsibilities are to resolve bigger issues of their companies, whose opinions carry enormous impact throughout their organizations and who can access the funds to make purchases.

Identify the Power

The first step is to find out who that person is. The number one barrier to selling at the top is often the salesperson. Whether you're afraid to rock the boat with your current contacts or you're afraid of asking difficult questions that may push you out of your comfort zone, it's interesting how many times the power person is not even identified. If you don't ever identify that individual, how can you put a plan in place to gain access?

The key to identifying the power begins with understanding your prospect's organization and buying process. You can certainly take steps to identify the key executives and managers in the organization through research and publicly available information. Many services also provide information specifically to sales professionals, so you can understand the hierarchy and official organization.

Beyond that, every company has a unique history, culture, and set of challenges, competitors and goals. More often than not, the company's approach to this is determined by the CEO and the company's executive team. As a salesperson wanting to earn your way to the top, you have a responsibility to learn as much about the company as you can. By demonstrating knowledge of the company's situation, you'll build your credibility in the eyes of the senior executive.

Remember, all companies have both formal and informal power structures and influences. Don't assume that the most senior person in the organization is always the individual who has the power. In your research, uncover the informal and political power bases and understand how decisions are made and executed.

It's important to find out what external factors are impacting your prospect. Focus on both the market and financial issues. Talk to employees, read the company's annual report, do a news search, and be a detective. Find out everything you can about the company and its strategy.

Triangulation is a process you can use to identify the ultimate decision maker. The concept is that you don't accept one person's view of the decision-making and procurement process as the whole truth. We ask multiple individuals for their perspectives:

- What is the process by which this decision will be made?
- Who is impacted by this implementation?
- What is their role in the process?
- Could anyone change this decision once it's made?

By asking a similar set of questions to multiple individuals, you will get a clearer picture of not only the actual power person, but also the entire process.

How Do You Gain Access to the Power?

Once power is identified, the next challenge is how to gain access. There are a number of strategies to consider when selling at the top.

- **Consider the executive's perspective.** Why would this executive want to meet with you? While you can articulate why you want to meet with the executive, you're not as clear on what's in it for him. Can you articulate concise, logical statements that would entice the executive's involvement?

  The most important elements in selling at the top are: credibility, professionalism, and the ability to position your capabilities as a solution to your customer's biggest issues.

- **Find a sponsor who can pave the way to the executive.** As insulated as senior executives are, there are always people who have access to them and whose opinion they value. A senior executive will be more likely to give you his time if someone he respects recommends that he talk to you or meet with you. By gaining access through a mutual contact, you not only increase the chance of having his attention, you also establish credibility for yourself and your message.

  Use common points of influence to get the senior executive's attention and interest. Make access through dealers, customers, suppliers and employees. Use your existing network to gain access and build enthusiasm and interest for your message. Ask them to arrange a meeting for you with the senior executive. If they won't do this, ask if you can use their names in the initial point of contact with the executive.

- **Bargain for access.** For those situations where you know you don't currently have access to power, consider bargaining for access. Use partnering strategies with your coaches and sponsors to negotiate access to the appropriate level. When a request is made of you for resources, time, testimonials, demonstrations or anything that would educate your prospect, use that opportunity to ask for something in return. Often a successful strategy for gaining access is to offer a peer-to-peer meeting and bring in one of your executives.

Finally, not identifying and gaining access to power in your sales cycles puts you at risk. Begin by being honest with yourself. Ask yourself: "Am I at risk of selling to someone who can't buy?" or "Am I at risk of wasting limited resources and time with individuals who can't ultimately do business with me?" and "Am I at risk for ruining my personal credibility by forecasting business that is not fully qualified?" ∎

Julie Thomas is president and CEO of ValueSelling Associates. For biographical and business information, see page 273.

Editor's Note: I am proud to count Gerhard Gschwandtner as my close friend and mentor. He is the founder and president of Selling Power magazine. In 1981, he wrote the magazine's first article in his garage office. Short on money, but big on dreams, he had no idea how to build a publishing company. A native of Austria, English is his third language. Despite the odds, Gerhard turned his dream into reality. Today Selling Power has circulation of over 120,000 in 67 countries. Here he shows you how to use stories to close sales.

The Story Close
by Gerhard Gschwandtner

Good storytellers are good sales closers. They know how to captivate the imaginations of their prospects and let the story illustrate the selling point in a most elegant and persuasive way.

The process of storytelling is mysterious and little understood by amateur salespeople. They often feel that telling a story may not be perceived as businesslike. Or they underestimate the tremendous psychological powers of a good story.

The three benefits of a good story are:

- **Stories relax.** Your story is bound to change the emotional climate of the conversation in a pleasant way. The more relaxed your prospect becomes, the more agreeable he will be to your proposal.
- **Stories captivate.** Your story will capture your prospect's full attention. Her mind will focus only on your story, and chances are that she'll forget her preoccupations about that purchase.
- **Stories drive home closing points.** The characters in a story will do the selling for you. All you have to do is set the stage, unfold the plot, and let the characters close the deal for you.

Here's an example of how a satisfied customer story can be used to reassure a prospect:

> "Mrs. Brown, I'm glad you mentioned that. You'll be pleased to hear that many of our customers have used this product for more than eight years without major problems.

"You may know Mr. Harvey Kirshner, the chairman of Interstate Inc. He was convinced that our machine would not make it through the first week on the job. [Pause]

"That was three years ago. He has since bought seven more. He told me just last month that buying our product was the smartest decision he ever made. I know that you'll be glad you made the decision to go with us. Shall we go over the details?"

Develop Stories that Close

The most effective stories that sell are unembellished, satisfied customer stories. They can help reassure your prospect, prove the value of your service, enhance the quality of your product, or lead to a larger order than you expected.

When you collect success stories, get every single detail you can. Describe the customer's struggle before he bought your product. Explain what happened when your product was first used. Record your customer's positive comments. Write out the details of your story, and be sure it's short, clear and interesting. Rehearse telling your story with family members or friends before you use it to close your sale. Write your sales closing stories on 3- by-5-inch cards. Develop at least five good sales closing stories.

Some psychologists claim that we tend to re-experience a sense of childhood wonder and amazement when we listen to a story. The astute storyteller uses this little-known fact to sell his ideas.

See how this satisfied customer story is used to justify the price:

"Mr. Smith, I'm glad you mentioned price because that's exactly why you should buy from us. Last week, I visited with Ms. Biddle. You probably know her from the Chamber of Commerce meeting, don't you?"

[Wait for reply]

"Well, when Ms. Biddle sold her machine, she got 80% of her original investment back. She had used the machine for over three very productive years. [Pause]

"You see, when you figure the total value of this machine, you need to deduct the resale value. Since our resale value is expected to be much higher, just as in Ms. Biddle's case, your total cost will be much lower.

"I assume that you're looking for a machine that maintains its value for a long time. Am I correct?"

[Wait for a reply]

"I'm glad we agree. When would you need delivery?"

Your Action Steps

Interview satisfied clients and record the interviews. Get their permission to play back their comments to new prospects. (Ask them to sign a release form—check with your legal department on how to obtain one.) Bring your interviews to a professional audio recording studio. Ask the sound engineer to edit your satisfied customer interviews in a series of short stories and splice them together so you'll end up with a single audio file. Let your recording tell the story of your success. ■

Gerhard Gschwandtner is founder and publisher of Selling Power *magazine. For biographical and business information, see page 265.*

Editor's Note: Mark Hunter has been in sales for over 30 years. After 20 years in sales management for three different Fortune 100 companies, Mark launched his own sales training company. He has since trained thousands of sales professionals and business leaders. His clients include American Express, BP, Coca Cola, and Unilever.

Shut up and Sell!
by Mark Hunter

Contrary to popular belief, to be a successful salesperson, it doesn't matter how much you know about your product or service. It also doesn't matter how much of an industry expert you are. It doesn't even matter how great your mother thinks you are. The only thing that really matters to be successful in selling is your ability to shut up and listen.

I'm sure you know how important it is to get the customer talking, so it's imperative that you have an arsenal of great questions to ask. Despite this knowledge, most salespeople overstate the amount of time they allow the customer to talk. The many interviews I've conducted over the years with customers and salespeople alike confirm this reality. Therefore, I suggest you take a step back and consider your sales presentation.

Keep it Short

To talk less means you have to ask questions that truly engage the customer. However, this doesn't mean you need to develop complex questions. Instead, the best tactic is to ask shorter ones. Long questions tend to result in short answers, while short questions will generally result in long answers. An example of a great short question is, "Why?" In my opinion, there isn't a better follow-up question you can ask after the customer has shared some information with you. Consider how your customers would respond to other short questions like, "Can you elaborate on that?" or "Could you explain more?" These shorter questions elicit detailed responses and that's just what you want. On the other hand, asking complex questions often tends to perplex customers. Because they're not sure what you're looking for, they're forced to respond with, "What did you say?" Questions should not be your way of showing your customers that you are an expert. Save that for your statements.

A Formula for Success

When preparing your sales presentation, you should not talk for more than 20 seconds at a time without asking a question. The question you ask should be one directed at the comments you've just made. By doing so, you're checking with the customer to see if he understood what you just shared with him. Again, this is something many salespeople overlook. They get caught up in sharing their expertise and the features of their products or services with their customers and forget all about what their customers are thinking. Even if your product or service requires a complex presentation, you should still follow this rule. Whether you're selling software, high value medical equipment, or technical tools, it's essential to check your client's understanding by asking a question every 20 seconds.

Be Prepared

Your goal on any sales call is to talk only 20% of the time. To help ensure that this happens, you have to plan ahead. Before you start developing your sales presentation, create your list of questions. Most salespeople spend a substantial portion of their time developing their presentations and, at the last minute, develop their lists of questions. Consider that if you expect to have a 20-minute presentation, you should formulate 40 questions (two questions per minute). Even though you may not use all 40, you'll definitely be more prepared. In addition, you'll be able to pick and choose which ones you want to ask. If you remember to ask short questions, you'll ensure that the customer is doing most of the talking. That way you'll learn valuable information that will help you better understand the customer's needs.

Up Your Questioning Ante

If you want to move your questioning process to the next level, ask at least 20 questions that will help your customer feel the pain his problem is causing his business. By doing so, he will be much more open to receiving your solution. For example, if you're selling computer backup systems, you might ask, "Can you explain to me what happens when your data is lost?" This short, concise question is designed to get the customer thinking about the risks he faces. Furthermore, the beauty of this type of question is that no matter what the customer's response is, some good follow-up questions will naturally arise.

By adhering to these guidelines, you will be able to see dramatic results in the number of sales you are able to close. As simple as it sounds, the more you shut up, the more you'll sell, and the easiest way to achieve this goal is by asking more, short questions. So, shut up and sell! ■

Mark Hunter is known as "The Sales Hunter." For biographical and business information, see page 266.

Editor's Note: For over 15 years, Colleen Francis has studied the business habits of the top 10 percent of sales professionals in organizations of all sizes from Fortune 500 companies to small businesses. She uses this knowledge along with her experience as a top producer in the technology and life insurance industries in her acclaimed sales training program. Her clients include large sales organizations like Adecco, Corel, Dow Chemical, and HelmsBrisco. Her insights will help you make an impressive opening statement.

Make Your First Impression Your Best Impression
by Colleen Francis

In my line of work, I hear a lot of opening statements. Some I hear during sessions with clients. Others come from unsuspecting salespeople who call me at work or home. Sadly, the majority seem designed to create resistance rather than relationships.

A great line opens doors, which can land you more business. A bad one will cause those doors to shut faster than you can say, "Hi, I'm Tim, and have I got a deal for you!"

I think the reason so many salespeople use such disastrous opening statements is that they spend so little time preparing what they'll say. Most sales experts say that we have between four and 30 seconds to create interest, yet many of my clients confess that they don't even begin to think about their openings until they're actually dialing the phone!

The little things can make the difference between success and failure. A few awkward or uncertain words, a mispronounced name, an inappropriate question or simply being under-prepared or long-winded can create a bad first impression, and cost you the sale. Something as simple as eliminating "How are you?" from your opening can yield as much as a 25% increase in your cold-calling success.

How do you craft a winning opening statement? First, recognize what's wrong with your existing opener, and then take the appropriate steps to correct it.

Get Rid of the Clunkers

Start by pruning your sales vocabulary. Say you finally get a decision-maker on the phone and you lead off with:

"Hi, this is _____ from _____. We're in the business of _____. Are you the person who handles that?"

I think you'll agree that this isn't exactly a killer opening. What makes it so bad? An opener like this announces your intention to try to sell something, triggering a defensive posture and a negative frame of mind—you know, the one that says, "Darn, it's a salesperson, how do I get him off the phone?"

Instead, determine the right person to talk to *before* you pick up the phone. Start by reviewing the corporate website, getting a referral or calling other departments (Sales, HR or the Help Desk) to determine the name of the decision-maker.

If you do call the wrong person, he'll let you know before you even have to ask. Avoid using an awkward clunker like this one and you won't jeopardize the relationship you're attempting to build. Remember, your job on your first call is to peak interest and get a dialogue going—*not* to sell something.

Tailor Your Opening

OK, so what should you do? When the decision-maker answers, go directly into something like:

"Hi Chris, this is _____ from _____. Our manufacturing clients tell us that we help them _____ by _____. How are you currently _____?"

Or:

"Hi Chris, this is _____ with _____. We work with (CEOs, IT Directors, etc.) to help them _____. I understand that you may be _____ and there's a possibility we may be able to help you _____. Does it make sense for me to ask you a few questions now to see if we should talk further?"

These statements are very generic. I suggest that you tailor or customize your opening with information you collect through conversations with other people in the company or by reviewing their websites or quarterly 10Q SEC reports (if their firms are publicly traded on a US stock exchange).

Touch on results in which they'll be interested. Scour the local and national newspapers for stories that include or affect your prospects and use that news in your opening. When you show that you know a little bit about your prospects, they'll be more likely to engage in meaningful conversations with you.

Remember: Potential customers will always be more impressed with how much you know about them than with how much you know about your product. Here are a few more specific examples of successful opening lines:

"Hi Chris, this is Colleen from ABC Staffing. We work with VPs of HR to help them find the right talent for their organizations quickly while guaranteeing the right skill match. I understand you're expanding your Toronto organization and there may be a possibility that we can help you with your recruiting. Does it make sense for me to ask you a few questions now to see if we should talk in more detail later?"

"Hi Chris. This is Colleen with ABC Fencing. Our manufacturing clients tell us that we save them money each year in lost and damaged goods by implementing secure perimeter fencing at their factory sites. How are you planning to secure the new plant you're building in Baltimore?"

One last note: If you're a new rep taking over a patch of existing clients in a territory, don't call and say, "Hi this is _____. I'm the new rep. Can we meet?" Instead, study the file, create two to three specific questions about the customer that show you're genuinely interested, and start your call with:

"Hi, this is _____ from _____. I was reviewing your file, and I had a couple questions about _____. Is now a good time to go over these with you, or should we schedule another time in the future to talk?"

Telling customers that you're the new rep puts your interests first. The statement above puts their interests first, which are always going to be more important (and more interesting) to them than yours.

Give your customers a chance to ask who you are. If they care, they will ask, giving you a chance to satisfy their curiosity with an answer they requested. Yes, it's a subtle change. But it makes a huge difference in how many positive relationships you build and how successful you become. ■

Colleen Francis is president of Engage Selling Solutions. For biographical and business information, see page 264.

Editor's Note: Dave Kahle's sales credentials are impressive. He's been the number one salesperson in the country for two different companies in two different industries. As a general manager of a start-up, he pushed growth from $10,000 monthly to over $200,000 in only 38 months. Known as The Growth Coach, Dave has been training sales professionals since 1988. This valuable lesson explains how to keep going in difficult times.

Staying Motivated in Challenging Times
by Dave Kahle

Sales is an emotional roller coaster, and unless you figure out how to manage those emotions and keep yourself motivated, you'll have a difficult time succeeding. This is particularly true during a downturn. The economy struggles and unemployment rises. Many companies cut back, there are fewer jobs available, and pressures to perform are greater than ever. It's easy to lose our motivation.

However, even though the world around us may be dreary and depressing, that in no way reduces our personal need to do the best we can. That means we all have a responsibility to stay motivated.

It is amazing what a difference a few degrees of attitude adjustment can make in our performance. Try this little exercise. Tell yourself these things: "Business is terrible. All of my customers are struggling. Nobody wants to see me, and when they do, it's just to complain." Now wallow in those thoughts for a moment, and note how much energy and enthusiasm you have.

Now, think the opposite: "I have great opportunities. My customers need me more today than ever. I have valuable solutions for them. It's a great time to have this job." Roll those around in your mind for a while. Note how much energy and enthusiasm you have.

As you reflect on this exercise, it's clear that your energy, enthusiasm and drive to succeed come as a result of your thoughts. Here is one of the most powerful truths known to mankind: *You can control your thoughts.*

Going Beyond "Positive Thinking"

Succeeding in difficult times depends a great deal on our motivation. Staying motivated requires us to take charge of our thoughts.

I've heard dozens of salespeople say, "I've tried positive thinking. It just isn't me." I agree that it is difficult to patch a bunch of positive thoughts on top of an essentially negative personality. The issue is deeper than that. Let's, therefore, examine the deeper issues.

At the heart of motivation lies a pair of powerful beliefs that you must embrace if you are going to successfully motivate yourself. Without a whole-hearted commitment to these foundational beliefs, all the techniques and tactics for self-motivation are like spreading wallpaper over crumbling plaster. It may hold temporarily, but it is soon going to deteriorate into a mess.

Here's the first foundational principle: You must believe that you can do better than you are now doing. The second is this: You must accept that it is your responsibility to do so.

It's simple and commonsense, but, the more I observe people and sales-people specifically, the more convinced I am that the majority of people do not share these core beliefs. Rather, they are in the habit of making excuses for their situation. They believe fate, not their actions, determines their success. They believe success is for someone else, not them. They never really grab unto the first of these foundational principles.

Others believe that they can achieve greater degrees of success. They embrace the first principle, intellectually, but they never internalize the second. They become content with their situation and remain in pre-established comfort zones. They look at their manager as the person who is responsible for their success, or lack thereof. Maybe it's their parent's fault, or their spouse's, or... the list goes on.

Whether you are struggling with a lack of energy that accompanies a bad day, or you're depressed and frustrated with your lack of progress on a larger scale, examine your core beliefs first. If you really accept these two principles, you have the keystone in place to become highly motivated.

Having said that, here are a couple proven techniques you can use to keep yourself motivated day-to-day.

Have a Compelling Purpose

Have something you are working to accomplish. This can be an important and compelling goal like saving enough money for a down payment on a house. When you are working toward something like that, your emotions of the moment tend to be a lower priority than your drive to achieve. If you are trying to make money for a home for your family, so what if you're tired or depressed? You get out and do it.

The same is true for having a compelling purpose. I believe that every salesperson should be able to articulate clearly his or her purpose in life. I once began a ten-week sales training program with a requirement that everyone write a two-sentence "life purpose." Why? Because it gives power and focus to everything you do. In your job as a salesperson, there will many difficult times when things don't go your way. You may lose a big deal, or be unable to get anyone to return your calls. At times like these, it helps to view them within the context of a larger perspective: your life purpose.

Choose Your Thoughts

Proactively put positive thoughts into your mind. Make a point of taking charge of your mind and the kind of thoughts you choose to think. Wise and thoughtful people for ages have discovered an extremely powerful principle: Your actions arise from your thoughts, and you can choose your thoughts.

Controlling and managing your thoughts is one of the basic tenants of Zen Buddhism, for example. In the Christian context, the apostle Paul said, "Be transformed by the renewing of your mind." Philosophers, educators, and thinkers of every generation conclude the same thing.

But the power of this truth is not reserved just for philosophers. Salespeople can use it as well. The reason you may feel depressed or anxious is because you are thinking depressing or anxious thoughts. Change your thoughts, and you can change your feelings. Change your emotions, and you can change your behavior. Change your behavior and you can change your results. It's not as difficult as it may sound.

Take Action

Do this: invest in a couple of audio programs filled with good, positive stuff, or find something at the local library. As you drive between appointments and on your way home from work, listen to those tapes or CDs. You'll find yourself thinking positive thoughts. Those positive thoughts will lead to a more positive attitude. That attitude will manifest in more focused actions. Those actions will lead to better results.

There is no limit to the amount of positive, educational material available to you. If you are not regularly exposing yourself to some of this, it is because you are choosing to *not* be motivated.

Succeeding in difficult times requires you to take charge of your motivation. Now is the time to take this most important step to becoming a true professional. ■

Dave Kahle is president of The DaCo Corporation. For biographical and business information, see page 267.

Editor's Note: Jim Kasper has more than 26 years' experience in sales, sales management, marketing and training. He's been an assistant professor of marketing at Regis University for over ten years. He explains how to handle an objection you'll hear more often during difficult times.

"I Don't Have the Budget"
by Jim Kasper

You've done your homework, the prospect likes what you're offering, and after all of your hard work, you see yourself walking out with an order. You're ready to close. Then you hear the dreaded, "I really like what I see, but I just don't have the budget." In a tough economy, this objection can happen all too often.

There are times when the customer really does not have a budget. The reasons for this may be:

- The customer may be too small to afford your services.
- It may be the end of the budget or fiscal year.
- Business may be particularly slow.
- Business may be good, but cash flow is slow.
- The company is cutting expenses to appease the analysts.

How do you determine if these are legitimate reasons when they come from your customer's mouth? Always ask open-ended questions about the budget as part of your normal fact-finding mission in the sales interview. By doing this, you bring out budgetary restraints at the beginning of the sales cycle, not the end. Preface your questions with the statement, "Ms. Prospect, I have a few background questions to ask you that will help us determine the most effective way to proceed." Then, ask:

- "Tell me about your fiscal year."
- "How has business been lately?"
- "What type of seasonality do you experience?"
- "When was the last time you made this type of purchase? How did it go?"

In other words, predetermine the fiscal condition of your prospect or customer before she uses one of these conditions as an objection.

Upon hearing, "It's not in my budget," consider the following suggestions to help you sell your prospect:

- **Establish a financial proposition.** A temporary personnel placement agency, specializing in the insurance industry, was approached by an insurance trade association to sponsor a member educational program. Although the association was a prime target for prospects, the cost of the program was thousands of dollars more than the firm expected. The small firm did not have the budget. How did the association close the deal?

  The insurance association representative asked the placement agency owner how many dollars the average insurance association member spent with the placement agency annually. Then the association representative figured it would only take three new customers to pay back the sponsorship fee. Next, the association representative helped the agency develop a plan to obtain six new customers by sponsoring the event.

- **Be a budget planner.** In January, a large financial services organization solicited proposals from several sales training firms. When the successful proposal was identified, their CFO realized the cost of the training was more than remained in the training budget for the fiscal year. The fiscal budget started in June. What did the successful sales training company do to close the financial institution?

  Realizing that the customer did not have the buget; the training company agreed to aid the financial institution in planning its next fiscal year's training budget. The training company literally became a planning partner with the financial organization.

- **"I guarantee it."** In today's fiercely competitive market, sometimes prospects play the "It's not in my budget" card just to see what concessions they can get out of the deal. When appropriate, and when you know who you're doing business with, try the guarantee approach. Many companies offer a performance guarantee to their customers calling for a product or service to meet a certain benchmark by a specific date.

Here's an example. A sales training company was asked to make a training proposal to a major electronic manufacturing firm. During the initial interview, the firm said that the training was not budgeted and they were looking for some creative approaches to "sell" the program to senior management. The training company then offered a guarantee that within 60 days, the program was to provide a specific R.O.I. If that R.O.I was not met, the cost of the program would then be refunded. When presented with that solution, management promptly allocated the funds.

Keep these suggestions in mind when you are presented with the no budget response:

- Never, ever automatically offer a price concession.
- Don't instinctively accept the response at face value; always probe for the hidden reasons.
- Ask yourself, "Can they really afford what I'm selling?"
- Ask the prospect, "What are your future plans to buy?"
- Ask yourself, "How badly do I want this business? When? At what cost?"

Following these guidelines will give you insight on your next step and help you determine whether to pursue the opportunity or withdraw and head down the road to your next prospect. ∎

Jim Kasper is CEO and founder of Interactive Resource Group. For biographical and business information, see page 267.

Editor's Note: Wendy Weiss is a leading authority on lead generation and new business development. For more than 20 years, in good economies and bad, she's helped businesses sell more by phone. Her clients include large sales organizations like ADP, Avon and Sprint. Use her advice to keep selling during difficult times.

Five Tips for Selling in Tough Times
by Wendy Weiss

In a recession, you cannot open a newspaper or turn on the television without hearing about the economy, the market, bankruptcy and tough times. It is a scary, depressing time filled with doom and gloom. What's happening with the economy? What will happen with your sales? With your business? With your job? Will you survive?

Let's face facts: we are in difficult economic times and things will probably get worse before they get better. At this juncture, business owners and sales professionals have only two courses of action available to them:

- **Option 1.** Tighten your belts, cut costs, increase discounts and accept lower sales revenues and a shorter, smaller bottom line. Hunker down and hope that you will survive till good times come around again.
- **Option 2.** Sharpen, refine and increase your prospecting and sales skills, and look for new opportunity.

Yes, look for new opportunity. While other business owners and sales professionals are busily tightening their belts, cutting costs, increasing discounts and accepting lower sales and lower sales revenue, opportunity is there for those who take action.

Most companies, including your competition, will be doing less and doing *with* less: They'll be cutting out marketing. They'll stop prospecting. They will discount. Moreover, they'll be scared to death to approach current customers for more business for fear of alienating and losing those customers altogether.

Because of the way most companies react to an economic crisis, this is actually a good time to build your pipeline, win new business and expand your market. The key to flourishing during difficult times is not to simply work harder; it's to work smarter.

Here are some actions that you can start today to insure that you maintain your sales and grow:

- **Increase your sales skills.** Prospecting and selling are communication skills and, as with any communication skill, they can be learned and improved upon. If you are not closing sales, it could be the economy; but it could also be that your skills need sharpening. Great sales skills will enable you to take advantage of the opportunities that do exist. Great sales skills will enable you to close sales even during difficult times. Conversely, not having the requisite skills will allow potential sales to slip through your fingers. If business is really slow, use some of that extra time for education.

- **Increase the number of qualified prospects you reach.** In difficult economic times many companies, business owners and entrepreneurs cut costs by eliminating marketing and prospecting efforts. This is a huge mistake. While this is probably not the time to be spending large sums of money on brand new initiatives, it is imperative to continue low-cost marketing and prospecting activities. Without prospecting, sales do not grow.

  One of the best and least expensive sales and marketing activities you can initiate is to use the telephone. Call potential new customers to introduce yourself. Call existing customers to sell them more products and services or gather referrals. Calling your customers has the added benefit of helping to maintain customer loyalty, which is imperative in times like these.

- **Make inroads on your competition's customers.** When times are tough customer loyalty is shaky. This could be the perfect time to increase your market share by targeting your competition's customers. Perhaps you offer another product or service that your competition does not. Perhaps your offering is less expensive or adds value in a way that your competitor's does not. This is an opportune time to introduce your competitions' customers to you, your company and your products and services.

- **Find new applications and markets for your products and services.** Can your products and services be used in nontraditional ways? Are there other markets that are potentially in need of your products and services? Now is the time to explore these new applications and markets. If you find that your traditional market is drying up, look elsewhere.
- **Find new ways to help.** The easiest sales to close are sales to existing customers. They already have a relationship with you. They know you and they trust you. Go back to your customers with new applications, add-ons and improvements for your existing products and services. Find new ways to help. Your customers will respond.

These five tips all have one thing in common: They require action. You cannot allow fear and anxiety about the economy to paralyze you. Instead, focus on what you can accomplish and take steps to do so.

In a difficult economy, it is imperative that you reach out to new prospects and to existing customers. Don't be one of the many who wait with their fingers crossed for the economy to improve. Instead, keep taking proactive steps to build your sales pipeline and generate sales revenue. This will help you weather any economic crisis and come out of it successful and well positioned for even more growth in the future. ■

Wendy Weiss is known as The Queen of Cold Calling. For biographical and business information, see page 274.

Editor's Note: Mark Hunter a.k.a. The Sales Hunter knows about landing "big game" accounts. He's spent 20 years working for three Fortune 100 companies where he managed sales territories worth more than $200 million. At one company, he directed more than 200 salespeople and $700 million in annual sales. He shows you how to respond when your prospect roars, "I want a discount!"

Price Cutting is for Sissies
by Mark Hunter

Sales is all about closing the deal, and in order to achieve that goal, a prospect and a sale professional must agree on a purchase price. At one time or another, we've all had our prices challenged. As much as we may like to consider ourselves great closers, in reality, many of us are sissies when it comes to this important skill. We may boast about never discounting our products, but when challenged on price, we fold faster than a cheap umbrella on a windy day.

Consider this scenario: You're on the verge of closing the biggest deal of your career. Doing so will put a nice, fat commission check in your hands and win you kudos from everyone in the company. Here comes the curve ball: the customer tells you he expects a discount and, to top it off, you find out about an equally qualified competitor who is willing to undercut your price.

You have two options: hold the line—don't reduce your price and keep your profit potential intact; or cut your price and take a lower margin for the sake of landing the big order. Which do you choose? The tendency for many salespeople is to concede to a discount. But, by being prepared as to why your product or service can fill your prospect's need, you can avoid caving in to the pressure of the moment.

Low Price Isn't Always the Best Option

To persevere, your self-assurance is critical. Be confident in what you say. More importantly, make sure your customer is certain of the benefits he will receive from working with you. He may be looking for the cheapest price, but what good is a low price if the product doesn't deliver? When the customer requests a price discount, respond by asking him how he intends to use your product or service, and what he expects to gain from it. Your goal is for him to express the pain he will experience if what he buys doesn't help him accomplish what he wants. You also want him to express the need he has for your type of product or service. Listen, and then explain how your product or service can alleviate that pain and best fill his need.

The worst thing you can do when a customer is looking for a price break is to give in. Unfortunately, if you can't confidently communicate your price, you will often cave in. To overcome this problem, you need to understand, in real terms, how your buyer can benefit from your product or service—from his perspective.

For example, if I'm taking a trip and my destination is 1,000 miles away, I have several options. I could hitchhike, which would cost me virtually nothing, but wouldn't guarantee when I'd arrive. I could drive my car, limiting my immediate costs to the necessary gasoline, but my trip could take several days. Or, I could fly, which would probably be my highest-priced option, but would be the fastest.

Your goal in selling should be to help ensure the success of your customers. You can see from my travel example that the cheapest option is not reliable, nor would it save time. In addition, most people wouldn't want to take several days to drive to and from their destinations. Therefore, because of the time it will save, the best option is to fly, even though it's probably the most expensive choice. Since time is of the essence in many industries, its value is worth the extra money. Cutting the price is clearly not beneficial or efficient for the client.

A Losing Proposition

Often salespeople will give a discount on an initial order because they believe they can make it up on the next order. However, there is no way to regain the lost revenue. Once the customer has accepted a lower price, that amount becomes his new level of expectation. Any other price is seen as an increase.

When a customer requests a discounted price, remember that giving one is an immediate reduction to your total profit. Depending on how drastic a price cut you are willing to give, you are ultimately the one taking the pay cut. Is that what you really want to do?

The Secret to Staying Confident

To hold firm on price you need to have a high level of confidence. One of the best ways to feel confident is by maintaining a full sales pipeline. This means that you have enough prospects and customers at each phase of your sales process so you don't worry about closing every sale. Your assurance comes from knowing that you don't have to close this deal if it means sacrificing on price.

Maintaining pricing integrity is a challenge. It starts by being self-assured and it extends not only to the service you deliver, but also to the expectations of the customer. Don't entertain requests for a discount. Be confident in both your price and the product or service you offer. Ensure that your sales pipeline is full by spending adequate time developing it at all phases of your sales process. Consider how your product or service can help ensure the future success of your customers. Don't believe the lie that you can make up your initial price cut on the next order. Without confidence in your price, you can say goodbye to your profits.

Remember, price cutting is for sissies! ∎

Mark Hunter is known as "The Sales Hunter." For biographical and business information, see page 266.

Editor's Note: A bestselling author, speaker and trainer, Jill Konrath is frequently featured in top business publications, including The New York Times, Business Journal, *and* Selling Power. *She shows you how to stand out from your competition.*

Winning the Battle of Commoditization
by Jill Konrath

The other day, I met with executives from two very different businesses. One firm sells products that cost a couple thousand dollars; the other sells services costing hundreds of thousands annually.

Yet both have one thing in common—in today's marketplace, their clients view them as commodities. Differentiation is difficult because truthfully everyone is offering pretty much the same thing.

So what can you do in this situation? It's a question most every organization is wrestling mightily with in today's rapidly changing sales paradigm.

Some tell their reps to stress their companies' great services. Unfortunately, since that's what everyone is saying, it's pretty ineffective. Others tout their technological superiority. But customers don't believe any one company can remain an industry leader for long. Product/service bundling is another option, but ultimately it drives prices down so much that only low-cost providers can survive.

Added value is another strategy companies are using in their misguided attempts to stay ahead of competitors. They offer free analysis, free delivery, free testing, free advertising or free anything. But pretty soon the freebies become the norm and profitability declines even further. You can only give away so much.

If you're like most sellers today, you're looking behind every nook and cranny to find that unique area of competitive differentiation that will set you or your company apart.

You may be begging your product development department for something that won't be immediately replicated by other firms. You may be screaming at your marketing team to get you qualified leads ready to buy your products.

Unfortunately, you're looking for salvation in all the wrong places.

You see, there is a way to consistently stand out from the crowd, be irresistible to prospective customers, and command premium pricing. You don't have to wait for marketing or product development or anyone else to save you. Nor do you have to pray for the untimely demise of your biggest competitors.

You see, the answer isn't out there somewhere. You can stop looking for that elusive weapon to gain advantage in the ongoing Battle of Commoditization.

Instead, go look in the mirror. The answer is *you*, the seller.

Absolutely no one can replicate you, your knowledge, your expertise, your problem-solving capability, your ability to create new options and solutions that didn't exist before.

Don't give me that baloney that you're only selling software or services or some sort of trinkets. That's old stuff! People can get that from anyone. They can go to Elance and get a brochure or website designer for peanuts. They can go to eBay to buy just about anything.

But they can't buy your brain!

Just ask Mark from a storage equipment firm in New Jersey. He recently emailed me to tell me that he was using my suggested approach to get into big companies and it was working like a charm. He was setting up appointments like crazy.

Curious to learn what he was doing, I contacted Mark and met a real pro. His company sells all sorts of filing systems. Everything he sells is available hundreds of places online. But Mark's brain isn't!

Several years back he was selling into the flavor and fragrance industry. These companies have thousands of teeny containers that they need to keep track of at all times. Rather than just selling these customers "storage stuff" he worked with them to develop software and laser pointers to keep tabs on these tiny samples. He figured out a way for his clients to process their orders that literally revolutionized their industry.

You see, he doesn't think he's selling storage equipment. He sees himself helping customers run their operations better. He uses his brain to come up with unique solutions to the challenges of their businesses that can't be replicated. He doesn't just add value, he creates it!

Another person who understands this is Tim from an experiential marketing firm in Austin, Texas. He realizes that it's all too easy for his services to become a commodity. So he focuses on the experience of working with him and his firm. What does this require? Nothing less than a laser-like focus on the customers he wants to work with; immersing himself in their businesses for months at a time, and concentrating on their competitors and marketplace trends.

Using what he's learned, he noodles over what his company can do to really make a difference. He plays with different concepts in his mind. When he finally meets with decision makers, he has an in-depth understanding of their problems and pains related to his offering. He has invaluable insights and ideas to offer that completely set him apart from his competitors.

Your personal expertise is what sets you apart today. Your ability to think for your customers is what makes you irresistible. Your creative genius in finding new solutions makes you indispensable.

Focus on *you*. Become the person that everyone wants to work with because you know so much that can help their businesses grow.

Become a value creator. When you do that, you'll never fight the Battle of Commoditization again. End of story! ∎

Jill Konrath is Chief Sales Officer of Selling to Big Companies. For biographical and business information, see page 268.

Editor's Note: Chris Lytle began his sales career by default. He interviewed with the general manager of his local radio station hoping to become the next Walter Cronkite. Instead, he was told they already had two newsmen and he could have a job in ad sales. Glad to get his foot in the door, he took it only to discover that sales was much more lucrative than news. Chris enjoyed a successful career in sales, sales management and radio station ownership before starting his own sales training company. Today he's trained over 100,000 sales professionals. His clients include ConAgra, United Way and Wausau Financial Systems.

Four Words You Don't Want to Hear
by Chris Lytle

Here are four words you really don't want to hear: "Send me a proposal."

If you've made a good presentation and the prospect has a problem you can solve, then you want the prospect to write you a check. That would be a better outcome than going back to your desk and writing a proposal, wouldn't it?

Too many salespeople stop selling as soon as a prospect says, "Send me a proposal." They take it is a buying signal and believe they've had a "great call." Whenever a salesperson tells me that it was a "great call," I know instantly that he didn't get an order.

"Send me a proposal" is either a buying signal or a stall. In either case, the fact that a prospect says those four words is not a reason to stop the conversation, pack up your briefcase and drive back to your office. Not without asking a few more questions.

How I Saved Myself From a Writing Assignment

I sell sales training. I'm on the phone with a person I haven't done business with for 10 years. I've just shown him my latest plan for developing his team of salespeople. He's excited about the process I've just presented to him. It's a way for his sales managers to run more powerful sales meetings. His top sales guy is on the conference call and is also supportive.

I should add that it's a $4860 decision, which in this prospect's world is relatively minor.

But then, my prospect says, "Send me a proposal on this."

"That's not a problem," I said. "I can lay out the terms and conditions in writing. You have seen everything I offer. Do you think it will help?"

"Yes, it definitely gives us some consistency in developing our team."

"And you have, or can find, the money?" I asked.

"If you can give me a couple of payments in the $1900 range, I can keep this off the corporate radar. I can sign off on it."

"Then, do you need a proposal or should I just send an invoice?" I asked.

"Send the invoice. We'll go ahead with it," he said.

With three more questions, I saved myself another writing assignment, solved my prospect's problem and closed a sale.

Have you ever written a proposal you didn't have to write? Worse yet, have you ever worked for hours on a proposal and then had the prospect quit taking your calls or responding to your emails?

"Send me a proposal" are four words that you don't want to hear. If you do hear them, ask enough questions so you know what they really mean.

The One that Got Away

I believe you learn as much from your failures as your successes. Most sales trainers don't want to admit they don't close them all. Let me share this failure and see if you can relate.

I guess I shocked a group of prospects recently. In the middle of a conference call, I said to them, "I give up." They were putting up a lot resistance to what I was proposing. There were three of them and I could feel that I was merely starting to argue instead of selling or solving their problem.

"Uncle," I said. "It's OK if you don't want to buy this. I give up."

It's interesting to observe what happens when you reject a prospect before he rejects you. One person on the call told me I couldn't quit, thus starting a new argument. I opted out. I felt bad that I couldn't convince them and good that I stopped trying to force the issue.

That morning, I had called another person who was "too busy" to talk to me even though we had an appointment. "I understand," I said. "Do you want me to quit calling you completely? It's not my intent to bother you or waste your time." This prospect "opted in" and we set up another meeting for the following week.

Pursuing someone who doesn't want to be pursued is stalking. I think there are laws against that.

Have you ever rejected a prospect before he rejected you?

Have you ever asked a prospect if he wanted to "opt out" of the process?

You don't have to close every deal to be successful. If a deal is not right for both of you, it's OK to walk away. ∎

Chris Lytle is President and Product Developer at Sparque, Inc. For biographical and business information, see page 268.

Editor's Note: Jim Kasper is a noted author and sales trainer with more than 26 years' experience in direct sales, sales management, sales training, and marketing. The founder and president of Interactive Resource Group, Jim's clients include Adaptec, AT&T, Corning and Honeywell. Read on and learn how to write a proposal that will seal the deal.

Creating the Winning Proposal
by Jim Kasper

As a professional salesperson, you expend a lot of energy creating favorable first impressions. You work hard at prospecting, making numerous cold calls and demonstrating strong questioning and listening skills during your initial sales interviews with prospective customers. Through your steadfast efforts, you're able to create interest for your product or service and move a prospect forward in your sales cycle. It's at this point that you look forward to setting the date for presenting a proposal.

You've now entered the proposal stage of your sales cycle. This is where you take all of the information you've carefully extracted from interviews and incorporate it into a formal proposal. Like most professional salespeople, you probably use a standard business proposal format. In many sales environments that we've seen, the proposal format is often overlooked even though it is perhaps the most important instrument in your sales cycle.

You need to ensure that your proposal format directly reflects your sales style and product/service position. If you have an upbeat, aggressive sales style, your proposals should mirror that style; they should not be "dry" or "antiseptic." On the other hand, if you operate in a technical sales environment, your format should focus more on the data and specification areas. If you're positioning your product/service as a quality high-end offering, your proposal should reflect a corresponding level of "polish." No matter what your selling style or position, there are rules to follow that will insure a strong, thoroughly read, widely distributed and understood proposal.

- **Critical content.** Test your proposal format by asking customers and prospects what they like and what suggestions they would offer to make it easier to read and understand. Check your proposal to ensure you've included the following elements:

  1. The project name, customer's name, customer contact name, date, your name, company, address, telephone, email, and website

  2. An objective: A summary statement identifying the objectives of the proposal

  3. An overview or brief description of the events that need to take place

  4. A timeline of events and suggested dates

  5. The proposition: Here's what I'm proposing to you, including specifications

  6. The pricing and terms page (near the end)

  7. A page on your company's background and your personal qualifications

  8. Professional references (other satisfied customers)

- **Speak the customer's language.** Your proposal should make extensive use of your customer's "shorthand" where appropriate. This shows him you were listening and have grasped his culture and environment. Good examples are using specific titles such as the Vice President of North American Laser Repair or specific names of internal departments and groups. Be sure to highlight the key points that the customer explained during your sales interview and, if possible, use graphs and charts to illustrate those points.

- **Show your professionalism.** Business proposals should be generated on your best paper stock. And don't ever let a proposal leave your office until it is proofed by someone other than yourself—someone who knows your business. Bind all proposals in a cover or presentation jacket. That lends a strong sense of professionalism to your prospect. Run as many original documents as needed for the customer and an additional copy for backup.

- **Focus on your customer.** Avoid loading up your proposal with quotes or references to products or projects you've delivered to other customers that don't focus on your customer. Instead, use information that is valid and applicable to that specific customer. While it may be impressive to include an extensive list of completed work delivered to customers, remember that the customer will likely lose interest if he has to read through too much material that doesn't pertain to him.

- **The fine print.** Many proposal templates we've seen include a statement of acceptance, typically appearing at the end of the proposal. This paragraph states that the customer accepts the proposal as presented, including the price and terms. Some companies have their legal counsels draft this paragraph to reduce the potential for litigation. An alternative is to confine the legal agreement to a separate letter of acceptance or in a purchase order given to the customer after a verbal proposal agreement.

   The final paragraph on the proposal price and terms page should state how long the price and terms are valid. This depends upon your industry sales cycle and pending cost increases. You should not state that the proposal is good for 30 days if traditionally it takes 60 days to run your sales cycle.

- **Delivery.** It's best to deliver as many proposals in person as possible. Remember your objective at the sales interview stage of the sales cycle was to get your customer to grant you the next appointment to deliver the proposal. Your presence shows the customer how important his business is to you by setting a tone of immediacy. It also speeds up your sale cycle by allowing you to address his questions and overcome his objections.

If you're unable to deliver your proposal in person, then overnight courier delivery or electronic delivery are your remaining options. Be sure to ask your prospect for his preference and if he requests electronic delivery, be sure to use a protected file format such as Adobe PDF and, in all cases, set specific times and dates for follow-up.

By following these steps, you won't lose a sale in the proposal stage. ∎

Jim Kasper is CEO and founder of Interactive Resource Group. For biographical and business information, see page 267.

Editor's Note: Dave Kahle is a selling expert with real-world experience, who understands and appreciates the problems salespeople face. He knows one of the biggest challenges salespeople encounter, especially in a downturn, is dealing with competitors. He shows you how to talk about them without being negative.

Dealing Effectively with the Competition
by David Kahle

Ever heard this statement before? "This would be a great business if it weren't for the competition!"

While you can't change the competition, you can certainly be responsible for your attitude and behavior toward them. What you say and how you act about the competition can have a bearing on your bottom line. An appropriate attitude and set of practices for dealing with the competition should be an essential part of every salesperson's repertoire.

Respect the Competition

Speaking badly about competitors, looking down on them, finding fault with them and generally disparaging them are common behaviors I see frequently among the companies with whom I work. It's easy to understand why. In sales meetings you're constantly told how your products stack up against the competition, what makes your service superior, and why your people are more experienced and more knowledgeable.

While your new product may contain some features that your competitor's does not, his product probably contains some features that yours lacks. While you claim your service to be superior, so does he. Your people are probably not more experienced and knowledgeable than his. Your competitor probably offers a sound business option to your customers. You need to bury those attitudes of superiority, and cast off that disdain for the competition. If your customers didn't think your competitors presented a viable option, they wouldn't be buying from them.

Don't Believe Everything You Hear

Occasionally customers complain about the competition or tell stories of how they messed up on some project. Rather than allowing this to confirm your smug view of the competition, take it with a healthy degree of skepticism. Understand that the people who share these stories with you are typically those customers with whom you have the best relationships. What you see as confidential information about your competitors' weaknesses may just be the natural human inclination to tell you what they believe you want to hear. Your friends want to find common ground with you, and your animosity toward the competition provides potentially productive soil to plow.

It's been my observation that many of those customers who are reporting on the flaws in the competition to you, are reporting on your flaws to them. Don't view everything you hear as 100% accurate.

Don't Speak Badly About the Competition, Ever

Disparaging the competition, speaking badly about the company or the individual salespeople, resorting to innuendo and snide comments, all of this says more about you to your customers than it does about the competitors to whom you are referring. It reveals you as small-minded, petty, smug and far more interested in yourself than you are in your customers.

This is something I learned the hard way, in one of the most embarrassing incidents in my tenure as a salesperson.

I was selling a piece of capital equipment, representing a product line that was 35% more expensive than the competition. However, the additional cost was justified in a far superior product. The competition had been experiencing a problem with one component of its system, the batteries easily worked themselves loose and disconnected. The competition solved that problem by using a rubber band to provide additional tension on the battery and keep it from jiggling loose.

I pointed that out to my potential customer, asking her how comfortable she felt with a product that was held together with a rubber band. My customer's response was:

"Do you know what I don't like about you?" she asked. I was floored and speechless. "You are so negative about your competitors." I turned beet red, stammered an apology and retreated quickly. That incident has stuck with me for decades.

Now the question becomes: If I don't want to speak badly about the competition, how do I present the advantages of my offer relative to the other guy's?

Here are four options:

- **Consider the competition's offer as irrelevant.** I believe this approach to be the most effective in the long term, because it focuses on the customer, not the competitor. If you have done an accurate, detailed job of understanding the full nature of your customer's situation, and have presented a solution that precisely meets the customer's requirements, what difference does it make who the competition is, or what the competition does?

  The issue is not the competition; it is your ability to meet the customer's needs. Your mindset, from the beginning, is not a bit focused on the competition, but rather is 100% targeted to completely understanding the customer's requirements. The conversation is not about how you compare to the competition, but rather how you meet the customer's needs.

  Obviously, this approach is not for every selling situation. It requires a commitment on the part of the salesperson to spend time with the customer in order to fully understand his needs. It assumes that you have the ability to shape an offer that meets the customer's needs. It requires a more professional self-image on the part of the salesperson, who sees himself as a consultant to the customer. If your routine is limited to asking for the technical specifications and then quoting prices, this approach is going to be outside of your reach.

  In the long run, however, it provides the ultimate response to the competitor's presence in your accounts.

- **Speak in generalized, not specific, terms.** It is more effective and more professional to speak in general terms about the general class of competition than it is to speak specifically about a particular company or person.

For example, if you want to make the point that you favorably compare to X company (that national competitor), say something like this: "Generally, large national companies are more concerned about their own financial performances than they are the needs of the local customers. Since we're local and family owned, we highly value every customer, and that translates into more personal and responsive service." Notice, you didn't talk about the competitor, you talked about "national companies," a general class of competition.

By generalizing any references to your competition you can point out your distinctiveness without being negative about any specific competitor.

- **Use questions, not statements.** It's far more effective to put questions about your competitor in the customer's mind, than it is for you to make statements about the competition. Remember, your comments are always suspect, because the customer knows that you have a vested interest in persuading him one way or the other. His observations, however, carry far more weight than anything you can say.

  Help the customer make his own observations by providing the questions he should ask. For example, don't say, "Y Company is a small local company that doesn't have the systems or technology to support you in the long run." Instead, say, "One of the questions you should ask of every vendor is this: 'What technology and systems do you have in place to assure that you will be able to support us for the long run?'"

- **Use tables and charts.** This is a commonly used technique to point out the differences between your offer and your competitors' in a detailed and professional way. Imagine a chart, with the salient features of your offer down the first row, and across the top your company's name, followed by Option A, Option B, etc., with the options representing your competitors. Then use a check mark to indicate the inclusion of that feature in each company's offering.

This can be a highly effective in pointing out the differences between your offer and your competitors' offers. In addition to the detail that it presents, the document itself is often prepared by your company, not by you personally, which means you are one step removed from being the source of this information. The problem with this approach is that the source of the information is your company, and you are always suspect.

Regardless of which one or combination of these approaches works for you, the discipline to deal with the competition in a professional manner is one of the hallmarks of the best salespeople. As a sales professional, you should think through and decide on an approach that fits for you. ∎

Dave Kahle is president of The DaCo Corporation. For biographical and business information, see page 267.

Editor's Note: Adrian Miller is a popular author, speaker and business consultant with over 20 years' experience. She's been through tough times before. This advice will help you keep closing deals.

The Sky is Falling!
by Adrian Miller

In an economic downturn, you can't pick up a newspaper or turn on your TV without being bombarded by doom and gloom about the economy. It's enough to make any salesperson want to hide under a rock until happier days return.

However, there is a silver lining in those dark clouds. Consider the warnings a call to action to prepare your business to ride the cycle. If you play your cards right during a downturn, you will not only keep sales up through the cycle, you'll also find yourself in an even better position when the economy begins to pick up. So, turn down the drone of financial doomsayers and start working this prime opportunity to increase your sales.

- **Stay close.** Stay close to your customers and prospects in tough times. Dazzle them with customer service. Be one step ahead of their wants and needs. Be proactive by anticipating their needs *before* they have to ask or remind you of something. Give them something for nothing. This doesn't necessarily mean a tangible item. Offer them valuable information, introductions, or some of your extra time.
- **Cross-sell.** Make certain that you are cross-selling all that you have to offer your customers. This is not the time to leave business on the table for your competitors to scoop up and perhaps even win your part of the business as well.
- **Focus on competitive advantages.** Remember that your key competitive advantages are valuable *only* if they equate to improvements in the situations of your customers and prospects. The bottom line here is: if you can't offer them an improvement, they have no need to change.

- **Become an advisor.** Be more than just a salesperson; instead develop meaningful solutions for your customers. Think out-of-the-box strategies. Get creative. Put yourself in the mindset of being a valuable resource for your clients.
- **Work harder.** Most importantly, when times are tough – work harder and smarter. Make more calls, utilize better touch-point management, and network, network, network!

Give these ideas a try and you'll be better able to weather the economic storm and even come out of it ahead of your competition. ■

Adrian Miller is founder and president of Adrian Miller Sales Training. For biographical and business information, see page 270.

Editor's Note: Kim Duke is an unconventional sales expert known as The Sales Diva. She helps women small business owners, sales professionals and entrepreneurs increase their sales in a fun and stress-free way. Savvy and sassy, she peppers her advice with humor and colorful anecdotes. Kim spent 15 years selling millions of dollars in advertising for the two largest television networks in Canada. I picked this story because in a downturn, everyone's a price squeezer. Here's how Kim handles them.

Is Your Customer Giving You the Price Squeeze?
by Kim Duke

A nasty little insecure habit I see in many business owners and salespeople is their fear of losing a deal. So, how does this habit show up? It's simple.

You have a customer or potential customer who asks for a proposal from you. By the way, you really want the deal and you'd love to work with this customer. In fact, you want it so bad you can taste it. (And you're already buying the new car with the commissions that you're going to make!)

So, you provide the proposal, quote your rate, and then something happens that honestly makes you quiver with fear.

It's when the customer says, "Company X said it could do the same thing for less money. Can you match those rates?"

Your vanishing commissions flash before your eyes. You see your new car drive off into the sunset without you and your revenue projections plummeting and crashing into the ground.

In a heartbeat you say, "Yes, I can," and you proceed to drop your rates as quickly as if you were holding a hot potato!

Years ago I sold advertising to a local high-end furniture store. The owner was a likeable guy and he was very proud of his expensive furniture line. He was also a notorious negotiator and had a reputation for bringing salespeople to their knees.

He wanted to do television advertising with me and he asked for a two-month air time proposal and he also wanted me to produce a new 30-second commercial for him.

No problem, we had worked with each other before. I knew what he liked and we had rapport.

The day I presented the proposal, we sat on some fabulous leather furniture. We discussed how it would benefit him and then he wrinkled his brow, and said:

"Kim, this looks wonderful but the other TV station has given me a proposal that's much cheaper. I need you to throw in the commercial production for free in order for me to go with you."

I paused for a moment, looked at him and smiled and said, "Bill, may I ask you a question?" He replied, "Sure."

I said, "If we take the price of the proposal off the table, which proposal meets your needs the best and will bring you the most customers?"

He replied, "Yours does. However, they are cheaper and they will throw the commercial in for free."

My gut was telling me something.

I then asked him, "Are your furniture prices artificially inflated or are you providing the best offer to your customers immediately?"

He replied sternly, "My furniture is top quality and I don't negotiate. We offer a fair price right away to our customers."

I then asked, "So if I were to come in today and ask you to give me this gorgeous leather chair for free because I was willing to buy the leather sofa—would you do it?"

He said, "Absolutely not."

I asked, "Why?"

He looked at me intensely and said, "That's one of the finest Italian leather chairs. It's worth every cent."

I looked at him and shrugged. "Bill, I'm a business person just like you. I offer a fair price immediately to my customer. What we're offering you can't receive from the other TV station. The production of the television commercial is not included in my price. So my proposal rate stands firm."

Bill looked at me and didn't say a word. (I think he was in shock!)

Then he said, "I have a confession to make. The other station brought back a second, lower proposal when they knew they were competing against you. So I guess they were planning on overcharging me the first time weren't they?"

No words needed to be said.

He signed a year-long deal with me and I totally shut out my competitor.

Are You Failing The Squeeze Test?

Listen. Do you know why customers buy on price?

They don't see any noticeable difference between you and your competitor. So, they start squeezing your proposal and the competitor's proposal just like they were standing in the grocery store squeezing oranges.

This is also reinforced when you drop your prices after being squeezed. In fact, your customer may even feel that you falsely advertised to him. You've basically told your customer that:

- Your initial proposal was a rip-off
- You're desperate for his business
- You aren't to be trusted in the future
- Your first proposal means nothing

Don't Put Yourself in a Position to be Juiced

So what should you do in this type of situation? Follow these easy steps:

- Understand the hot buttons of what your customer is looking for and establish his budget ahead of time, if possible. (Don't be bringing in the Package A, B or C plan—that's for wimps.)
- Position your company with something unique that will actually mean something to your customer.
- If you know your rates are fair, then don't fold when faced with the price squeeze.

In negotiation, it isn't about one party getting everything and the other party feeling cheated. In a successful negotiation both parties feel satisfied.

If you drop your rates to win the deal, you'll actually resent your customer because your profit margins have been slashed. This isn't exactly going to give you the warm fuzzies and you'll end up providing second-rate customer service and an inferior product.

If the deal is worth negotiating, then make sure your customer gives up something in order to receive a discounted rate. Or else he has to make a commitment to something bigger or longer term.

You also have one last choice (which happens to be my favorite). I stick with my rate (which I know is fair), I tell my customer why my rate is higher than my competitor's price and then I tell him how I can solve his problem in a unique way.

And then? I also show him that I'm willing to walk away. Remember in the world of selling, walking away shows confidence, honesty and that you have a backbone.

You'll lose a few customers for sure, usually the ones who weren't going to be good customers for you in the long run. However, you'll end up attracting a much higher level of customer (and more of them) in the end and no one will feel like he's been in the juicer. ■

Kim Duke is CEO and founder of The Sales Divas. For biographical and business information, see page 264.

Editor's Note: The founder and publisher of Selling Power *magazine, Gerhard Gschwandtner has more than three decades of international sales and marketing experience. His advice on how to develop a prospecting plan that works is pure gold.*

See New Faces, Win New Opportunities
by Gerhard Gschwandtner

If you're looking for ways to manage your territory so that you get a full day each week in front of new prospects, here's a roadmap. But it's up to you to implement, implement, implement. No magic bullet here. Just solid, sensible strategy.

No matter how often you tell yourself you're going to start setting aside time for prospecting, no matter how many planners and time management programs you buy, you always seem to end up with too few hours in the day. And it's always the hours you set aside to make cold calls and meet with new prospects that get short shrift.

If you're not following through on the prospecting commitments you've made to yourself, the problem may not be lack of time but something else entirely: You haven't devised a strategy for prospecting, and you've failed to quantify the value of your prospecting activities.

The first step in developing a successful prospecting strategy is to identify potential customers in your territory and organize them, according to one senior sales representative, who arranges prospects in a comprehensive yet simple manner, classifying each prospective customer by his potential and projected sales volume.

The next step is to keep track of and manage your activities in a way that makes sense for you. Don't assume you must invest in the latest digital technology if you're more comfortable with a paper planner and careful notes. Regular reports to management and reminder e-mail messages to salespeople keep everyone focused on the prime targets. But if this level of detail isn't your cup of tea, adapt the process to fit your personality.

Once you've developed a workable tracking mechanism, you'll be able to quantify exactly how much time you've put into each sale and into each nonproductive lead. You'll know what percentage of sales you get from each type of customer, and you'll be able to define how much each prospect is worth to you.

This knowledge will allow you to easily set appropriate goals for the week, month, and quarter and will help you determine why you're not as successful as you'd like to be, even though you're working as hard as you can.

When you know your activity is more likely to yield dividends, it's easier to make prospecting a priority. At the same time, though, keep your perspective and think of the initial sales call as a fact-finding mission where you can gather and update your information on the account and begin to determine how to best position your product, your company and yourself.

Get the Most Out of Your Territory

Every sales territory is a potential gold mine, but whether you strike it rich depends on targeting your efforts to tap into the richest vein of customers. The best way to accomplish this is to plan your days, weeks, and months to keep your territory delivering maximum sales. Here are a few suggestions:

- **Start big, then narrow.** Begin with your goals for the next month, and then plot them out. From there develop your weekly plans and, from those, your daily schedule. At the end of each day revise as necessary so that you're concentrating on the most productive accounts in the most efficient manner possible.

- **Do your homework.** Existing customers and hot prospects should be your top priorities, of course. A prospect won't just volunteer information, however, so before setting your appointments, do some research to help gauge each prospect's temperature. Information gathered ahead of time will also give you a sense of how long a prospective call should take.

- **Resist temptations.** The attraction of a big customer or opportunity that's well out of your way can be enticing, but don't give in. If the opportunity evaporates upon your arrival, you may have wasted half a day or more chasing a red herring. Instead, find a day in the future when you can make that prospect fit your schedule and not throw you off your plan.

- **Go far to near.** Whenever possible, schedule the appointments that are farthest from your office first, and then work your way back through the rest of your calls. As the day draws to a close, you can race toward the finish like a thoroughbred on the home stretch. ■

Gerhard Gschwandtner is founder and publisher of Selling Power *magazine. For biographical and business information, see page 265.*

Editor's Note: A sales strategist and business advisor, Jill Konrath speaks frequently to corporate sales forces and industry associations. Jill shares some insights here on establishing value.

Is Your Value Proposition Strong Enough?
by Jill Konrath

A value proposition is a clear statement of the tangible results a customer gets from using your products or services. The more specific your value proposition is, the better. In difficult economic times, your value proposition is critical to your success.

Most people and companies have lousy value propositions. They're weak—and I mean really weak. Often they're simply a description of the offering's features or capabilities. Or they're filled with self-aggrandizing puffery.

Here are a few examples of weak value propositions:

- It's the most technologically advanced and robust system on the market.
- We improve communication and morale.
- We offer training classes in a wide variety of areas.
- My product was rated the best-in-class by leading authorities.

You're probably saying, "So what?" That's exactly what most customers think when you share a weak value proposition. They've heard lines like that a zillion times before and don't believe you one little bit. Besides, you haven't shared what's in it for them—and that's all customers care about.

With today's tight economy and overburdened decision-makers, you need to have a strong value proposition to break through the clutter and get their attention. That means you need a financially oriented value proposition that speaks to critical issues they're facing. By including specific numbers or percentages you get the decision-makers' attention even faster.

A while back I was having lunch with the president of a half billion dollar division of a major corporation. She told me that if someone called her and said he could reduce her waste by just 1%, she'd meet with him immediately.

Now a 1% saving seemed miniscule to me, so I asked her why. She told me that she knew exactly how much her company spent on waste—and it was a big chunk of change. Every penny she saved would go right to her bottom line as more profits.

Strong value propositions deliver tangible results like:

- Increased revenues
- Faster time to market
- Decreased costs
- Improved operational efficiency
- Increased market share
- Decreased employee turnover
- mproved customer retention levels

Documented success stories make you believable to prospective buyers. So how does your value proposition look? Can you describe what you do in terms of tangible business results? Do you have documented success stories?

Or do you need to do some work to enhance your value proposition? If it's not strong enough yet, don't despair. Most people and companies have a much stronger one than they use. They just get caught up describing *what* they make or *how* they do things. Here are some things you can do right now to enhance your value proposition.

- **Brainstorm with your colleagues.** Review your marketing material and what you say to customers to try to get their attention. If you're not talking tangible results, keep asking each other, "So what?" So what if it's an efficient system? So what if we have a replicable process? So what if it's high quality?

  By asking "so what" questions over and over again, you'll get much closer to the real value you bring to customers. If you're a sole proprietor, do this exercise with a group of other small business owners.

- **Talk to your customers.** Your existing customers are your best resources to find out what value you bring. Tell your customers you need help understanding the real value of your offering and you'd like a chance to learn their perspectives.

Most people are scared to ask their customers about this. It took me awhile before I was willing to risk this, but what I learned was eye-opening. Not only did it change my value proposition, but it also changed my offerings and self-perception.

Don't let another day go by with a weak value proposition. A strong one literally opens the doors of major corporations for you, while a weak one keeps you on the outside. ∎

Jill Konrath is Chief Sales Officer of Selling to Big Companies. For biographical and business information, see page 268.

Editor's Note: Lee Salz is a featured columnist for Sales and Marketing Management Online and the host of an Internet radio show, "Secrets of Business Gurus." His secrets for overcoming price objections are money in the bank.

The Secret to Overcoming the Price Objection
by Lee B. Salz

OK, the title of this article is false advertising. There is no secret to overcoming the price objection. The truth is that the price objection cannot be overcome. That's because it isn't intended to be overcome. It's meant to be resolved through thought facilitation by a salesperson. The salesperson's role is to help the prospect work through the price concern as opposed to attempting to overcome it.

It's Not Really an Objection

First, can we agree that it isn't really an objection? It's a concern. I know that many sales books call it an objection, but it's not. It's an attempt by prospects to resolve financial questions in their minds. People want to feel good about decisions they make and that's why they bring up their concerns.

The mistake many salespeople make is that they think they understand the prospect's concern when the price issue is initially raised. A fatal flaw, indeed! The truth is that the cause for this concern isn't initially known. A myriad of possibilities could be causing the prospect to express his concerns about price such as:

- Is it a question of how much use he will get of the product?
- Is it whether or not he can afford it?
- Is it that he saw a similar product at a cheaper price?
- Or is it a salesperson being hypersensitive to the mere mention of price?

Without knowing what's causing the price concern, you can't possibly help the prospect work through it. Let me share a personal example: I live in Minnesota where owning a boat is commonplace. To me, however, it's expensive. It isn't the price of the boat, or the cost of maintenance, or even the price of the slip. It's the fact that the season for boating is so short that

I don't feel I would get enough use out of it to justify the financial investment.

On the other hand, I bought Peg Perego motorized cars for my three kids. Each one had a $300 price tag on it. Expensive to some, but cheap to me. Why? Because I'm rich? Hardly. No, it's because my kids use them, a lot! From my perspective, they're worth every penny. If I get significant use out of something, I can justify the price in my mind. At the other end of the spectrum, like most parents, I have also bought tons of toys in the $20 price range that have been used once, maybe twice. After that, the toys are never touched again. To me, that's expensive.

Some other price concerns center on whether or not prospects can financially afford the product. A good salesperson helps prospects recognize the options available to them for financing the purchase.

Same Thing, Lower Price

In other scenarios, the prospect has seen the same product, or a similar one, at a lower price. The mind tries to turn everything into an easy-to-understand commodity. When I worked in employment background screening, prospects would compare a $9.95 database search with a comprehensive courthouse search. The comparison of the two was apples to oranges. The strong salespeople were able to explain the difference in a way that led prospects to see that they needed the comprehensive search. The $9.95 search can be perceived as very expensive since you rarely catch any bad guys with it.

All Sales Do Not Come Down to Price

The worst case is when the salesperson does not believe that his product is worth its price tag. If this hits home for you, I highly encourage you to sell something else. If you don't believe in your price, I guarantee you that no one else will either. If you believe that all sales ultimately come down to price, help me understand this:

- Why doesn't everyone buy generic drugs?
- Why do people buy bottled water when they can get it for free from the tap?
- Why doesn't everyone drive a Yugo?

- Why are people buying satellite radio when there are plenty of good stations available for free?
- How come most people have cable or satellite television when they can get a dozen stations for free?
- Why isn't everyone shaving with a single-blade disposable razor?
- Why isn't everyone drinking generic coffee?
- Why isn't everyone fighting to sit in the last row at the ballgame?
- Why do people even go to a ballgame when they can watch it comfortably for free in their living rooms?
- How did your company manage to get any clients at all?

I think you get my point: people will pay more if they feel the purchase is worth the price. Maybe you can't afford the product you're selling. That's a completely different issue. There's a great expression to illustrate that point: "Don't spend the prospect's money." You don't belong in his shoes, so don't put yourself there. You never truly know a person's financial situation.

Look, no one wants to get ripped off, and everyone wants to brag that he got a good deal. So, if you can master the facilitation of the discussion around the pricing concern, you will inherently have more sales. ∎

Lee B. Salz is president of Sales Architects. For biographical and business information, see page 272.

Editor's Note: Tough times don't deter Leslie Buterin. She loves a challenge. Several years ago, a CEO challenged her to find a way to overhaul his company's sales process to focus on reaching executive level decision-makers. Despite a paralyzing fear of cold calling, Leslie invested two years of her time to develop the system and teach it to the CEO's sales staff. She was so successful she launched her own consulting company teaching others how to reach top decision-makers.

Learning to Speak "Executive"
by Leslie Buterin

Cold calling high-level decision-makers takes a shift in thinking, a rewiring of your brain. Why? Because according to our experience with thousands of sellers, more than 87% of sales professionals still hold onto, and take action based on, three beliefs that actually sabotage cold calls made to executives.

First, the majority of salespeople think they need to announce the name of their companies as a way of gaining credibility when cold calling prospects. This is simply not true; it is unnecessary information for executive-level decision-makers. In fact, if the prospects have had unpleasant experiences with your industry, your company name will only serve to conjure up the bad feelings associated with those experiences.

Second, many sales professionals believe they must speak as fast as they can to make their points about their products or services within the limited time they have the prospects on the phone. They hope to get in a phrase or two that will hook the prospects and keep them engaged in the call. Again, not true.

Prospects really do not care about what product or service you have to offer. If they have any familiarity with your product or service at all, they will use this information to pigeonhole you and send you down the ladder to the person who handles "that sort of thing."

Third, many sales pros still persist in taking the long road. With ferocious tenacity they cold call the low-level decision-makers of an organization and painstakingly look for in-house introductions to the people at the top of the company.

Wrong again. This does not work because most of those low-level decision-makers walk in fear of the high-level decision-makers. They do not know what to say to those guys, let alone have the intestinal fortitude to approach them. In the unlikely event these low-level decision-makers do get into the executive suite, they want to use that time to make their own cases with the top decision-makers, not yours.

So, what's a cold-calling sales pro to do? Think about the words of Kevin Davis in his book *Getting Into Your Customer's Head*. According to Davis, "The traditional self-focused selling approach is no longer effective because today's new buyers are unwilling to follow you. They don't want to be 'sold.' They want to make educated decisions. To make a sale, you must join them on the buying path."

Here's how top-selling professionals apply Davis' big thought to cold calling. They know it is of utmost importance to learn the language spoken by those in the executive ranks. The way to speak in terms that are meaningful to top decision-makers is by answering one or more of their top three questions, which are:

- How can you increase their revenues?
- How can you decrease their expenses?
- How can you improve their communications?

So, how do you speak to executives and get them to listen to you? Come up with a rock-solid value proposition. Sales pros know this one phrase is an important key to getting in the door. Trouble is, they don't know how to come up with one statement that differentiates them from the competition and at the same time compels prospects to say, "Let's meet."

Take a Lesson from Your Happy Clients

To develop your value proposition, start by taking the time to interview your happy clients. They are your most important sources for the words that will get your cold calls opening doors to the executive suite.

How is it that the words of your happy clients hold so much power? Because your clients' words are the very words that are most meaningful to your prospects. Let's break this big thought down with a brief example. What follows are changes in language made as a result of coaching calls with clients. As you read, ask yourself which you would be most interested in hearing about:

- "Sales training" or "Doubling your sales revenues with three changes to your cold calling practices"
- "Reducing your combined telecommunications costs" or "Cutting your monthly telephone and Internet connections expenses by 50% or more"
- "Life insurance" or "A reduction of your tax liability by more than 20%"

What makes these phrases so successful? The value propositions are crafted using words of happy clients, and they stay away from industry speak. The psychological triggers that work frequently become clear only after you've identified the phrases that work and separated them from the phrases that do not.

Stifle Your Industry Speak

Here's what one of my clients learned using this process. He sells telecommunications products and services. His clients, who use and love his services, want Wal-Mart-like, everyday low prices on phone and Internet connections. When these clients heard the word "telecommunications" they confessed that one word alone conjured up images of time-consuming and labor-consuming implementation programs; heavy investments in equipment; and big dollar signs. As soon as the big-dollar word, "telecommunications," was uttered, they were not interested; their brains shut down. They never even heard him say his purpose was to reduce their expenses!

Turns out, the phrase "telecommunications cost" is pure industry speak—unwelcome language that triggers negative connotations in prospects' minds. Of course this is not at all what my client intended to convey. How did he find this out? By interviewing clients and learning that everyday decision-makers think and speak in terms like telephone and Internet connection expenses.

Talk to your clients and you will find that they will highlight certain benefits. Do not be surprised if they come up with benefits that never crossed your mind or easy-to-understand language that demystifies what you are selling. Then, use their words to craft your very own killer value proposition that will get you in the door for face-to-face meetings with decision-makers.

Learning executive speak is not a massive undertaking and getting comfortable with the lexicon of high-level decision-makers is well worth the time you invest. Why? Because you can attract their attention and stand far above your competitors when you take the time to learn the language of your prospects. ∎

Leslie Buterin is founder of Top Dog Consulting. For biographical and business information, see page 263.

Editor's Note: Paul Johnson's been a sales success since he won his first award at the age of 24. A noted author, sales trainer and speaker, Paul's clients include ADP, AutoNation and Nortel Networks. In difficult times, buyers will pressure you to cut your prices. Paul explains how to close the deal without resorting to discounting.

Earn Top Dollar Even in Tough Times
by Paul Johnson

When buyers see list price, they expect discounts to follow. Every dollar you discount is a dollar of pure profit you're giving away. Every effort you make to remove discounts can reap rich rewards. By changing the way you address the relationship between pricing and discounts, you can stop giving away heavy discounts and escape the commodity pricing pressures in your business.

Here are four simple techniques you can use to wring every dollar you deserve out of your next sale:

- **Amplify the pain.** First, find and amplify your buyer's pain. Before any discussion of price, your buyer must be truly motivated to make a change. In other words, make sure the buyer understands just how much it's costing him to not implement your solution.

The life insurance business has used this approach for years, because nobody wants to think about dying. The agent asks the prospect to think about all of the aspects of being inadequately insured. He asks: "Do you have enough money set aside right now to pay for a decent burial?" or "How will the mortgage be paid next month?" or "Who will pay for the children's education?" These types of questions heighten the awareness of the buyer to the gravity of his decision, which increases the perceived value of the solution as well as creates a sense of urgency to make a positive decision.

But wait, not all buying decisions are pain-oriented. Many buying decisions are tied to gain of some sort, whether financial, power, prestige, or comfort. Still, these gain motivators can be made even more effective by bringing in the pain elements. All you need to do is consider the flip side with the prospect.

For instance, if you're considering a new mattress on the basis of increased comfort, what will happen if you don't get the mattress? Will you, or do you now suffer from back or joint problems? Will you wake up tired, drag through your day, and be unproductive at work? Will you waste more time sleeping than you need to, because of the lack of quality sleep?

When you consider questions like these, the new mattress is no longer a luxury. Instead, it becomes a necessary tool that will cost you many productive hours at work and negatively affect your relationships if you fail to have it. With pain, you now have a motivated buyer with a sense of urgency.

- **Quantify the problem.** The next step for maximizing your selling price is to quantify the buyer's problem. Often the buyer will need a little help with this. Some things are easy to quantify. For example, what would it cost if a company's website goes down and visitors can't access company information or conduct transactions? That may be easier to quantify than putting a dollar figure on what a bad night's sleep might cost you the next day.

You can quickly quantify any situation by going through a best-case, worst-case or likely-case scenario. For instance, the best-case situation for your website to go down would probably be in the middle of the night, perhaps on a weekend. You'd lose some traffic, but only a very small percentage compared to overall weekly traffic. The worst-case situation might be to lose your website right after your company is featured on CNN. While this could happen, the probability is rather small. Now, it's easier for the buyer to understand that a likely scenario could be to lose his website during a normally heavy traffic time, perhaps midday or early evening. With such a likely scenario clearly in mind, it's easy to understand how financially painful the loss would be.

- **Package your solution.** A third tactic for maximizing your selling price is to package your solution. Don't price out components separately, but show a single price for fixing the buyer's problem. The price should include all of your offerings that are necessary to deliver the complete fix.

Once you've bundled your solution for a single price, it's hard for your buyer to shop elsewhere. The more of your offerings your buyer needs, the more difficult it will be to find another source who can duplicate that same set of offerings. Buying them à la carte from multiple sources will almost always prove to be more difficult, if not more expensive.

I'm amazed at how many companies believe they have to provide line item pricing because their buyers ask for it. Of course they ask for it! That's so they can nitpick each item and squeeze out a bigger discount. Most companies are a little high on some items and a little low on others, but still offer a great overall value. Your prospect will never point out the underpriced items, but you can bet he'll grind you on the ones that are a little high.

- **Pick a proud price.** As you set the price for your offering, the last thing to consider is the cost of the problem the buyer quantified earlier. Remember that you are presenting a neatly wrapped solution to a buyer who's motivated to solve a painfully expensive problem. His problem should be a lot more expensive than the price you're asking, preferably by a factor of three or more. Feel free to name your price, and pick a good one!

Your price shouldn't be exorbitant, but it doesn't have to be the cheapest in town. You deserve to make a good buck relative to the problem you're fixing. This is no time to be shy and leave money on the table. If you haven't been able to point out how the buyer's problem is costing him much more than the price of your solution, don't be surprised when you don't get the order.

To earn top dollar for what you offer, you'll need to amplify your buyer's pain, quantify his problem, package your solution, and make sure the cost of his problem is always much higher than the price of your solution. It's worth working a little harder to defend your pricing because discounting eats away at your profit and commissions. Use these techniques and you won't have to give either away anymore. ∎

Paul Johnson is founder of ConsultativeSelling.com. For biographical and business information, see page 267.

Editor's Note: A legend in the sales training industry, Tom Hopkins began his business career at 19 selling real estate. He was anything but successful, that is until he invested the last of his savings in a three-day training seminar. He quickly became an avid student of sales training. At the age of 27, he was a millionaire. During his last year in real estate, he sold an average of a home a day. Today he runs a highly successful sales training company.

Objections Equal Desire
by Tom Hopkins

When I was still a bit green in my selling career, I had a dream. In it, I went into a home to sell my product to a married couple and they were so helpful. They thoroughly enjoyed my presentation. They agreed to everything I mentioned. They didn't ask any questions or make any objections. They even helped me fill out the paperwork. The whole transaction was completed in record time. I walked out their door with check in hand, several qualified leads and two very happy people waving goodbye. What a wonderful dream. Somehow, I don't think I was alone in having a dream of that sort. Most new salespeople think that's what selling is like. Unfortunately, some veteran salespeople keep looking for that dream to come true, as well.

Selling this easily can be achievable. If you remember these seven key steps, the sales process can also be a dream. The steps are: prospecting, original contact, qualification, presentation, handling objections, closing and getting referrals. Take note though, that handling objections is a normal step in any sale. It's human nature to object, hesitate, stall or procrastinate when making any decision that separates a customer from his money. A customer has to feel absolutely confident that what he is buying will give him all the benefits he wants. The customer has to be comfortable with the value he is receiving for his hard-earned dollars. I know that's true about me, so why should I expect my prospective clients to be any different?

Learn to Expect Objections

My success rate in sales increased tremendously when I expected to hear objections instead of being afraid to hear them. When I began to listen for them, I was amazed to learn that I was hearing basically the same three or four objections in nearly every selling situation. That's when I began doing some serious analysis. I spent a few hours thinking about each of those objections. I wanted to know why my prospects were saying those things and what I could do or say to help them get comfortably past their objections.

I began by putting myself in their position and discovered most prospects were objecting because of one basic emotion—fear. They were afraid to make an irreversible decision. They were afraid to make a commitment with their money. They were afraid the product wouldn't live up to their expectations. They were afraid I was a "take-the-money-and-run" salesperson whom they'd never be able to reach again when they had questions or problems after they bought the product.

Realizing that, I began to make some changes in my presentations. I eliminated words from my vocabulary that provoked fear, words such as "monthly payment" and "contract." When you hear the phrase monthly payments, you visualize yourself writing out yet another check every month when you pay bills. That's certainly a negative image, isn't it? I began replacing the term monthly payment with monthly investment. Do you see the difference in your own mind when you hear the term investment? It's much more positive, isn't it?

The term contract brings to mind something legally binding, something you should have your attorney look over, something you'll have to go to court to get out of. I came up with several alternative words for that term so I could intersperse them throughout my conversation without raising my prospect's defense barriers. I now use the terms paperwork, agreement or form. Aren't those much softer, less threatening terms? Try using them in your next presentation.

For those salespeople who still have a certain amount of fear of their own when they hear an objection, let me explain what objections really are. Besides being a normal part of the selling sequence, objections are defense mechanisms. They are ways for the buyer to tell you that you're moving too fast. They are ways the buyer tells you that he needs more information before he can feel confident about going ahead with the investment.

Always remember, the prospect is not objecting to you, personally. He is objecting to some aspect of the product or service that he is not yet comfortable with.

Here are some dos and don'ts for handling every objection you hear:

- **Don't argue.** If this sounds silly to you, good. You already know this. But, even though you know it, do you fight with your clients in the back of your mind? If you do, eventually it will begin to show. When potential buyers object, they're asking for more information. If the salesperson gets upset and sarcastic or applies pressure, he is, in essence, killing the sale. If the salesperson wins the argument, the prospect is beaten and will often find a way to get back at him. Usually, by buying from someone else.

- **Don't attack your customers when you overcome their objections.** Put space between your prospects and their objections. By this I mean that you must be careful to separate your prospect from each objection as it comes up, so when you discuss the objection, you don't hit the prospect in a vital spot.

Learn to develop sensitivity to how your prospects feel when they voice their objections. Be concerned about helping them save face, not determined to prove them wrong. If you start fighting their feelings, their negative emotions will always take over.

You've worked so hard to eliminate negative, fear-producing images thus far, so don't blow it when you hear an objection. Objections simply tell you where their interests lie. Take advantage of that information to learn what you must emphasize, eliminate or change before they'll buy.

For example, if a man buying tires for his wife's car expresses concern about the safety or reliability of the tires, he's concerned for his loved ones. You would then sell security. If you harp on the low cost of the tires, instead, he'll realize you're not paying attention to his concerns and you'll most likely lose the sale.

- **Do lead them to answer their own objections.** A true professional always tries to maneuver prospects into answering their own objections. Most prospects will do just that given time and a little more information. After all, deep down they want to go ahead. They wouldn't waste their time objecting to something they didn't want to own, would they? ■

Tom Hopkins is chairman of Tom Hopkins International, Inc. For biographical and business information, see page 266.

Editor's Note: Kendra Lee is an award-winning author, sales consultant and trainer who specializes in gaining access to small to medium sized companies. She explains how to use anxiety-promoting questions to motivate your prospects.

Are You Keeping Your Customers Up At Night?
by Kendra Lee

Effective consultative salespeople know how to keep their customers up at night. The salespeople know how to get into their customers' heads by asking questions that will force them to think about the issues that are important to their businesses. It's up to you to become the conscience of their businesses.

True, not all your customers want to be reminded of the difficult challenges that may be confronting them; but, by filling this role, you will enhance your credibility and value to your customers. You'll be the person who attracts their attention and keeps their interest because of your ability to get them to focus on the important issues at hand, the issues they cannot overlook.

For example, one of my customers, an executive, was concerned about the fact that only 19% of his salespeople were making their quotas. At the same time, he saw an opportunity to greatly improve their revenue position based on the fact that 76% of the remaining salespeople were regularly within 20% of their quotas. Last November he told me that he wanted to make it a priority to find a way to get the salespeople, who were within easy reach of their quotas, to achieve their sales goals.

As his sales consultant, I have stayed in touch and prodded him. But even though he always says helping his salespeople reach their quotas is a priority, he hasn't taken any action to achieve his goal. It seems his many business priorities have gotten in the way. I then asked him one very well thought out question:

"Why was he avoiding taking action when he had already quantified the lost revenue this situation was causing?"

Based on my question—one that certainly got his attention and made, by his own admission, for some sleepless nights— he and I have established a plan of action that he's now implementing. Without the prodding and attention I displayed, the opportunity to find a way to increase revenue may have been lost while he continued spending money and time—and losing revenue—on the wrong sales strategy.

In my situation, the question to ask was fairly obvious, but it's not always easy to know the most effective and strategic questions to ask. With this in mind, there are three thought-provoking questions you can ask that will cause your customers to pause and give a situation serious consideration:

- **What are the strategies you're not focusing on?** This question will cause your customers to think about what they may be overlooking or not giving enough time and attention to. People frequently lose sight of even the most basic strategies for success, and you can help them become grounded again.

- **What is the return on investment you're not getting, but should?** This question will help your customers consider if they're achieving the results they expected, and if not, why not. It's an excellent way to address any problems or issues before they become unmanageable.

- **What is causing the biggest problem—your people, processes, or budget?** This question will help your customers pinpoint their biggest challenges and help them develop a plan to resolve the situation.

Once these questions are presented, it's critical for you to continue to follow up on what's been asked. You may make suggestions and recommendations, but until you see your customers take action, don't let them off the hook, and don't let them try to provide easy answers, otherwise nothing will be accomplished. Your interest and attentiveness to what's being done might cause some discomfort for your customers, but by following through, they will realize the benefits of the exercise and the benefits of having you on their teams. ■

Kendra Lee is president and founder of KLA Group. For biographical and business information, see page 268.

Editor's Note: Joe Guertin began his training career when an advertising sales client asked him to share his selling philosophy at their sales meeting. Joe was happy to oblige, and a new career was launched. Today, Joe is a leading sales trainer, specializing in developing new business and selling value versus price. Here are some of Joe's prospecting secrets that will bear fruit in the toughest economic times.

Plan, Execute, Win!
by Joe Guertin

The most successful and profitable salespeople are constantly finding new ways to fill their business pipelines. Now is the best time to get out there and start building new business.

Imagine your selling cycle as a pipeline. Make new contacts and you send them into your sales development pipeline, where you'll work with them on fact-finding and brainstorming. You're getting to know them and they're getting to know you. They come out the other end when they buy. Now, if there aren't enough prospects in the pipeline, and a business slowdown occurs, you're stuck. There goes your commission check.

When a slowdown occurs, most of us will blame time. Even people who are good time managers find it difficult to do it all when it comes to maintaining current customers. With all the contact and administrative time required it's hard to be effective prospectors.

But the top performers know that's just an excuse, so they do what it takes ahead of time to avoid the empty pipeline problem. Their strategy is based on three clearly defined steps:

• **Have a plan**. The essential elements of the plans of all the top performers include having a goal, a prospect list and the means to measure their progress.

The 20-4-1 Rule says that for every 20 prospects called, only about four will eventually entertain serious proposals from you, and only one out of those four will buy right away.

We can argue the justifications of specific numbers, but the lesson is this: Not every prospect called is going to buy immediately, so plan to talk to as many prospects as possible.

Another part of your plan is creating a list of target prospects. These are what we call future customers. Don't just list top-of-mind names, invest some time and do a little digging via business publications, online resources or networking to create a larger, more balanced list of large, small, short-term and long-term prospects. Then measure your progress. Some companies will measure the number of new prospects visited on a weekly basis, or the number of presentations made.

During peak times, sales professionals sometimes use cluster contact systems. For example, they send mass mailings that include articles and handwritten notes to all the prospects in the pipeline, keeping themselves and their companies at the top of each prospect's mind.

- **Set aside business development time.** One of the smartest ways to discipline yourself is to isolate blocks of time every week for new business development. Treat that time like you would an appointment with your best customer, and schedule other activities around it.
- **Exert personal discipline.** You're busy; everyone's busy. Yet, peak performers make the time to keep growing. Business development will be unsuccessful if it's only an occasional thing. Your existing accounts may be exhausting your time now. Adding yet another activity may seem to hinder your ability to serve them. Challenge yourself, be disciplined and every week when you fulfill your plan, reward yourself.

I made a reference to successful and profitable salespeople earlier. Here's why: When you have a steady stream of prospective customers, you're going to present and negotiate with a calm, clear mind, and be far less likely to suffer from Midnight Urgency. You know what I mean, that feeling of waking up in the middle of the night thinking, "I'll do *anything* to get that order!"

Your confidence will help you close more sales while your integrity stays intact.

Work your plan and keep your pipeline filled. You'll feel better about your sales career, sleep great at night and make a ton of money, too. ■

Joe Guertin is president of The Guertin Group. For biographical and business information, see page 265.

Editor's Note: In her 15 years as a top-producing sales professional, Colleen Francis negotiated with some pretty tough customers, including the U.S. government. She explains how preparation in nine specific areas is your key to success.

Preparation Equals Negotiation Success
by Colleen Francis

Mediocre salespeople are notoriously bad planners. It can be said that they habitually "play" more than they "practice." They go into most sales interactions unprepared, thinking they can "wing it" and negotiate "off the cuff." Top negotiators know differently. Top performers know that in order to successfully negotiate with clients they must plan carefully or risk being left vulnerable. Without proper strategy, your opponents will use your lack of preparation to their advantage. In other words, you are likely to give up more than you intended because you didn't have a plan.

Here are nine areas of planning to consider before you start negotiating with a client:

- **Determine your goals.** Negotiation is the art and science of reaching an agreement that meets your goals and the goals of your client. Your strategic goals create the measure you judge yourself by at the end of the process and they need to be set before the negotiation begins. Your goals also will act as your guide during the negotiation, supporting everything you say, every move you make and every agreement you reach. Carefully planning your strategy in advance will ensure you reach the goals that you and your company want to achieve. Remember that all goals should be set using the S.M.A.R.T. formula (Specific, Measurable, Attainable, Realistic and Time bound).

- **What's your BATNA?** What will happen if you do not reach an agreement with your client? Two of the biggest negotiating dangers are being too committed to gaining an agreement and being unduly pessimistic about what will happen if the negotiation fails. In my experience, most salespeople are overly committed to reaching an agreement (sometimes at the expense of all profitability) when they have no other options. Do yourself a favor. Ensure you have at least three opportunities waiting to close (or negotiate) for every one that you're currently negotiating. These three other qualified opportunities are your Best Alternatives to a Negotiated Agreement (BATNA) because they ensure you will never feel desperate to close business. The willingness to walk away is the most powerful leverage you can have during a negotiation. You'll only feel able to walk away, if you have something else waiting for you. Yes, you understand me correctly; prospecting is the key to negotiating success.

- **What is your position?** Specific goals for your negotiation can be called positions. Positions are simply statements of what you need to get in order to accept the deal. You should take some time before the negotiation to document what you want to get, need to get and what would be nice to get out of the interaction. Writing down these positions will make them clear in your mind and will help you focus the discussion. While you're at it, it's good practice to guess at what the client will want and intend to get as well.

- **Hide and seek.** In addition to positions, we all have other things we want to hide from (or avoid) and seek in the negotiation. Often, these are more hidden or political things. For example, your client may want to save face and you may want to augment your reputation. You may want to avoid exposing conflict inside your own company and the client may want to avoid including certain colleagues in the process. During your preparation it's valuable to ask yourself what you and the client seek, and want to avoid.

- **Find the missing link.** So, you know your goals and positions, and you have made an intelligent guess about your client's goals and positions. Now is the time to find the link between the two. Linking your goals to your customer's goals is a key to effective selling. A negotiated agreement is only profitable if it satisfies all parties. The best way to accomplish this mutually profitable relationship is to focus on finding the missing link between your objectives and your client's. Of course it's difficult to do this successfully if you don't know what your client's goals are. Think of this as a sales challenge: The better qualified your client is, the more you know about him and understand his goals, the better prepared you will be for the negotiation. Great negotiators start preparing for the negotiation at the start of the sales cycle and never stop!

- **What's your bottom line?** Your bottom line is the absolute, last resort and final offer on each key issue. It's your walk-away point. Setting a bottom line before you begin negotiating is important because it makes it easier to resist the temptation of agreeing to an unprofitable deal. Setting a bottom line protects you from seller's remorse and it makes it easier for others to participate in the negotiation with you because you've provided a negotiating framework. There are some downsides, though. The most notable is that having a bottom line can discourage creativity and may limit your ability to capitalize on new information revealed during the negotiation. Be careful not to set your bottom line too high. It's easy to overestimate the value of what you're selling, especially if it's personal.

- **Identify your trip wire.** The best negotiators set a trip wire for every negotiation that will indicate when they're close to their bottom lines. Your trip wire is established to ensure you don't enter into agreements that you will later regret. Establish a trip wire by identifying an outcome that's slightly better than your BATNA and bottom line, but far from your ideal bottom line. When a trip wire is triggered during a negotiation, commit to taking a break and thinking about the situation before accepting the deal. The last thing you want is to be forced into taking a deal that's worse than your trip wire. As a last resort, accept your trip wire and an acceptable end to the negotiation, *only* if you're able to receive something in return.

- **Where are you weak?** No one likes to admit he's not perfect, especially a salesperson! The truth is, no negotiation argument is perfect and yours is no exception. Everyone and every negotiation argument has at least one vulnerability. Your weakness is that spot that threatens the achievement of any one of your goals based on a real or perceived vulnerability in your argument. Don't ignore or brush off a perception. Your client's perception of you is the reality in which you negotiate. When planning for a negotiation it's wise to consider your weaknesses and plan for effective responses.

- **Giving concessions.** The first concessions you give always need to be "non-monetary," in other words, something that does not sacrifice the price of the product. If the client will not accept a non-monetary concession, then it may be necessary to give him a price break (monetary concession). For your point of reference, a concession is the act of granting, yielding or surrendering a right, privilege or gift. Your treatment of concessions will determine your success or failure in a negotiation and long-term relationship building. Always remember the cardinal rule: no free gifts!

Sure, it may seem daunting to prepare for a negotiation. That's because salespeople usually don't like the thought of getting to work! According to CSO Insights, just 10 minutes of prep can increase your effectiveness by up to 42%. Knowing that, doesn't it make sense to spend a little time thinking and planning before your next negotiation rather than simply jumping in unprepared? ∎

Colleen Francis is president of Engage Selling Solutions. For biographical and business information, see page 264.

Editor's Note: Jon Brooks has over 12 years' experience in sales and sales management. He began his career as director of inside sales for Telogy Incorporated, a high-tech financial services company. Jon grew the inside sales organization to upwards of 50 people across four different inside sales teams. He was responsible for 300% revenue growth in just twelve months, accounting for $45M in revenue. Today Jon is a principal in Brooks Dreyfus, a specialized sales consulting firm that helps companies improve their telesales efforts. He outlines a key recession-busting strategy: luring customers away from your competition.

Steal Business Away from Your Competition
by Jon Brooks

Displacing a competitor from his accounts can be a very difficult task. At the same time, displacing a competitor can be very lucrative for salespeople and an extremely profitable way for your company to increase its market share. To be successful, you should be careful in your approach and message to the competitor's client. Below are a few sales tactics to steal the business away from your competitor.

When your prospect mentions he's using your competitor, don't become confrontational or use that as a reason to end the conversation. He's expecting you to do that. Instead, take an approach that acknowledges and aligns with what he has said. For example, "I can understand you buying Competitor X's software for your specific needs. I'm sure I'd do the same thing in your situation."

This response may feel very odd because it sounds like you're telling your prospect to buy from the competition. In reality this response doesn't encourage him to purchase from the competition but instead validates the actions the customer has already taken. This unique approach will raise the curiosity level and lengthen the phone conversation you can have. Most importantly, it places you in an affable position with the prospect, not a confrontational one.

Likes and Dislikes

From this point you should move into a tactic we call "likes and dislikes." Simply put, first ask the customer what he likes about the competitor and then ask him what he doesn't like about the competitor. When you get to the point where you're asking about things he doesn't like, it's crucial that you phrase the question in a positive manner. For example, "What can Competitor A improve on?" That question is much better than, "What do you not like about Competitor A?" As you can see, the word "improve" is positive and the phrase "not like" is negative. Taking a positive approach will reflect well on you and your company. Additionally, it will likely allow you to continue building a relationship in future conversations.

Now you can try to displace your competitor with information about the client's likes and dislikes. You want the prospect to realize two key facts:

- Everything he likes about the competitor, you also do extremely well (if not better).
- Everything he doesn't like about the competitor you ensure does not happen with your customers.

Again, this is a very basic overview of the outcome you are hoping to accomplish. How you achieve this outcome is not as simple as telling the prospect, "I also like what you like and dislike what you dislike." It takes a well planned approach that revolves around the information you obtained during the call. Make sure during your conversation to write down detailed notes of everything the prospect is telling you. This information will be the cornerstone for structuring your solution (better than the competition's solution) to meet the client's needs.

Create a Problem

Another tactic you can use in subsequent calls is called "creating a problem." The basic premise behind "creating a problem" is just that, to create in the mind of the prospect—a problem with his current supplier.

To understand how this tactic works you need to go back to a very basic understanding of how a sale occurs. A sale occurs when a prospect believes that a salesperson can provide a solution to his need. What prevents a sale from occurring are "concerns." These concerns can range from price to simply not liking the salesperson. Anything that prevents a need-based sale from occurring is considered a concern. When a customer purchases a product from someone, ideally all of the customer's concerns should be alleviated. If a customer has no concerns, there is a smooth passage from the need to the solution (or in layman's terms, a sale takes place). If you can create concerns in the mind of your prospect, those concerns may jeopardize his relationship with your competitor. The more concerns you create that hit his "hot buttons," the more likely their relationship will ultimately fail.

The competitor will be blindsided by concerns that he must now try to solve. If he cannot alleviate those concerns, his client may leave him and come to you! Imagine what's going through the mind of your competitor, "I thought I closed this customer, why is he constantly calling me with concerns?"

You can take many different approaches to creating concerns. We think the most effective approach is to ask questions based on what he has already told you. Specifically, those areas he would like his supplier to improve upon. To accomplish this, take the points he's already mentioned and phrase them in the form of a question. The major advantage in phrasing these points in the form of a question is that the customer creates the problem, not you. Rather than you telling your competitor's client that he should have a problem with his current supplier, he tells himself. Continue to expand on those points in greater and greater detail. Here's a simplified example of how this conversation might go:

Salesperson: "Mr. Jones, you mentioned that you wish (Competitor A) had better customer service. Can you expand on that?"

Competitor's client: "I wish they would get back to us sooner when our software is not working properly."

Salesperson: "You're right. It's important to be extremely responsive in those situations. What are the negative effects of not having your software work properly?"

Competitor's client: "Well, it can cost of thousands of dollars because our employees are unable to work."

Salesperson: "Nobody can afford to lose thousands of dollars waiting for software to be fixed. Can I send you some information on how our product has a guaranteed 99.9% uptime? This ensures our clients don't lose the kind of money you're talking about."

The first conversation is just the beginning. Continue to expand on these points in greater detail on future calls. These are "hot button" concerns that the prospect has raised about your competitor. Continue to remind him not just about his concern, but more importantly the negative outcome it has on him. When a prospect understands the entire negative impact his concern is having, he will be much more likely to displace his current provider and buy from you!

Don't flatter yourself by believing that you can convince the prospect to ditch your competitor and come to you on the first call. Displacing the competition will take time. As with all sales, begin by closing the customer on very small goals and progress the relationship to bigger goals. For example, your first goal may be to close the customer on getting him to tell you information about his company. Or maybe it's as simple as having him write your name and number down for future reference. These goals may sound trivial, but they bring you one step closer to winning business from the customer. One small step multiplied by dozens of competitor's clients will put you far ahead of fellow sales reps and the competition. Ultimately it will lead to more and more sales. Remember, great rewards come to those who are patient. ∎

Jon Brooks is a founding partner of Brooks Dreyfus Consulting. For biographical and business information, see page 262.

Editor's Note: Julie Thomas knows about selling in tough times. She spent over 16 years successfully selling in the technology field, rising from sales rep to vice president of worldwide sales development at Gartner Inc. In a fast-declining minicomputer industry, she not only met her quota, she exceeded it. Julie credits her success to the ValueSelling training she received. She liked it so much, she ended up buying the company! Her advice will help you negotiate successfully in a down economy.

Negotiating to Win
by Julie Thomas

In today's hyper-competitive markets, prospects are more risk-averse than ever. Many prospects focus on every aspect of every purchase to prove that they are getting the best possible deals. Often they have "professional purchasers" who are fully responsible to get the best deals possible. At the same time, your goal is to establish enough value to minimize the cost discussion when it's time to close the business. As a seller of goods and services, your company's profits are directly affected by your ability to meet your customers' needs while meeting your own goals.

Sales is the business of relationships, and like any relationship it requires give and take. We typically expect the give and take, also known as negotiating, to happen during proposal and contract discussions; however, in reality, we continually negotiate throughout the sales process—on everything from picking a time to meet to determining who will participate in a demo to hashing out the terms and conditions of a contract. Negotiations are most productive when conducted objectively, and at the right time.

Here are a few points to remember when negotiating with prospects:
- Understand the "need" behind your prospect's position. In any negotiating situation, your responsibility is to understand your prospect's criteria—as well as your own— and ethically create positive outcomes for all parties involved.
- Know your empowerment level; you could find yourself in dangerous territory with either your company or prospect if you commit to things that are outside your control.

- Define what constitutes a "win" for all parties. Here, it's critical to consider what you want as well as what your prospect wants.
- Be clear about what you can negotiate and what is non-negotiable. For each of us, there are non-negotiable items that are not open for discussion or compromise. It's important that we understand them and are clear about what we're willing to negotiate.
- Maintain composure; respond rather than react and maintain a high level of rapport every step of the way.
- Finally, know your "walk-away" position; some deals are simply not worth what you are being asked to give up.

A key to successful negotiating is to understand when to negotiate in the first place. Negotiating components of deliverables, terms or pricing before the prospect is actually "sold" on your solution will cause you credibility problems. It's important not to negotiate until you have clearly shown the prospect what his world will be like after he acquires your product or services. Establish both business and personal value for the individuals you are working with. Also, understand the prospect's process for purchasing so that you are not caught in a position of multiple negotiations with multiple individuals.

There are typically three things to negotiate at the end of your sales cycle: deliverables, terms and conditions, and pricing. Your price is always a function of your deliverables and your terms and conditions. As you prepare for your negotiation, there are three key strategies that can help you through the process:

Strategy #1: Trade-offs

A successful negotiation means balancing the needs of both parties. With trade-offs, your objective is to meet both parties' needs by trading items from one category with items in a second category. For example, you may be willing to reduce your price if you can make a change in terms or deliverables.

How it might sound:

"If you want this product shipped to multiple locations, are you willing to accept different payment terms?"

Strategy #2: Embellishments

This strategy requires you to add incremental value in one category when you can't make a trade-off to accommodate the prospect. For instance, you may throw in deliverables that have little cost to you but are have value to the prospect.

How it might sound:

"If we expand the training class from 15 to 20 people, are you willing to move forward today with the terms and investment we have discussed?"

Strategy #3: Compromise

Compromise involves finding the middle ground in the same category. Splitting the difference on price, payment terms or a specific deliverable could be examples.

How it might sound:

"If we can split the difference in payment terms between net 10 and net 30, can we move forward today?"

Think about a current sales cycle that's nearing the closing point. First, analyze all areas of your qualification process to confirm that you have a truly qualified prospect. If you find that you're not working with a qualified prospect, re-engage on the sales cycle rather than the negotiation.

Next, prepare for any potential negotiation by identifying both the prospect's and your own ideal position. Make a list of what is non-negotiable from your perspective, and another list of what you think your prospect might require to move forward. From these two lists, develop potential win-win negotiating strategies using the aforementioned strategies:

- Trade-offs
- Embellishments
- Compromises

Negotiating for success requires planning and strong communication skills. Being prepared for the negotiation with solid ideas and strategies will put you in a position of strength! ■

Julie Thomas is president and CEO of ValueSelling Associates. For biographical and business information, see page 273.

Even though time is precious, we sometimes let it slip away. When the going gets tough, the tough need to be more productive. This article identifies a few of the time bandits that steal our time. Imagine if you had three more months per year to sell. That's the amount of time that can be restored when you make a commitment to focusing on work for a full eight hours per day, as Michael Johnson explains.

Fighting the Time Bandits
by Michael Dalton Johnson

Work eight hours a day. That's it. The rest of the day is yours.

You can get a lot done in eight hours. In fact, eight hours is an eternity. If you don't believe this, fly coach for eight hours seated next to a crying infant. You'll get a keen understanding of just how long it is.

Consider the time you devote to productive work as your "Golden Eight." Golden because time is indeed money especially if you are in sales.

Working a solid, focused eight hours can be difficult. Every day, time bandits knock on your door. Members of this mob include personal phone calls and texting, bull sessions with co-workers, checking personal email, looking for lost things (highly productive people have clean and well-organized desks), personal errands, long breaks and longer lunches...the list goes on.

It all adds up. Research shows that, on average, salespeople waste two hours a day. This works out to be a startling three months a year! How much can you sell in three months?

By far the biggest time bandit is the Internet. While the Web is an indispensable business, communication, education, and research tool, it is also highly addictive. Like most addictions, it can devour your precious time, energy and productivity and, by extension, your income.

Take it from a recovering Internet addict; if you are serious about increasing your productivity, you will avoid these Internet time bandits:

- **Social Networking.** Sure it's fun to share photos and news with friends and family but it also diminishes your productivity. Do it after hours.

- **Online Videos.** That hilarious video of the cute little kitten playing ping-pong is a must see... but not during the Golden Eight you've devoted to work.
- **News and Blogs.** Offering lively writing, lots of photos and tempting links to other sites and news items, these are powerfully addictive. Stay off them during work.
- **Shopping.** The Internet is open 24 hours a day. Shop before or after work hours.
- **Surfing the Web.** There's a lot out there to see. It's interesting and entertaining but a pointless drain on your precious time.
- **All That Other Stuff.** Online games, auctions, adult sites, chat rooms, job sites, dating sites, vacation and travel sites are all major workplace no-no's.

Carpe Diem! Each morning take a few moments to write down what you want to accomplish that day. This does not have to be an hour-by-hour work plan. It can simply state the work activities that will give you the highest return on your time. Allow yourself a little flexibility, but follow your plan.

You'll be on your way to much greater productivity. You'll enjoy the feeling of knowing you've put in an honest and productive eight hours. You'll look forward with much greater appreciation to the 16 hours left for rest, relaxation, friends, family and maybe a little time on the Internet. ∎

Michael Dalton Johnson is founder and president of SalesDog.com. For biographical and business information, see page 267.

Editor's Note: Joanne Black is one of America's leading authorities on referral selling. Her clients include Alliant Resources Group, Charles Schwab, and Wells Fargo Bank. With more than 30 years' experience in sales, sales training and consulting, Joanne has sold her way through some pretty tough times. Learn eight ways to attract new business in a difficult economy.

Get More Referrals, Attract New Clients and Decrease Costs during a Recession
by Joanne S. Black

Salespeople sell. It's what we do—to many different kinds of businesses in any and every economy. A stagnant economy can kick even the most seasoned sales pro in the knees. It becomes more difficult than ever to sign up new clients—or even to get potential clients to take the time to talk to us.

The reality is that every salesperson can land great clients, even in tough times. Every salesperson can make more money, even in a lagging economy.

Despite what we hear and read, economic upswings and downturns have been the norm throughout history. The extended period of growth and prosperity we experienced between the early 1950s and 2000 was an aberration. Hard to believe, isn't it? We got so used to an upward growth curve, albeit with a few minor downturns, that we never thought we'd hear pundits say that things haven't been this bad since the Great Depression.

Many salespeople feel paralyzed when clients stop buying and their pipeline dries up. Clients cut advertising, travel, training, marketing, and discretionary expense line items. Salespeople think that since there's nothing they can do, they should do nothing. But "nothing" is futile thinking.

It's time to take action!

There are as many business rules as there are businesses, but a few tenets are always key, in any economy. Economists agree that the companies that will not only survive, but thrive through tough economic times, are the companies that invest in themselves—with strategic marketing programs, new sales approaches, or accelerated business processes.

As a salesperson, you need to invest in yourself. What if you could reach your market, accelerate sales, retain your loyal customers, and attract new business without increasing your cost of sales—while decreasing your sales time?

Here are eight "killer steps" to attracting new business in a volatile economy.

- **Broaden your perspective and narrow your focus.** Step back and develop strategies for your sales territory that will separate you from the competition and will create a leap in demand for your products and services. Just like looking through the lens of a camera, you see the broad landscape first. Then, you adjust your lens and focus on a specific image.

  You need to do the same for your book of business. Look at the big picture, focus on a specific strategy, and go for it. Don't let anything distract you. One approach is to assemble an informal group of advisors and get their input and creative ideas. Include people who have differing points of view from you. This is not easy, but it's critical.

- **Be nimble and innovative.** You'll never have all the facts. Make quick decisions—whether to go after a new market, put a new twist on an older product, shift your selling strategy, or build a new alliance. Be fearless and make tough choices. Get rid of your sacred cows. When the economy slows, the pace of your decision-making must speed up.

- **Dazzle your current clients.** Don't ignore your current clients at the expense of new business, because they are your best source for new business. Call your clients. Find out how the economy is impacting their business. Offer to help in any way you can. Send them an article, put them in touch with someone else in their situation, or even offer to provide a service with no fee. Yes, no fee. Now is the time to help. Period. Do whatever it takes.

- **Prioritize wisely.** The most important activity for any salesperson is to do what's "closest to cash" the first thing every single day— whether it's following up with a prospect, writing a proposal, or closing a deal. Most of us get buried in email every morning and surface a few hours later. If you do what's "closest to cash" first, it won't matter if other things on your to-do list don't get done. They're just not that important.

- **Become the expert.** Companies hire experts because they can't afford to make mistakes. They want to be assured of results for their business. Position yourself and your company as the expert with a specific product or in a specific market niche. This is counter-intuitive—especially in a tough economy. We often think if we don't mention everything we do, we will miss an opportunity. The opposite is true. The more narrow your focus, the better your market position.

- **Stay connected.** Woody Allen said, "Eight percent of success is showing up." You need to show up. You need to be visible. If you want to get more business, you have to network like crazy. Attend a minimum of one event a week. Pay for it in advance. You never know who you will meet and what you will learn. Never let your network go down. Go to the events where your clients go. Networking is an essential referral-marketing activity.

- **Don't cut price.** There's a lot of chatter about cutting prices in a lagging economy. Yes, clients will negotiate on price. That's their job—to build business while watching the bottom line. How many times have you submitted a proposed price to a client, and had them say, right off the bat, "Great! Where do I sign?" It doesn't happen. We always want to get the best deal, so why wouldn't our clients?

  If you must adjust your price, then adjust the scale of your project or the deliverables as well. Always get something in return and write it into your agreement. Instead of cutting your price, consider how to "get in and get started." Divide your offering into smaller chunks, get results, and create traction.

- **Commit to building your referral business.** Referrals are always terrific, but they mean even more in a lagging economy. When you receive a qualified referral, you typically land a new client between 70 and 90 percent of the time. Additionally, you are pre-sold, your selling time decreases, credibility increases, and you ace out your competition.

There is no other business development process that can claim these results. Yet, more than 95 percent of salespeople don't have a targeted referral strategy—with a written referral plan, weekly referral goals, and ways to track and measure referrals.

Referral Selling: Get Started

Getting started with a referral selling strategy is straightforward. Follow these tips and you will get more referrals. You will attract new business. You will get more clients. You will accelerate your sales.

1. **The List.** Make a list of everyone you know—current clients, past clients, peers, neighbors, service providers, friends, past co-workers, professional association members, volunteer groups, etc. You should have at least 100 names. Prioritize the list by starting with the people that you know best. You are not asking these people for their business; you are asking them to refer you to people they know.

2. **Goals.** Set a goal and decide how many people you will contact each week. Arrange in-person meetings if at all possible.

3. **The Ideal Client.** Tell your referral sources that you build your business through referrals and would like their help. Describe your ideal client and ask for one or two people who meet your description.

4. **Referral Sources.** Ask your referral source to make the introduction. Without an introduction, it's not a referral—it's a cold call.

The only budget you need to worry about during a recession is your time... your time to ask for referrals. It's a recession-proof strategy! ■

Joanne S. Black is founder of No More Cold Calling®. For biographical and business information, see page 261.

Editor's Note: Jim McCormick is not only an accomplished speaker, author and business executive, he's a world-class skydiver. He holds five skydiving world records and has jumped over 2,800 times including jumps from 31,000 feet. Needless to say Jim's not afraid to cold call. Fear of rejection holding you back? Take the plunge and read on.

How to Succeed at Cold Calling
by Jim McCormick

There it is. That darn phone. And you have to pick it up and call someone you don't know. You need to make some cold calls.

The first thing to know is this—the longer you put off picking up the phone and making that first call, the heavier that phone gets. Give it enough time and you'll swear the phone weighs 500 pounds when you try to lift it.

How do you overcome the understandable fear of cold calling? I've been skydiving for years. In thousands of jumps, I've learned some valuable lessons that apply to lots of things, including cold calling. Let me share some insights with you that I've reaped from all those skydives. Here are a few simple suggestions to make you more successful at cold calling.

You Have to Believe in What You're Offering

You have to believe in the product or service you are offering. You have to know you are selling something of value, something that will assist the person or organization you are calling.

If you are not sure of the benefits you are offering your prospect, you need to sit down and think about them. Ask yourself, "How will this person or his organization be better off if he buys what I am selling?" "How will he sell more, operate better, be happier? "

This is vital! Do not bother going on to the next steps until you have this really clear in your mind. You will be wasting your time. You have to be absolutely convinced, deep down, of the value of your product or service.

Now if you are stumped on this one, get some help. Ask some colleagues or friends for their thoughts on the value you are offering. If you do all this and conclude there really is not much value in what you are offering, then move on! You will never be a success at selling something you don't believe in. And life is too short to spend your time doing it.

It's similar to skydiving. If you do not believe in yourself and your equipment, you have no business being in the plane. You owe it to yourself, and your prospects, to only sell something in which you truly believe.

Change Your Perspective

When I was getting certified to take people for their first skydives, I was required to put on the student harness and ride on the front of an experienced instructor—just like my students do now. This was required because it is critical that I understand the student's viewpoint. Experiencing a jump from the student's perspective has definitely made me a better instructor.

It is the same for cold calling. You have to put yourself in the buyer's shoes. In your mind, trade places with your prospect. Ask yourself, "What would make me say, "yes?" Also ask yourself, "What would make me say, "no?" You have to appreciate the buyer's perspective to effectively sell to him.

It may help to ask people you have already sold why they said, "yes." What made the difference to them? You'll gain valuable insights that will help you better understand your prospects' perspective and make you more effective.

Shake Off the Rejection

When you are cold calling, you will experience rejection; it is unavoidable! Here is the important thing to keep in mind: It is not about you! Your prospect is not rejecting you. He is rejecting the product or service you are offering. He may just not need it right now. Or he may be so overwhelmed with challenges, he just cannot focus on what you have to say. He is not rejecting you! He does not even know you.

Rejection is a part of life, so is an occasional sub-par performance. I have walked away from many skydives very disappointed in my performance; but you have to shake it off and keep going. If I allowed my disappointment to get to me, I would eventually stop jumping, and that would deprive me of something I truly love.

It is similar with cold calling. If you allow the rejections to get to you, they will profoundly impact your effectiveness. When you get the "no" answers, the terse responses, or even the hang ups, you have to be able to say to yourself, "Oh well, their loss. I'm sorry they're not able to take advantage of the wonderful product or service I am offering right now. But, I am going to keep calling to find people who will"—and mean it.

Accept the Fear

No one likes being rejected or hearing "no." That is normal and OK. It is easy to allow the desire to succeed to lapse into a desire not to fail, which can then turn into fear.

Don't worry, being fearful of rejection or failure is natural and appropriate. What is important is that you do not play games with yourself. If the fear is there, don't try to fool yourself into thinking otherwise. Don't deny it.

Until you accept the presence of the fear, it is in charge. When you accept its presence and the fact that it is likely affecting you, you take a great deal of the power away from the fear.

Keep Dialing

You build momentum with each call. When you stop dialing, you lose it. Set things up so you have plenty of prospects to call before you get started and do your research in advance. When it comes time to call, do it with a vengeance! The sooner you make the next call, regardless of whether it is a sale or not, the better. You build momentum. One sale will lead to another.

If the last call was not a success, it is even more important to pick up the phone again right away. The longer you wait, the more likely it is to get to you. Get started.

Cold calling will always be challenging, but you can make it more pleasant and be more successful at it by following these steps. Now get started. The sooner the better! ∎

Jim McCormick is managing principal of TakeRisks.com. For biographical and business information, see page 269.

Editor's Note: Alan Rigg has more than 20 years' hands-on experience in sales and sales management. As a sales performance expert, he's consulted with hundreds of sales organizations in a variety of industries. He's authored two books on applying the 80/20 Rule in sales and is a sought-after speaker and seminar leader. His advice will help you handle premature price objections.

How to Delay Talking about Price Until You've Identified Value
by Alan Rigg

Talking about price is an important step in the sales opportunity qualification process. After all, if a prospect can't afford your price, is he really a valid prospect? Do you really want to invest your valuable time trying to sell to him?

That said, it often does more harm than good to discuss price before you and the prospect have determined whether your product or service can provide value. Just about any price sounds high when it's quoted in a vacuum. Yet, that very same price can sound very reasonable, or even cheap, when compared to the quantified impact of a prospect's business problems.

What is a Quantified Impact?

Just about every product or service can solve specific problems for your prospects. Your mission as a salesperson is to ask questions to determine whether a prospect has any of the problems that your products or services can solve.

Once you determine a prospect has one or more of the business problems you can solve, your next step is to ask questions to uncover how each problem impacts the prospect's business. Then you should ask questions to encourage the prospect to quantify his business problems, associating dollars or percentages and time frames with it.

Here are several examples of quantified business impacts:
- Our top-performing salespeople produce $200,000 more net profit per year than our average-performing salespeople.

- [Problem] Generates an extra million dollars in operating costs in a six-month period.
- [Problem] Increases our administrative expenses by 22% per month.

Close More Sales with Quantified Impacts

How? If the quantified impact of a business problem exceeds the investment required to fix the problem, a buying decision is easy to justify. The larger the difference between the impact and the required investment, the easier it becomes to close the sale. If the quantified impact is a multiple of the required investment (for example, a quantified impact of millions of dollars versus a required investment of thousands of dollars), the buying decision becomes a "no-brainer."

To make your case, your prospect must be the source of the numbers. Why? In general, prospects don't trust salespeople. Many have dealt with salespeople who were more interested in making sales than they were in providing value. Plus, prospects recognize that salespeople have a vested interest in building a convincing business case that can be used to support a buying decision. This causes prospects to discount any quantified impact information that salespeople provide. However, when the prospect is the source of the information, he perceives it as unquestioned truth. This makes learning how to ask questions to quantify the impact of business problems a valuable skill indeed!

What do you do if a prospect asks for the price of your product or service before you have had a chance to uncover the quantified impacts of his business problems? Depending upon where you are in the process, you might respond in one of the following ways:

"Bill, I promise that I will provide complete pricing information before we finish our conversation today. However, at this point I don't even know:

- …anything about your business. What does your company do?"
- …whether you have any of the kinds of problems we address." (Then ask a qualifying question that will help determine whether the prospect has one or more of the business problems that your products or services can solve.)

- …whether it even makes sense for you to consider buying anything from us." (Then ask a question that will help the prospect quantify the impact of a specific business problem that has been identified.)

In my experience, the prospect will be willing to defer the pricing conversation. In the rare case where the prospect refuses to answer your questions and continues to push for price, you might say something like:

> "Bill, at this point we don't have anything to compare the price with. My experience has been that a price quoted in a vacuum always sounds high. Would you agree?" (Allow prospect to respond.)

> "If we can't establish value, would any price convince you to buy?" (Allow prospect to respond.)

> "Could we spend a little time trying to figure out whether [product or service name] will produce value for you?"

The Prospect May Not be Willing to Engage in a Value Discussion

This is especially likely if your product or service is seen as a commodity. If that's the case, you will need to decide whether you want to try to win the prospect's business based upon price. However, remember that this situation is the exception. In most situations the prospect will be willing to defer the pricing conversation and answer your questions.

The key to successful price discussions is first determining whether your product or service can provide value. This value creates a frame of reference against which price can be compared.

To determine value, ask questions to discover whether your prospects have any of the business problems your products or services can solve. Then, ask questions to identify how each business problem impacts the prospect's business. Finally, ask more questions to quantify the impact of each business problem. The greater the quantified impact, the better your price will look in comparison, and the greater your chances will be of making a sale! ∎

Alan Rigg is president of 80/20 Sales Performance. For biographical and business information, see page 271.

Editor's Note: Dave Stein is an internationally recognized sales expert, bestselling author and popular columnist. For two decades, Dave worked in the technology sector for Fortune Systems Corporation, Datalogix International, and Marcam Corporation. In 1997, he founded his sales consultancy, serving clients like Hewlett Packard, Kronos, Oracle, and Siemens. Most recently Dave co-founded a sales training evaluation company, ES Research.

An Alternative to Discounting
by Dave Stein

Last minute discounting has become so prevalent that many companies have come to depend on it as their default sales strategy. Employing a go-to-market strategy of being the lowest cost provider is one thing, but dramatic, tactical discounting on every deal will erode your company's margins and leave you digging a deeper and deeper hole in which your company will ultimately bury itself.

I don't want to give you the impression that discounting is never appropriate. I can think of three scenarios where it's required:

1. **When a company has mispriced its offering.** Let's face it. Times have changed. Competition is fierce. And yes, as much as we don't like to admit it, prices and fees have been forced down in some markets. If everyone else is now selling what you sell for $1.00 and you're still selling it, just as you always have, for $2.00 and you can't prove you can deliver a dollar's worth of additional value for the customer, your pricing is too high—way too high. Call it a discount, or call it a price adjustment, in this situation you've got to face reality and sell your products at a price the market will bear, or you won't sell very much at all.

2. **As a token concession to close the deal.** I don't see a problem with "rewarding" a buyer for signing an order within your timeframe, for example. Understand, I would much rather provide other concessions that don't cost my company money and don't let my customer think that whenever I'm going to ask him for an order, I am going to give up part of my margin and commission. But I do live in the real world and

understand that for my clients, pricing concessions are sometimes required to get the deal signed.

3. **When you haven't done an adequate job of selling the unique business value your product or service will provide the customer.** My clients will tell you I am never happy in a situation like this, but if you haven't done the best selling job, and there's some room for a discount, and you need the deal, discounting may be better than losing the deal on principal.

How Do You Avoid Discounting?

To succeed in business-to-business sales today, you must sell business improvement, not products or services. That means differentiating yourself from your competition in the unique value you, your products and services, and your company can provide to help your customer achieve his corporate, divisional, business unit, department, or government agency goals.

Have you transitioned into the mode of creating customer demand by targeting accounts, getting in before they know they have a need, and establishing yourself as a knowledgeable, trusted, and patient advisor? If not, you'll continue to be on the receiving end of all sorts of one-sided customer demands, mostly taking the form of answering requests for information, doing presentations, demonstrations, fighting the constant battle against having your offering commoditized by the customer, and being on the receiving end of strong demands for discounts.

We've been taught over the years to bundle our products and services where possible to provide the customer with a single investment number. That way, we were told, he can't nickel and dime you, and can't slice up your offering so he can say no to pieces he doesn't want or need. But now times have changed and when you think about it, that's exactly what you want to do. If you sell products or services that can be componentized, sold in pieces or modules, or in phases, you're potentially in good shape.

Scenario

You know your competition is going to come in with a substantial discount, just like he has before. Your sales effort must include:

- Assuring yourself that the customer is not making a decision solely or primarily on price. This question must be asked again and again of key decision makers.
- Getting agreement from the real buyer that you understand his business objectives and that your offering can help him achieve those objectives. This method doesn't work unless you're dealing with the real buyer.
- Finding unique areas of additional value (on top of his existing requirements) that you can provide through the capabilities of your product or service offering.
- Management support for potentially selling part of your offering now, and the rest later rather than selling the whole thing at a discounted price.

In cases where you know your competitors will be discounting, you'll need to offer several investment options to your customer. Alan Weiss, the consultant's consultant, suggests providing three opportunities for your prospect to say yes.

If you offer your prospect three options to buy, let's say for the sake of labels, Platinum, Gold, and Silver, and you've done a good job of selling the business value of your offering, you can avoid having to concede more than a nominal discount.

Your plan here should be not to discount, but rather to back value out of your proposal to meet the prospect's desired investment level. Presenting three options lets you do exactly that. The customer gets to determine how much he wants to invest and he will enjoy the resulting ROI associated with that level of investment.

Here are the three options:

The Platinum Option

- Gets the customer what he needs (and wants);
- Highest level of investment. You might ask for a 10%-30% premium over the Gold level for this option, depending on the value you believe you can deliver to the customer;
- All the features, modules, components, and capabilities available. Your best resources;
- Quickest time to value;

- Priority service—a special 800 number, top of the queue, 24 x 7 x 365;
- The highest ROI; and
- Other perks, such as quarterly meetings with your CEO, special invitation events, input into your product development plans.

The Gold Option

- Gets the customer all of what he needs (and a few wants);
- Budgeted level of investment. This is aimed right at the prospect's budget level;
- Most/many of the features, modules, components, and capabilities;
- Proven, talented and dependable resources;
- Quick time to value;
- An attractive ROI; and
- Other perks, such as quarterly meetings with your VP of Service, and special invitation events.

When your prospect tells you your competition has come in with a very low price, you discuss calmly with him the fact that you have an option (the Silver option) that will provide him with what he needs at a competitive price. You will already have differentiated yourself from the competition in a number of areas: understanding the customer's business, industry, opportunities, challenges, competitive and customer pressures, and you will have built rapport with the real buyer. In addition, you've professionally educated your prospect on the risks that befall companies who depend on tactical discounting to win.

The Silver Option

- Gets the customer most of what he needs now, and the rest in "phase two," next quarter or next year;
- The lowest level of investment, aimed at 10%-30% below the Gold level, depending on how severe a discount the competition is going to offer;
- Some of your total array of features, modules, components, and capabilities. The rest can be purchased later;
- Talented and dependable resources;
- Reasonable time to value; and
- An ROI that meets his corporate requirements;

What will the customer do? He may tell you he wants your Platinum option at the Silver price. If you've done an effective job selling the business value of your product or service and built a relationship with the real buyer based upon trust, you can look him in the eye and tell him it just isn't possible. What will he do then? My clients tell me that more often than not, he'll go for the Gold or Platinum option. ∎

Dave Stein is CEO of ES Research Group. For biographical and business information, see page 273.

Editor's Note: Considered the grand master of telesales training, Art Sobczak publishes a popular newsletter on prospecting and selling by phone. I still have some 13-year-old issues on my bookshelf from the days when I had a large telemarketing division in one of my publishing companies. It was good stuff then, and it still rings true today. Art doesn't just tell you what to do. He clearly outlines how to do what you need to—in this case, how to help prospects understand the dollar value of your solution.

Show Them the Money!
by Art Sobczak

Once into his questioning, the sales rep asks, "So you're finding that the last stage of the manufacturing process is a challenge?"

Prospect: "Well, yeah, we're having to do a few repetitive tasks to get it done."

Rep: "We have software that can make that job easier and it's only five thousand dollars."

Prospect: "Five thousand just for making that part easier. That's crazy."

So what happened here?

The sales rep uncovered a problem. However, he was so eager to talk about how his product solved that problem, he failed to continue walking the prospect down the path to realizing what the problem was costing him. He didn't see the problem as being painful enough in the short or long term.

For most business-to-business transactions, it's all about the money. The return on investment.

It's pretty simple: You will always sell more when you help the prospect or customer understand the cost of the problem or potential problem, and then the payoff of the solution and/or the result of taking action.

"Dollarize" the Situation

In his great book, *How to Become a Rainmaker*, Jeffrey Fox calls it "Dollarizing." He says, "Rainmakers don't sell fasteners or valves or washing machines or double-paned windows or tax audits or irrigation systems or training programs or golf clubs. Rainmakers sell money! They sell reduced downtime, fewer repairs, better gas mileage, higher deposit interest, increased output, decreased energy usage, more wheat per acre, more yardage per swing."

When you analyze it, we buy things because the price we pay for something is perceived as being less than the dollar value we attach to the result. Our job, then, is to be sure the prospect realizes that the value of the result is high and the price is low.

The classic book, *SPIN Selling* uses the term, "Implication Questions." It's taking a problem that a buyer perceives to be small (or nonexistent in some cases) and building it up in a problem large enough to justify action.

Using the earlier example and dollarizing with implication questions we could get a different result.

Prospect: "Well, yeah, we're having to do a few repetitive tasks to get it done."

Rep: "What do you have to do?"

Prospect: "In the final stage, one of the operators has to go back and re-input the command codes to keep the line moving."

Rep: "Please explain."

Prospect: "He has to leave his main station, move over to the other console, input the codes he already put in, and then go back to his position."

Rep: "How often is that happening?"

Prospect: "Geesh, over a hundred times a day?"

Rep: "Isn't that slowing up the line and cutting down production?"

Without belaboring the point, you can see where the rep is going with this—ultimately, he would get the prospect to tell him exactly how much lost production is costing the company every day!

Extrapolating that out over the course of a year might mean hundreds of thousands in lost profits. Now then, wouldn't that $5000 software be a no-brainer?

Monetize and Quantify

Whenever you uncover a problem, a pain, or a desire, attach numbers and dollars to it. For example,

- "How much is that costing you?"
- "How many?"
- "How often does it happen?"
- "What are the other expenses involved?"

There are hundreds of questions that could apply. Matter of fact, you should define them for yourself.

Your Action Step

Pull out a legal pad. At the top of the first page, describe a result of your product or service, such as, "High quality plastic, meaning fewer returns due to defects." Then, list all the possible costs of returns due to defects for a customer, such as customer service phone time to take the call, cost of replacement part, all shipping costs, return of defective part, possible lost sales because of poor quality, and more. Finally, develop questions designed to get your prospects and customers talking about the problem. Take it further and brainstorm for the possible answers, and your next questions to keep them talking, and attaching costs to the problem, and the payoff for a solution. Rinse and repeat. Start new pages for each of your results.

Just think of what lost sales might be costing you now, and how much more you could make by doing this. ■

Art Sobczak is president of Business By Phone, Inc. For biographical and business information, see page 273.

Editor's Note: Jeb Blount has more than 20 years' experience in sales and marketing. He has coached, trained and developed hundreds of sales professionals. A bestselling author and popular podcaster, Jeb learned this invaluable technique from his father, a famous trial lawyer.

The Missing Step in Your Sales Process
by Jeb Blount

Jennifer was nervous. She had just given the final presentation to the decision-making committee from a Fortune 500 manufacturing company she'd been trying to turn into a customer ever since she received the RFP nine months earlier. As she got into her car and pulled out of the parking lot, she knew something was wrong. Up until the presentation she felt that her rapport with the key contact was strong, and her relationships with the other influencers in the account had also seemed solid. But for some reason, her presentation had not generated the enthusiastic reaction she had anticipated. She racked her brain, going through the checklist of issues she had uncovered, but couldn't think of anything she had missed.

Two weeks later, Derek, the director of procurement from her prospect called to break the news that the committee had signed a contract with her competitor. As the news sunk in she felt like the wind had been knocked out of her. How much time had she spent working on this account? She had put more effort into this one than any other account in her pipeline, spending months gathering information, visiting locations, and interviewing people up and down the company's chain of command. This hurt. Stammering, she asked, "Why did you choose them over us?"

Derek, who had grown to like Jennifer, tried to let her down easy. "Jennifer, we think you and your company are great. We especially like you and really appreciate all of the time you spent with us. You helped us learn things about our business that we didn't know. But, at the end of the day, we felt like your competitor had a better invoicing and billing process that would allow us to manage our costs across multiple divisions. If it helps any, I was in your corner. I just think your competitor did a better job presenting his solution."

Jennifer was stunned. Her company had a far superior billing platform than her competitor. She knew this was important but thought, based on her interviews, that waste reduction was a higher priority. She tried to explain this to Derek, but it was too little too late. Apparently, her competitor had known that billing was a big issue and dedicated a large portion of his presentation to invoicing and billing solutions.

A Sales Lesson from a Lawyer

My dad is considered by many of his peers to be one of the top trial lawyers in the United States. During the summers, when I was growing up, he would often take me to court with him. It was during those trips, while watching him and others that I learned something important about lawyers. In court, when presenting or selling their cases to the jury, attorneys never ask questions for which they don't already know the answers. In other words, by the time they get to court (despite what you see on TV), there are no surprises. They make their cases to the juries systematically using evidence and witnesses that have been vetted through pre-trial discovery and depositions. They have even taken time to research the jury members to gain a clear understanding of what is important to each of them.

Learning this lesson as a kid paid off for me as a sales professional. As I applied the pre-trial discovery process to selling I found that I closed more deals, negotiated better terms and conditions, and developed stronger relationships. And, I was almost never dealt surprises during presentations or closings. In fact, while I was anchoring my relationships, and strengthening my cases, my competitors were running around trying to learn top secret closing techniques that would magically deliver the deals.

The real secret to closing is working with qualified prospects and executing the sales process. Once you're working with a qualified prospect or customer your sales process generally will cross through three or four major steps—depending on your product or service. Those steps are Discovery (or information gathering), Presenting, Closing, and in some cases Implementation and Transition. Of course there are many sub-steps, but these are generally acknowledged as the major parts of the sales process.

However, I believe there is an additional step that most trainers and 80% to 90% of sellers leave out. This is the step I learned from my dad. Executed correctly, this one step, with the exception of qualification, will have a greater impact on your closing ratio than any other in the sales process. In this step, which comes after Discovery and before your Presentation, you sit down with your prospect or customer (sometimes this means multiple people in an account), and confirm and verify the information and problems you have uncovered. In the Confirmation step you allow your prospect to correct any mistaken assumptions you've made, fill in any gaps, and most importantly you allow him to prioritize the issues that are most important to him.

Usually this step only takes a 15- to 30-minute conversation over the phone or in person and is set up like this, "Hi Bob, this is Jeb Blount, SalesGravy.com, thank you for taking so much time with me to help me understand your needs and issues. I can't wait to present my solutions at our meeting next week. Before I do that though, I want to be sure that I don't waste your time with unimportant things. Since I've uncovered a lot of opportunities to help you I was wondering if I might have 15 minutes of your time to review my assumptions just to be sure I'm on track to help you get what you want. Would 3 p.m. tomorrow work for you?"

This simple act sets up an informal meeting during which Bob confirms my assumptions, prioritizes what's important to him, and tells me exactly what I need to do to close him. It shows him that I care about his needs and concerns, demonstrates my commitment to excellence, and gets me in front of him one more time before the presentation, which further strengthens my relationship. I also know none of my competitors will take this extra step.

Using the Confirmation step, you go into your presentations with no surprises. You know exactly which solutions to present, which problems to solve, and on which hot buttons to focus your attention. You systematically make your case and wow your audience with your knowledge and understanding of their business issues. By the time you get around to signing the contract, closing the business seems almost anti-climatic because closing wasn't something you did or some cheesy technique you used, it was simply a result of understanding clearly what was important to your customer and building an ironclad case for your solution. ∎

Jeb Blount is founder and CEO of SalesGravy.com. For biographical and business information, see page 262.

Editor's Note: Anne Miller is an internationally respected author, speaker and seminar leader who teaches salespeople and business leaders how to use metaphors to convey complex ideas and get the sale. Her clients include American Express, Yahoo!, Dow Jones, The Blackstone Group, and Northrup Aircraft Division.

Words Matter: Make What You Say, Pay!
by Anne Miller

"The difference between the right word and the almost right word is the difference between lightning and a lightning bug." – Mark Twain

Words matter. A group of people were shown a picture of an automobile accident and asked, "How fast were the cars going when they _____?" The word that was used to fill in the blank differed among the members of the group. The words that were used were: "bumped," "contacted," "hit," "collided," or "smashed." The people who were asked the question, "How fast were the cars going when they smashed?" gave the highest estimates of speed. The difference in a single word led to the different reactions.

Let's take another example. You want to describe someone who became very angry when he heard some news. You could say any of the following and be correct, but depending on the words you used, your message would have a different impact on your listener.

- John became very angry when he heard the news.
- John exploded when he heard the news.
- John erupted like a volcano when he heard the news. His verbal outpouring, like hot lava, scorched everyone in his path.

Words Make You Money

Everyone is scrambling to find new ways to sell more effectively. Products are updated, materials are redesigned, and sales processes are changed. Any or all of these strategies may in fact increase business. However, there's one area you could improve that's overlooked by most salespeople—language. Improve your word power and you will increase your selling power. Two particularly effective word tools are metaphors and analogies.

Years ago, I used an analogy to compete for and win the presentation skills training business of a leading ad agency in New York. I was up against every major firm and consultant in the city, including one that specialized in doing presentation work with agencies.

When confronted with the fact that I had no ad agency in my client base, I responded, "That is correct. However, you just won the DHL account. How much overnight courier experience did you need, to have the right to do DHL's advertising? Let me suggest, none. You would learn the dynamics of that business the way you learned the dynamics of all your other accounts in the insurance and beer industries. DHL executives just had to be sure you were the best ad agency for them. Isn't that right?"

"True," replied the executive vice president.

"The same is true with me," I continued. "I'll quickly learn the dynamics of your ad agency the way I have learned the dynamics of my other clients in the aerospace, investment banking, and consulting worlds. You just need to be sure I know everything about presenting. And I do," I said these last three words staring into her eyes.

As the truth of the analogy gradually dawned on her, all the executive vice president could manage to say was, "Oh." I won the business and went on to earn many thousands of dollars from the company over the next several years—all because of this carefully thought out analogy.

Language and Business

In this culture, the concept of words as serious sales tools (or weapons, depending on your metaphor of choice) may seem silly. However, I would argue that it is precisely because of our cultural trends that the people who use language with precision, creativity, and thoughtfulness will have a distinct competitive advantage and triumph at the end of the sales day, with or without pretty new support materials.

There is a golden opportunity awaiting the articulate salesperson in a culture where the art of language has deteriorated. Language is being corrupted and debased by at least four factors:

- Meaningless sound bites: They are now down to as little as 15 seconds.

- Lazy "valley speak": "Like, this product is really good, because like it saves you all kinds of time and things, and like, you know, it's competitively priced, uh, and also… ."
- Anemic vocabularies and clichés: "great" "awesome," "cool," "unique," "blue chip," "bible of the industry," "Olympic gold." Most clients tune this out.
- Commoditized descriptions: "We provide unparalleled customer service, innovative solutions and strong follow-up to help you grow your business." (Just once I'd love to hear someone say, "We provide lousy customer service, vanilla solutions, and haphazard follow-up," just to see how the client will react.)

This meaningless mess of what passes for communication is compounded by the overwhelming amount of additional commercial information that comes at your clients daily from the press, the Internet, billboards, super-market floors, shrink-wrapped buses, the backs of taxi cabs and even bath-room doors. No venue is safe. Escape to the movies? Theatres show commer-cials before the movie and, in the movies themselves. (No doubt we will one day hear, "And the Oscar for best product placement in a drama goes to… .)

Are Words Really That Important?

What words do you use to describe what you do, how you do it, and what the benefits are to your clients?

- In the few seconds you have on the phone or in a voice mail message, what words do you use to earn an appointment or a callback? When was the last time you taped yourself to rate the effectiveness of the individual words you typically choose to use?
- When you open a business discussion, is every word designed to engage?
- When you present your ideas, are they articulated in the most appealing way or are they filled with clichés and bland language? For example, do you say, "This program is a very powerful one that will help you build your business," or do you say, "This program will unleash the creative powers of your staff to sell more business than you ever thought possible"?

- When you're discussing your client's needs, are your questions crafted to elicit the best information while at the same time creating a comfortable, conversational environment for your client?
- When you address questions and objections, are your responses strategically phrased so that your client isn't put on the defensive?
- When you move the sale forward to the next step, do you use non-pressuring language?

Words matter. Put some thought and care into them. It won't cost you anything except a little thinking time. The result can mean the difference between a "yes" and a "no." ■

Anne Miller is the author of Metaphorically Selling. For biographical and business information, see page 270.

Editor's Note: Dan Seidman is the creator of the Sales Autopsy website where he performs postmortems on sales horror stories. A speaker, author and trainer, Dan has over 25 years' experience in sales and sales management. He shows you how to close a sale by teaching your prospect a lesson.

Teaching Consequences to Your Prospect
by Dan Seidman

When I first taught this concept of consequences at a car dealership, I returned a week later to hear some great stories of reps who were not only having better dialogues with prospects, but were earning quicker closes as well.

One salesman had asked a man who wandered into the store during the day if he sold for a living. On getting a yes, the rep said, "Can I ask you a question? Are you ever embarrassed to have prospects see your car?"

The buyer launched into a story about his strategy for parking his old beater vehicle far from the front of a business he was calling on. He didn't want his prospects to see his car, or worse, to expect the prospect to ride with him, should they go to lunch.

This man who wandered into a car dealership was suffering from the evil impact of his old, beat up automobile. He wasn't there to attain the benefits of a new car. The rep I had trained focused in on the bad, rather than the benefits. Bad refers to the problems a new car solves, not the good things a new purchase offers.

And in the rep's words, "I closed that guy faster than anyone I'd ever dealt with."

How? He used the most effective selling strategy in existence today— teaching consequences to prospects.

The psychology of consequences is rooted in how we grew up and learned to make decisions. Let's begin by viewing my sales presentations—before and after I started teaching consequences to my prospects.

Before

As a recruiter, it was my job to pitch outstanding candidates to employers looking for salespeople. I attacked the marketplace like hundreds of other recruiters in Chicago. Our phone calls, thousands of them each week, all sounded like this:

> Dan: Hello (decision maker), I understand that you're looking for a salesperson, and I would like to share a great one with you. She has hit 150% of her quota the past three years, is trained by Xerox, which you know is outstanding, and she has made President's Club—that's top 10%—for her firm the past two years. What an excellent addition she'd make to your team. (I was about to get hit with any of a dozen objections.)

> Decision maker: We don't pay fees to headhunters. We require a college degree. She'd need 10 years in selling. She hasn't sold in our industry. I already have plenty of candidates from my ad in the paper. It's late in the interviewing process. If she's doing so well, why is she looking? And so on.

It was the beginning of a verbal arm-wrestling match. Except it didn't matter if my larynx was stronger; the prospect could always just hang up the phone. Selling by pitching this way was exhausting, discouraging, and demeaning. There had to be a better way for my energy and my ego.

After

I'll never forget the first time I used consequences. I created a list of questions that pointed to the impact of the missing sales rep problem. Here's how the conversation with that first sales manager evolved:

> Dan: Hi, John, I heard you had an open territory, how's it going?

> John: Well, I'm very busy interviewing people now.

Dan: Good, hope you find someone. So who's covering that open territory?

John: I am.

Dan: In addition to managing your other people and all your other work?

John: Yes.

Dan: Oh. no, that's probably not taking too much extra time from your day?

John: No, it's not really affecting my days, I just work into the evening. (He laughed; he's establishing rapport with me.)

Dan: Since you've been doing the work of this missing person, is your family OK with the extra hours you're putting in?

(After a long pause)

John: You know what, I haven't been home for dinner in two weeks. And my wife is a great cook!

I continued, asking other consequence questions, like "Do your competitors know that these accounts aren't being visited?" "Is the missing person costing the company much money?" "Is this costing you money?" The situation was being framed by the trauma caused by the missing sales rep.

Five minutes into the phone call, he asked me if I had anyone for him to see. Imagine that! I hadn't presented a product or service to him. I hadn't presented any benefits I could offer. There wasn't even a hint that I had a solution for his problem. But he knew one thing about me that was true: I knew his situation, his personal experience, almost as intimately as he did. So who was better qualified to help him—me, or the other pushy parrots calling to "present" candidates for the job?

There is a way to sell effectively and uniquely today—if setting you apart from and ahead of the competition matters. You must learn to teach consequences to your prospects.

How does that work?

Your agenda on a sales call will be to help your buyer discuss and take ownership of the company and the individual negative impact of the way he or she does business without or until the time he implements your product or service and solves his problem.

Here's how I look at the use of consequences from the buyer's point of view: He's going to write the sequel to his current tale of trouble. Essentially, that buyer can choose the ending to his story. You'll help him script that conclusion.

Getting to this on a personal level during the sales process takes some time, rapport, and good questions. You need to invest the time and show concern for the prospect's situation in order to generate true rapport.

Here are some insights on teaching consequences to your prospects:
- You do a lot less talking;
- You don't have to be able to "handle objections" since you offer nothing to object to;
- You know what the real trouble is—it's not a missing salesperson. It's all the aggravation—corporate, financial, and most of all personal—to the person dealing with the problems that can be fixed with your product or service.

Here are some insights on using feature-and-benefit selling:
- You play the numbers game, so luck becomes an important part of your income;
- You sell on price, so your best potential earnings are often at risk;
- You sound like every other salesperson out there, so you're not memorable.

One of the strange things about using consequences is that the buyer doesn't know what strategy is being used. He gets caught up in the concerns being discussed. On the other hand, in a feature/benefit presentation, the buyer is painfully aware of what you're trying to pull because it's what the buyer always experiences with salespeople.

The Workshop

The best way to equip you with the most effective language to use with prospects is to begin with the traditional feature/benefit approach. Most organizations already have literature that was designed based on benefits. This will provide us with a launching pad that we'll move away from as we use selling words that propel us—and our earnings—sky high.

I'll use a basic example, automobile sales, to get you comfortable with this practice of altering words in print and in person.

5 Benefits to Buying a Car Today

- Prestige of owning a new car
- Cool color
- 0-60 mph in eight seconds
- Rides and handles like a dream
- 100-year warranty

5 Problems your New Car Solves Today

- Can't take a client to lunch in my car
- Old look says that I'm not successful
- Dangerous to merge in traffic
- I feel every bump in the road
- Surprised by what breaks down every month

Here's a sample list of consequences you'll be looking for:

Corporate

- Irrecoverable or squandered revenue, market share, or marketplace status
- Fear about the company's future
- Angry shareholders
- Embarrassment to customers
- Sending a bad or wrong message to customers and/or employees
- Mistrust of a company's offerings and products

Individual

- Ruined advancement opportunity or obstruction of career path
- Reduced or lost income potential
- Loss of personal prestige
- Corporate doubt about abilities

- Inefficient work processes that increase workload and steal time from family
- Wasted efforts to close business or build business
- Family frustration over work issues

Sit down and begin to design questions that stir up this pot of consequences. You'll want to ask the prospect for his initial feelings about what the trouble is, then say things like, "So, does this also mean... consequence?" or "Wow, who's going to deal with... consequence?" or "That's not good if... consequence."

Remember: You want to begin with the company consequences, then move to the personal.

These steps form your path to closing more business. Learn to walk your prospect down this trail and you'll have conversations you've never before experienced in selling. You'll gather rich information that will help you gather more riches for you and your family. ∎

Dan Seidman is the creator of SalesAutopsy.com. For biographical and business information, see page 273.

Editor's Note: Rochelle Togo-Figa has more than 25 years' experience as a top-producing sales professional. As a sales coach and trainer since 1995, she's worked with clients from major companies like American Express, Met Life, Philip Morris, Crain's Business Publications and Yellow Book. You'll profit by using her seven-step process to closing sales.

Seven Key Steps to Closing Every Sale
by Rochelle Togo-Figa

When clients tell me they're not bringing in the sales they want, one of the first questions I ask is, "Are you asking for the business?" Their response is usually either, "No, I don't know what to say," or "What if I ask and they're not interested?" Well, if you don't ask, you'll never know where you stand with your prospects.

The close is the crucial moment of decision in the sales process when the prospect decides whether to enter into a business relationship with you, or not. Closings are so painful for many salespeople that 50% of all sales calls end before they ask for some sort of commitment to the next step.

Let me share a story with you. Jim and Ron were friends for more than 25 years and golf buddies for nearly the same amount of time. They had grown up together, were as close as brothers celebrating each other's personal and professional business successes over the years. One day while they were teeing off, Jim turned to Ron and said, "Ron, how come after all the years we've known each other, you've never given me any business?" Ron turned to Jim and simply said, "You never asked." This response may sound surprising but it's true. The most common reason business owners don't get the business is that they don't ask for it. It's as simple as that. If you want the business, you must ask for it.

Let's take a look at seven key aspects to closing the deal.

- **Be prepared.** There are a number of questions for you to answer before you can ask for the business. When you can answer "yes" to these questions, you're ready to ask the closing question:
  - Does the customer want what I'm selling?
  - Does the customer believe in me and my company?

- Can the customer afford my product?
- Does the customer fully understand what my product is?
- Have I prepared and practiced my closing techniques?
- Am I prepared to remain silent after asking the closing question?
- **Use Trial Closes.** Throughout the sales meeting, look for opportunities to get agreement from the prospect. Repeat back to the prospect what he has told you. Tie it back to benefits. For example: "Don't you agree, it's going to give you the financial security you said earlier is so important to you?"

  Checking in with him throughout the meeting and getting agreement allows you to use the information as you prepare for the close. If your prospect agrees, you can bring him back to that at the end.

- **Assume the sale.** From the moment you walk in and sit down with the prospect, assume the prospect wants to buy your product. If he's willing to meet with you, he must have some interest in what you're selling. If you continually assume the sale over and over in your own mind, you'll project that confidence during your meeting with the prospect. Here are a couple example statements you can make before the prospect buys:
  - You'll be happy you decided to buy it.
  - You're going to love how it looks in your home.
- **Ask pressure-free closing questions.** As the prospect gets closer to making a decision to do business with you, his level of anxiety increases. This is an uncertain time for the prospect in the decision-making process, and the sale can go either way. The way to keep the sales door open and lead the prospect to doing business with you is by asking pressure-free questions. The magic word that makes a question pressure free is "if." "If" removes risk and pressure from the question. The prospect will respond freely as there is no commitment to be made at this time. Here are a couple examples:
  - If you were to go ahead with the purchase when would you need delivery?

- If you were to decide to buy how many would you like?
- **Ask closing questions.** Don't break your momentum now. Here are a few questions you can ask potential clients to reach an agreement:
  - Are you ready to get started?
  - Shall I draw up a contract?
  - Do we have a deal?
  - Let's take a few minutes now so I can walk you through the agreement.
  - Let's set up our next meeting and I can go over the plan with you then.
  - Shall I finalize the details?
- **Be quiet!** After you've made your recommendation, and asked all your closing questions, remain silent. Allow your prospect to respond first. He's listened to your presentation and probably needs a couple of moments to absorb the information and make his buying decision. Take a deep breath, be quiet and wait for the prospect to speak first.
- **Decide on the next steps.** Whether or not you've closed the sale, be absolutely certain that both you and the prospect understand what happens next. Before you end your meeting, take out your calendar and set up the next meeting, or the next call. Never leave a meeting without knowing the next step.

Follow this step-by-step process and you'll be on your way to closing more deals. ∎

Rochelle Togo-Figa is the creator of The Sales Breakthrough System™. For biographical and business information, see page 274.

Editor's Note: In 2003, Craig Elias won a million dollar prize in venture capitalist Tim Draper's Billion Dollar Idea contest. His winning idea? An Internet-based lead exchange service for sales professionals called InnerSell. Craig shares another moneymaking idea with you: using "trigger events" to connect with prospects.

Shorten Sales Cycles by Capitalizing on Trigger Events
by Craig Elias

One of the biggest challenges in prospecting is when you get what sound like positive buying signals, but your close ratio is low, and your sales cycles are still long.

If people tell you to call back in a few months, and when you call back, you're not getting the results you expected, capitalizing on the following Trigger Event strategies can both dramatically improve your close ratio and shorten your sales cycles.

When you cold call someone, in an attempt to sell him something, you're interrupting that person's day. The dominant instinct is always going to be for that person to find any reason to get off the phone and get back to what he was doing before you interrupted him.

Your goal is to maintain your poise and get past that first 15 to 30 seconds of the initial call, which is always going to be a little bumpy.

But the reason you're riding out those first 15 to 30 seconds is not so you can try to turn the person into a short-term prospect on the spot!

Actually, you're trying to discover if this person has experienced a Trigger Event. If there has been such a Trigger Event you want to find out what it was and when it happened. The Trigger Event could have taken place quite a while ago, it could have happened only recently, or it could still be on the horizon.

These Trigger Events typically fall into one of three categories:

- **Bad Experience:** The buyer has a bad experience with a product or service, with people, or with a provider. This is something that happens on the current provider's end. For instance when a product is upgraded or replaced, very often, the new product creates dissatisfaction because it does not meet the buyer's expectations. To spot these opportunities keep your eyes and ears open for competitors who announce an upgrade/replacement of their products or services, such as Windows XP to Vista.

- **Change/Transition:** There is a change or transition in people, places, or priorities. This is something that happens on the current buyer's end. For instance a buyer changes at one of your prospects and the relationship that existed between the current supplier and the buyer is diminished. To spot these opportunities keep your eyes and ears open for changes in people within your prospect list, like an email you send to a buyer on your prospect list bounces back to you.

- **Awareness:** The buyer becomes aware of the need to change suppliers for legal, risk-avoidance, or economic reasons. This is something that happens on your end. For instance when you help a prospect understand that buying from you is less risky than continuing to buy from his existing supplier. To spot these opportunities, keep your eyes and ears open for situations where the perceived risk of inaction (continuing to buy the existing solution from your competition) becomes greater than the perceived risk of taking action – buying a new solution from you, for example announcing you have recently won a big customer or a big contract leverages the tendency of companies to imitate their competitors because they view it as risky not to.

During the first minute of your call, use the opportunity to understand which of the following three buying modes the buyer is in:

- **Status Quo:** The buyer is completely happy with what he currently has. There has not been a Trigger Event in the recent past, but there may be one on the horizon. You may think this person is a waste of time and you may want to move on to the next person on your list. Actually, if this person has money, authority, and influence, this is a great long-term opportunity. A strategy for this type of call is to start the relationship-building process. I would also suggest that you check back on a monthly basis to see if a Trigger Event has recently happened.

- **Searching For Alternatives:** This person is unhappy with what he has, has spoken to several suppliers, and probably already has a favorite.

A Trigger Event took place a while ago, and he's already taken action on it. You may think that this is a short-term opportunity because the buyer is actively talking to a number of potential suppliers. This is in fact probably a medium term opportunity because it is highly likely this buyer already has a first choice! Selling to buyers under these conditions typically results in a lower close ratio and a longer sales cycle, which is exactly the problem you are experiencing. A strategy for this type of call is to position yourself as the buyer's second choice so you are called first if the buyer's current favorite falters. You should check back every other week to see where you stand.

- **Window of Dissatisfaction**: A Trigger Event has recently taken place and this buyer knows that what he's currently using is no longer sufficient, but he hasn't done anything about it yet. Because he tells you to call back in two months, four months, or six months, you make a note to do that and move on to the next person on your list. Wrong response! This is actually a short-term opportunity, because the buyer is not talking to your competition yet. When you call back a few months later, even if you call a few weeks early thinking it will give you an edge, it's very likely he will already be talking to your competition. The strategy for this type of call is to identify the business opportunity and pursue it immediately. As much as possible should happen on the initial call, with your next contact taking place in the very near future. You must find a way to push a little bit and learn more about the Trigger Event, then try to set a near-term course of action.

As it stands, most salespeople are focusing on those buyers in Searching for Alternatives who are already talking to their competition (and missing the biggest opportunities) those buyers who are in the Window of Dissatisfaction, who recently experienced a Trigger Event and have not started talking to your competition yet. That's why your numbers are as bad as they are; that's also why your sales cycles are so long.

Salespeople need to do a much better job of 'staying on their feet' for the first 30 seconds or so of the call. That is long enough to ask a couple of questions that will help them learn whether the person has:

- Not experienced a Trigger Event in a long time
- Experienced a Trigger Event a while ago and is already doing something about it
- Recently experienced a Trigger Event and has done nothing about it yet

Once you learn if, and when, a buyer has experienced a Trigger Event you can apply the appropriate strategy. When you do that, and focus first on those people in the Window of Dissatisfaction, who recently experienced a Trigger Event and have done nothing about it yet, you will have a much higher close ratio and you'll have much shorter sales cycles! ■

Craig Elias is the creator of Trigger Events Selling™. For biographical and business information, see page 264.

Editor's Note: Tom Richard is a syndicated weekly business columnist and sales speaker. Tom began his successful sales career in high-end retail, before moving to outside sales. His company presents sales seminars, CSP certification training, and sales coaching for both individuals and teams.

Who Are You Competing Against?

by Tom Richard

You probably think that your biggest competitor is a big-name chain store, a recognized brand name or a specific salesperson. While it's true that sometimes a customer's choice boils down to either buying your product or someone else's, this isn't always the case. Sometimes, the customer's real choice is between buying your product or simply doing nothing at all.

Knowing that your customer doesn't have to buy the product at all will change the way you look at the sale. If a purchase doesn't seem to be noticeably enjoyable or easy, your customer may opt out of buying it. When this happens, your customer's reluctance has become your new competitor.

Learning to shape your approach to the particular needs and emotions of your customer will help make the transaction smooth and enjoyable. Here are some tips for discovering your customer's emotional reasons to buy and using them to stir his motivation to act on that desire now.

- **Make buying enjoyable.** Customers enjoy buying products, not having products sold to them. Nobody likes to feel persuaded, pressured or suckered into making a purchase. People enjoy spending money when the decision to buy is theirs, and when they are in control of getting the things they need or want. Build up the customer's buying experience to make it enjoyable for him.

- **Focus on the customer, not the product.** The strength of the sale is in discovering why your customer came to you in the first place. Your customer wants a solution to his problem. Understanding your customer and his problem is much more important than listing reasons why your product is better than your competitor's.

- **Reveal the benefits of acting now.** Most customers understand that if they decide not to buy, they will not enjoy the benefits of using your product. So, talk about the customer's individual buying motives for the purchase. Draw on his desire to enjoy your product and create an environment where he will feel comfortable gaining it immediately.

- **Ensure a smooth transaction.** If the process of buying seems like a hassle, your customer will be tempted wait out his decision and do nothing. Eliminate any unnecessary steps that make the act of purchasing long and painful. Reduce as much of the technical paperwork as you can and try to make the decision to buy the last decision he will have to make. Simplifying the transaction will make his experience easier and more rewarding, making his experience with you more enjoyable.

- **Eliminate the risk.** Customers will be less likely to act on their desire to buy if the purchases seem too risky. Do anything you can to help make your customer's decision to try your product an easy one. You can allow him a grace period in case he changes his mind, or establish a guarantee to comfort and reassure him of his decision. Product trials are another way to gain your customer's trust in you and your product. Once the risk of the purchase is gone, your customer will feel comfortable acting on his desire to have your product.

- **Follow through after the purchase.** Reassure your customers of their decisions by supporting them throughout the life of your product. This needs to be more than a manufacturer's warranty and more heartfelt than telling them about your company's 97% satisfaction rating. Be personal. Be sincere. Prove to them that their continued happiness is your goal.

Understanding the specific decisions your customers face will help them feel comfortable buying from you. When you use a tone and message that encourages them to take action, they will feel motivated and will have no excuse to wait. They will enjoy the immediate benefits of their purchases, and you will enjoy the lasting benefits of the sales. ■

Tom Richard is an author and sales trainer. For biographical and business information, see page 271.

Editor's Note: Adrian Miller has more than 20 years' experience as a sales trainer and consultant. Her clients range from Fortune 500 companies to small businesses in a wide variety of industries, including financial services, publishing, manufacturing, accounting, biotechnology, legal, healthcare and technology. She shares her ideas for succeeding in an economic downturn.

When the Going Gets Tough, the Tough Start Selling
by Adrian Miller

With a slow economy comes a fiercer, more competitive market that will require you to set yourself and your products apart from your competitors. It's easy to make excuses for poor sales performance in an economic downturn, but a successful salesperson will find opportunities to increase revenue. Here are a few ideas to help you reach your goals:

- **Set goals and plan accordingly.** When the economy turns sour, don't put yourself in a position of scrambling for business. Take a look at your target market to reevaluate how you've done business in the past and determine how your customers' needs have changed as a result of the economic climate. Once you have an understanding of these fundamentals, you can set realistic business goals and charge forward to meet them.

- **Invest in training.** In a down market, you will be competing against the best and the brightest. It's imperative to have cutting edge knowledge and experience to take the lead. Play it smart and invest in ongoing training even though it may seem counterintuitive to be spending money during a bad economy. You'll find the return to be well worth the investment. Don't hesitate to inform your clients of any up-to-date information you may have learned. They will be impressed that you are taking the initiative.

- **Networking strategies.** Networking can be a powerful tool for developing new business relationships. However, not every gathering has the potential for making quality contacts. Selectivity may be in your best interest when it comes to attending networking events. This will ensure that you have a target audience filled with potential customers. Remember that your ultimate goal for the event is to make contacts. Successful salespeople are assertive and able to introduce themselves without being forceful. By the end of the event you should have a list of contacts. Whatever you do, don't make the ultimate mistake of forgetting to follow-up.

- **Don't wait for your clients to call you.** Existing clients are your best resource. Customers are all too often lost because their salesperson never took the time to follow-up after the initial sale. Staying in close contact with them builds trust and long-term relationships. It's important to keep clients up-to-date on new products and marketing materials. However, it's also vital that you keep yourself current on the ever-changing needs of your clients. The doors to new sales and cross-selling opportunities will open by just listening.

- **Ask for referrals.** A referral is commonly thought of as the highest form of compliment you can give a sales professional. However, customers rarely provide a referral without being asked. Most often, it's up to you to take the initiative to ask for additional contacts. All too frequently, sales professionals are afraid to ask, don't feel they have a good rapport with the client, or simply forget. The proper timing of asking for a referral can depend on the situation. It is appropriate to wait until you build a relationship with the client, although, it might be acceptable to ask if you know the client is excited about a recent purchase. Don't be discouraged if a referral doesn't have a need for your product or service. It is possible they will in the future or know someone who does.

Most importantly, keep a positive attitude and don't let a slump get you down. ■

Adrian Miller is founder and president of Adrian Miller Sales Training. For biographical and business information, see page 270.

Editor's Note: Jim Domanski has sold through good times and bad. He is considered one of the leading experts in the field of business-to-business tele-sales consulting and training. Jim's expertise comes from 10 years in the trenches selling phone systems for Bell Canada and more than 17 years advising companies on how to sell using those systems. His clients include American Express, Shell, SAP, and GlaxoSmithKline. Author of four books on tele-sales strategy and tactics, Jim demonstrates how to make the perfect follow-up call.

Eight Essential Tips for Making a Perfect Follow-Up Call
by Jim Domanski

In many ways, a follow-up call to a prospect is more challenging than a cold call. Typically, the follow-up call is what really gets the sales cycling rolling. It's where value truly begins to manifest itself, substantive information is gathered, and the relationship begins to develop. It is absolutely vital that you have superb follow-up strategies and tactics so you can make the most of the moment. Here are eight tips for making a perfect follow-up call:

- **Get a commitment for the follow-up call.** Perhaps the single biggest mistake sale professionals make is not establishing a specific date and time for the follow-up call at the end of the initial call. Vague commitments from prospects ("Call me next week") or sales professionals ("I'll send the proposal and follow up in a couple of days") result in missed calls, voicemail messages and ultimately a longer sales cycle. All you need to do is ask for a follow-up date and time. For instance:

  "I'll be glad to write up the proposal (quote, whatever) and email it to you. What I would like to recommend is that we set up Tuesday, the 19th, at say, 8:45 a.m. to review it in detail and determine the next steps, if any. How does that sound?"

  If this isn't a good time, recommend another time. If that doesn't work, get the prospect to establish a date and time.

Creating a deadline is a simple but extremely powerful tactic—use it.

- **Build equity and be remembered.** After every call to a first-time prospect, send a thank-you card. Handwrite a message that simply says, "John, thank you for taking the time to speak with me today. I look forward to chatting with you further on the 16th. Kind regards. . . ." No more, no less.

In today's fast-paced world, a handwritten card tells the client that you took the time and effort to do something a little different. This registers in the client's mind and creates a degree of equity in you. It differentiates you and is remembered, and it gives the client a reason to be there when you make your follow-up call.

If you don't think a card will get there in time, send an email with the same message. Just be aware that an email does not have nearly the same impact as a handwritten note.

- **Email a reminder and an agenda.** The day before your follow-up call, email your prospect to remind him of your appointment. In the subject line, enter the words: "Telephone appointment for March 19 and article of interest." Note that the subject line acts as a reminder but because it's vague enough the prospect will probably open it. There's a hint that maybe the date and time has changed.

Your email should confirm the date and time of the appointment and then briefly list your agenda:

"John, the call should only take 10 minutes. We'll review the proposal and I'll answer any questions. And then we'll determine the next steps, if any."

Notice how the words echo those used when the follow-up was initially set. In particular, notice the trigger phrase ". . .the next steps, if any." The "if any" helps reduce some of the stress or concern a first-time prospect might have. Often a first-time prospect skips out on the follow-up call because he's worried that he'll have to make a commitment. This is natural. If a prospect senses an easy, informal, no-pressure type of phone call, he's more likely to show up on time for that call.

- **Add value in a P.S.** Notice the reference to an article in the subject line or your email. At the end of your email, add a P.S. that says, "John, in the meantime, here's an article I thought you might enjoy regarding. . . ."

The article may be about your industry, the market, a product or better yet, something non-business related that you had discussed in your initial call. This creates tremendous value even if the client doesn't open it. Why? Because you took the time to do something extra. This helps the client remember you and gives him yet another reason to take your follow-up call.

Of course, this means you have to do some homework. Start looking on the Web for articles of interest and value relative to your market and industry. Keep a file of these articles because they can be used over and over again.

- **Call on time.** Don't start your relationship on the wrong foot. Call on time. Never, ever be late with your follow-up call. Not even by a minute. The promptness and respect you show on a follow-up call reflects on you, your company and your products.
- **Avoid the opening statement blunders most reps make.** Many reps stumble and fall by using these routine follow-up opening statements:
  - "I was calling to follow-up on the proposal."
  - "I'm calling to see if you had any questions.'
  - "I just wanted to make sure you got my email."
  - "The reason for my follow-up call was to see if you had come to a decision."

These opening statements are not only poor, they are commonplace and do nothing to make you stand out. You are perceived as yet another run-of-the-mill vendor looking for a sale, you need a little more pizzazz.

- **Build a follow-up opening statement that gets through the clutter.** There are four simple steps to creating that pizzazz. First, introduce yourself using your full name. Second, give your company name. Step three is where you differentiate yourself: Remind the client why you're calling and what prompted the follow-up call in the first place. This means going back to your initial cold call and reminding the client of the pain or the gain that was discussed or hinted at in your previous call. For instance:

"Phyllis, this is Michael Sacks calling from BVS Training. Phyllis, when we spoke last week you had two concerns. First, you indicated that you were concerned about having your current online training program renewed automatically before you had a chance to review it in detail, and second, that there were several modules whose content was questionable."

Michael reminds Phyllis why she agreed to this call. He does this because he knows that clients are busy; that they forget; or that the urgency of last week may not seem so urgent this week. Remind your client of the irritation and then move on to step four, the agenda:

"What I would like to recommend at this stage is two things. First, we review those modules that have you so concerned, and second, we'll take a closer look at the current contract. Then we'll determine the next steps, if applicable. How does that sound?"

Clients like clear, concise agendas. They want vendors who are organized and don't waste their time. They want sales professionals who take control and move the calls forward. This gives them confidence.

Finally, notice how Michael repeats a theme that he established in the first call and in his follow-up email. He indicates that they will "determine the next steps, if applicable." It's a nice touch and reduces client resistance.

- **Be persistent, be polite, and be professional, but don't be a pest.** If you follow this formula, about 70% of the time the client is there to take your call. But, that leaves 30% who are not there for one reason or another. If the prospect is not there, leave a message so that he knows you called on time. Say:

"Hi Phyllis, it's Mike Sacks from BVS Training calling for our 8:45 appointment. Sounds like you might be tied up for a few moments. I'll call back in 10 minutes if I haven't heard from you. In the meantime, my number is 555-1212."

Next, call in 10 minutes, exactly. If the prospect is still not there, leave another message:

"Hi Phyllis, it's Mike Sacks from BVS Training following up on our 8:45 appointment. Looks like you're still tied up. Please give me a call when you're free at 555-1212, otherwise I will call you later this morning or early this afternoon."

So far you've been persistent without being a pest. Now, give the prospect a chance to call. A good rule of thumb is half a day. Four hours is plenty of time for the prospect to call you and more importantly, it doesn't make you seem desperate or annoying. Here's what you can say if you have to call again:

"Phyllis, it's Mike Sacks from BVS Training. I called a couple of times today but as of yet we haven't been able to connect. When we last spoke you where concerned about the contract expiration date and the content of some of the modules. I'm sure you don't want that date to come and go, so my number is 555-1212."

Notice how the professional reminds the client of the call but does not make her feel guilty or embarrassed by using the phrase "...but as of yet we have not been able to connect." Also notice that the rep reminds the client about their earlier conversation and the pain the prospect was experiencing. In effect, he wants Phyllis to think "Oh yeah, that contract is nagging me. I'd better get back to him."

If that doesn't work make four more follow-up calls spaced three business days apart. This shows persistence but the calls are spread far enough apart that the client doesn't feel like she's being stalked. If there's no response by then, you probably won't get one but at least you took a good stab at it.

Having solid follow-up strategies and tactics will separate you from the dozens of other sales professionals who call the same prospects as you. This gives you a distinctive edge. Make the most of your follow-up calls and watch your sales grow. ∎

Jim Domanski is president of Teleconcepts Consulting. For biographical and business information, see page 264.

Editors Note: Maybe it's not the economy; maybe it's you. Settling for the same tired, stagnant sales pitch could be costing you sales. Do an honest personal assessment and think about how you can improve your pitch. Ressurect your enthusiam and listen more closely to learn what your prospects really need. With a winning presentation, you'll close more sales, no matter what the economic indicators may say.

Refresh Your Pitch and Close More Sales
by Michael Dalton Johnson

Dozens of elements go into a winning sales presentation. Some are obvious, such as creating rapport, establishing value, and asking for the sale, while others are much more subtle.

Because these quick refresher tips primarily focus on style and personality, they fall into an "easier said than done" category. To really benefit from this advice, you'll need to give it some serious thought, do an honest self-evaluation of your "pitch personality," and make the required improvements. If you find you are particularly weak in one area you may need to get additional advice or training.

- **Be enthusiastic but don't overdo it.** You represent a great company with a fantastic product or service and you're naturally excited about it. Excitement is contagious. Show your enthusiasm and you will make more sales. Caution: don't overdo it. Over-the-top breathless enthusiasm comes off as contrived and will increase buyer resistance.

- **Honest down-to-earth communication closes sales.** Above all, respect your buyer's time and intelligence. Memorized, long-winded or lame, rapid-fire sales pitches kill deals. Make eye contact and speak to your buyer as if you were talking to an intelligent yet uniformed friend. Do not be too formal. Use your buyer's name from time to time, but not excessively. Communicate in an honest, open, confident and matter-of-fact manner. Smile.

- **What's your body saying?** It's important that you communicate positively with your body language. Surprisingly, this is true even when talking on the phone. Lean slightly forward and show interest in the conversation. If you naturally talk with your hands don't stop. Remember, the buyer is subconsciously picking up on your body language. Make sure yours is conveying your interest in the buyer, along with your confidence in and passion for your product.

- **Focus on benefits.** Never forget that it's all about the buyer, not you. Your pitch must resoundingly answer every buyer's unspoken question: "What's in it for me?" Choose key benefits that you feel will be most interesting and important to your buyer. Don't rattle them off like a laundry list early in the conversation, but introduce them into the natural flow of the dialogue. Keep benefits uncomplicated and easy to understand. Buyers are interested in the bottom line. They are remarkably uninterested in why you joined your company or your organization's vision statement. If the conversation veers away from benefits, subtly bring it back. As the conversation comes to an end, summarize the benefits and ask for the sale.

- **One size does not fit all!** If you are delivering the same basic pitch over and over, you are undoubtedly losing sales. Take a lesson from the U.S. Marines and "improvise, adapt, and overcome." This requires listening and reading your prospect. You must always be thinking on your feet and adapting your pitch in real time to what you are hearing from your buyer. It's no easy feat, but those who master this skill close far more sales than those who don't.

- **Accentuate the positive.** Which do you think sounds better to a buyer? "Our product will save your company 2500 a month" or, "You will save your company 30,000 *dollars* a year with our product." Obviously, the second statement is more compelling because 30,000 "dollars" is far more dramatic than 2500 even though they amount to the same savings. More importantly, "You will save your company...," makes the buyer both intelligent and a hero. Buyers want to save money. Buyers like to make smart decisions. Buyers love to be heroes.

- **Ask questions and listen up.** You've heard it a hundred times: stop talking and make more sales. Effective listening will give you most of the answers to your qualifying questions without even asking them. Ask questions that get your buyer talking. You will quickly learn about your customers' needs, what their hot buttons are, and how to gain their interest and confidence. Simply put, when your customer talks, you sell; when you talk, you lose.

Making a sale is a lot like playing a winning chess game. You rarely win with a brilliant move early in the game, but rather later after gaining an accumulation of small advantages. Listening to your prospect gives you those winning advantages. ■

Michael Dalton Johnson is founder and president of SalesDog.com. For biographical and business information, see page 267.

Editor's Note: D.M. Arenzon is known as "Mr. Cold Call." He earned the nickname when a prospect he'd been calling picked up the phone saying, "Hey, it's Mr. Cold Call." The name stuck. Arenzon calculates he has made over 80,000 cold calls to date. He is an author, speaker, trainer and cold calling pioneer. He explains how to set yourself apart when calling prospects.

Do What Most Cold Callers Rarely Do and Close More Sales
by D.M. Arenzon

How much do you really know about your prospects before you call them? Do you know anything about their industries? Do you know the names of their competitors? What kind of challenges are they facing from their competitors? How much more attention would your prospects give you on the telephone if you knew just one more detail about their companies or industries?

One of the main reasons sales reps don't make sales is because they know absolutely nothing about their prospects before they pick up the telephone. Why is this happening? Perhaps, they are equating quantity with closing sales. Yes, it's important to make outbound calls, but what's even more important is how much research you do before you make that first telephone call.

When you incorporate what you have learned about your prospects' companies and their industries into your telephone conversations then you are letting your prospects know that you really do want to help them. The question you might ask is what specific steps can you take to understand your prospects' lines of business and their industries? Below are four practical ideas that you can use to separate yourself from other sales reps who might also be cold calling your prospects:

- **Cold Call by Industry.** If you really want to master the industries of your sales prospects then only make cold calls in those industries. Think about it; if you made 10 calls a day in the same industry five days a week for one month, can you imagine how much you will learn about that industry? Can you imagine how much more you could bring to the telephone call? Rather than sounding like just another cold caller, you will soon be viewed as an expert in your field. If you take more time to learn about your prospects' industries you will be able to ask better questions. Better questions will always close more sales!

- **Industry Associations and Trade Publications.** Find out the main industry associations and trade publications in your prospects' industries. As you peruse these mediums, learn about the major challenges facing those industries. Based on what you have learned, you can incorporate your findings into your cold calls and offer your prospects multiple solutions. Solutions will always close more sales!
- **Study Your Prospects' Companies' Websites.** Spend a few minutes on your prospects' websites to learn more about what they do, how they do it and why they are market leaders in their industries. If you see an audio or video demo of their products or services then check them out. If you see a list of client testimonials then read each one to find out more about their customers. Check out their most recent news releases and if there are management biographies then read them! If you take the time to understand how your prospects do business then you will always close more sales!
- **Get to Know Your Prospects' Competition.** How can you capture your prospects' attention? Let them know what their competitors are doing and what they may not be doing. Do an online search and locate similar companies in their industries, study them and offer your results to your prospects on your cold calls. Offer ideas on your calls about how you can help them take market share away from their top three competitors. If you can come up with one good idea to help them take market share then you will always close more sales.

Research is your key to making more sales and without it you are just another sales rep making cold calls. A sales rep who makes 100 calls per week will never do as well as a sales rep who embraces a research mindset and makes only 25 to 50 calls. Quantity does matter, but quality is what will set you apart from your competition and make you money! ∎

D.M. Arenzon is known as "Mr. Cold Call." For biographical and business information, see page 261.

Editor's Note: A pioneer in the coaching profession, Keith Rosen has been featured in Selling Power, The New York Times, The Washington Times, Inc. Magazine, and The Wall Street Journal. He explains how to resurrect lost accounts.

Opening Closed Doors
by Keith Rosen

As a salesperson you've decided the time has come to strengthen your business relationships, attract more customers and advance your career.

You began reviewing the list of prospects who said no to you in the past. Sure, they may have turned you down before, but you know that change always occurs—in the economy, in technology and in your prospects' businesses. If your approach is merely to touch base and see if they are in better positions to make purchasing decisions, you have the same plan as every other salesperson.

Before making your next contact, spend some time evaluating the history of the account. Chances are there were things you missed during your initial interaction that cost you the sale. Uncovering these areas you need to strengthen, realigning your thinking and then developing a unique strategy to follow will enable you to generate the results you are seeking. Here are a few ideas:

Determine Why They Didn't Buy

This is better done immediately after you are turned down, but it is also a good way to get back in front of someone. The key is to get your prospects to speak with you openly. This can be difficult, since many prospects feel the need to disguise the truth to avoid hurting your feelings. Instead, they use generic reasoning, such as high prices, no need to change current vendors, no budget available or bad timing.

Uncover the real reason by asking questions about their new goals, the problems they're facing with their current vendors, products or services, etc. This often leads to a conversation about the potential purchase of your product or service that you would never have opened up otherwise. Ask questions such as, "If you could create the ideal solution/product/service, what about your current product/service would you like to improve or change?" Or, "What solution would my product/service have to offer that would motivate you enough to explore working with us?"

Do Your Homework

It's not enough to simply understand the problem and provide a solution. You also need to anticipate your prospects' future needs. Where do they rank within their respective industries and how does that compare to the past? What changes are expected for their industries? Will the economy or technology have an effect on their businesses? What are some of the problems they're facing now? How will utilizing your product/service help alleviate these issues? Read up on press releases, annual reports or articles on the company. If you want to create a new purchasing opportunity, determine your prospects' current as well as future needs—needs that your prospects may not even be able to identify themselves.

Get Their Attention

What is the prospect's primary motivation to listen to you another time? Determine a particular advantage that your product/service offers him. To stimulate the prospect's attention, develop a short, concise message you can send him (letter, email, etc.) or deliver in a conversation describing the specific problems that can be solved or results that can be expected through utilizing your product/service. Be creative. There are probably dozens of features you could promote. It's up to you to uncover the one that would motivate each prospect to speak to you again.

Here's an example you can use to open up the conversation: "After reflecting back upon our prior conversation, I have some new ideas that I'd like to share with you regarding how our product/service may actually complement and enhance what you're currently doing." Or, "I was thinking about another client who was in a similar situation as yours and thought that you might be interested in hearing about how we were able to defuse the challenges he had."

Become a Resource

When following up, don't simply call to follow up. In other words, stay away from calling with the intention of seeing if he's received your information or to check in to ask if he has any immediate needs for your product/service. Take some extra time and weave in a compelling reason for your call. How can you deliver value to him? Is there something timely that you can share with him about your product/service or about his industry? Is there something newsworthy that you can discuss that applies to him like a success story about one of your clients?

Determine how you can contribute to the growth of a prospect's business aside from the product or service you're offering. It could be supplying him with a free newsletter or educational seminar, a better service plan or connecting him with other people in your circle of influence that can contribute to the success of his business. Create a contest among your staff to develop ideas that will add value to your product/service without increasing your prices or fees. More service and value at a perceived lower price creates a new interest. Adding value to your product or service at no additional cost to the customer is exceeding your customer's expectations.

Start Selling Results

Feature and benefit selling is a dying strategy. Most companies are no longer in the business of selling products, but of providing solutions. In order to provide a solution, you must first understand the problem. Prospects are more interested in what the end result or advantage your product or service will produce for them as opposed to what your product does. It can be greater productivity, lower overhead, monetary savings, or an increase in their quality of life. What problems are solved by your product or service? What end result or value will they experience from what you are offering? Can it be quantified?

When cold calling, following up or networking, are you providing the prospect with enough of a compelling reason to want to speak with you and learn more about your product or service? If your reasons are not powerful enough to move someone from a state of inertia to interest or action, here's your opportunity to give him an overhaul.

Interview past and current customers. Ask questions up front to get a complete understanding of your customer's position and why he bought from you in the first place. What would make him look great in terms of how he is evaluated in his job? Remember, people buy based on their reasons, not yours. You can then look ahead and create a strategy that will accurately pinpoint how your product or service can help your future customers and the measurable results they can expect.

Stop Chasing Dead Ends

Are you making too many follow-up calls? Whether it's because of a stubborn attitude or reluctance to accept that a sale is truly dead, salespeople sometimes spend too much time chasing accounts that simply do not qualify as potential sales. This should have been detected during the qualifying stage of your selling process. If it was not, ask questions to determine exactly where the prospect stands. When discussing the possibility of earning a prospect's business, it's crucial that you give him the opportunity to not only say "yes" but "no" as well. Getting turned down can make you feel rejected, but it also allows you to move on to more promising prospects. ■

Keith Rosen is president of Profit Builders, LLC. For biographical and business information, see page 272.

Editor's Note: Steve Marx sent us a copy of his book, Close Like the Pros, *with a post-it where he wrote, "Always be a partner–and so will your prospect!" this interesting philosophy infuses Steve's practice of "interactive selling." You'll get a taste of it here as he shows you how to partner with your prospect to close the deal.*

The Truth About Closing
by Steve Marx

Salespeople often work themselves into a frenzy about the close. The run-up to the presentation involves revision after revision and rehearsal after rehearsal. The day is preceded by sleepless nights and the hour by sweaty palms. The bigger the price tag, the sweatier the palms and the more preemptive is the entire process of preparation. And a sales manager who asks about that upcoming presentation every day for a week only amplifies the anxiety.

OK, so maybe I oversold it. But you know there's a lot riding on the submission of a big proposal, and you have to take it darn seriously. It takes a lot of your time and attention—your bandwidth, to use the latest jargon—and you know that a big mistake could deep-six the whole thing. Where might the mistake be? The price? The delivery schedule? The installation process? The payment terms? The third-party supplier? The measurement or monitoring? Who knows?

You should know. You can know.

The truth about closing is that it never happens all at once. Your effort to make it happen all at once—to focus all the decisions into one document and one day—is like trying to push an elephant through the eye of a needle. You're defying nature, asking for the impossible. It's why the prospect almost invariably says... all together now (because all of you know what the prospect almost invariably says)... "I need some time to think about it."

The prospect knows what you, too, should know. You're not asking for a decision; you're asking for a set of decisions.

Unless all you're selling is a simple commodity, for the prospect to give an overall "yes" to what you're proposing, he has to be able to say yes to each element, each aspect of the proposal. He has to think through all the

angles, not just the pieces and parts you presented so clearly and persua-
sively in your formal proposal, but a lot of other issues and considerations
known only to him. These little decisions are interdependent and many of
them must happen in sequence in order for you to get the yes you're seeking.
So, of course, he "needs some time to think about it."

If you looked at closing as a process rather than an event, you'd have
fewer sleepless nights and sweaty palms, and your prospect would need a lot
less time to say yes. The truth about closing is that it never happens all at once.
The notion that it does is a myth that probably developed because we
assemble all the pieces and parts into a single document called a proposal.
But the world's best salespeople know that the proposal document should
not be a collection of decisions to be made, but rather a summary of decisions already made!

The world's best salespeople have relocated the proposal from the middle
of the sales process to the end. Rather than gather up all the decisions to be
made at once—as if that were even possible—sales pros work shoulder to
shoulder with their prospects to build the plans. They recognize that the
big yes they're seeking is really a string of incremental yeses. (Just think back
to the last time you bought a car… was it one decision or a string of decisions, starting with "I guess I really need to replace this thing?")

The first decision your prospect must make, of course, is the decision about
you and the value you might have for him. Plenty of salespeople recognize
this as a separate decision, but they fail to see all the other little decisions along
the way to the big yes. If you're selling a tailored solution of any kind, a
product or service that involves customization or configuration or application or installation, the details are numerous. If your proposal gets any detail
wrong, it could upset your applecart. If you get several details wrong, you
won't even get a call back from that prospect.

All those details represent risk, and opportunity. Your opportunity—the
one that's missed by most but perfected by the pros—is to work interactively with your prospect in developing the proposal. Don't develop it by yourself, or using only your staff. Work together with your prospect and his
staff. Let each aspect of that configuration or customization begin life as a
hazy idea or a trial balloon, and let it be modified, tweaked, honed, or if necessary, rejected.

Take the mystery and the risk out of the process—for you and your client. Turn the close from a looming giant mountain into a series of no-sweat molehills. The pros sell interactively, and often get their yeses before ordinary salespeople get their maybes. They spend less time working on the prospect—and more time working with the prospect. Selling interactively often happens fast, with frequent conversations and collaborations, some in person, some by phone, some through email. By the time it's all on paper, the prospect has already vetted, solved all the problems, and approved everything.

Your prospect really does "need time to think about it." Your job is not to take that time away from him, but simply not to deliver the proposal until he's put the time in and built the proposal with you. ■

Steve Marx is founder of The Center for Sales Strategy. For biographical and business information, see page 269.

Editor's Note: Author of How Winners Sell, *Dave Stein is a recognized business expert featured in* Fast Company, The New York *Times, Business Week, Inc., Fortune and* Forbes. *Use his powerful strategies for gaining control with prospects, even when you're dealing with tough buyers.*

Seven Ways to Get Control of the Sale in a Demanding Market
by Dave Stein

Buyers are grappling for control—total control. The indicators are every-where: reverse auctions, tougher purchasing agents, consultants getting paid big bucks to shield salespeople from potential customers, more demands placed upon salespeople, thicker RFPs, pricing up front, more tightly scripted presentations and demonstrations, and less information available to the sellers.

If you take a moment to think back to the deals you've won and those you've lost, I'm certain you'll agree that your chances of winning a deal where you had no influence on the circumstances were less than even. If there are five contenders for a deal you have less than a 20% chance of winning. Since one or more of your competitors probably has some control or influence over that company's buying process, you are in a highly disad-vantageous position.

It takes a good measure of courage (one of the critical personality traits of great salespeople) not to blindly follow the demands of a prospect. Admittedly that's hard to do when you have a slim pipeline, a product or service that isn't rated number one, your company has little name recogni-tion or you come into a deal late.

Here are just a few strategies for gaining and maintaining some control over the customer buying process:

- **Ask for it, early.** A long-term, mutually beneficial customer rela-tionship begins with win/win right from the start. In fact, the begin-ning of the customer's evaluation process is when he needs you the most. He wants you to answer an RFP? As a condition, ask to meet with the executive from whose budget that investment comes. He wants a presentation to a committee? In return, you get to speak with each of the committee members in advance of the meeting to assure you understand the issues, expectations and objectives.

Is this risky? Sure, but I'd rather take the risk and push the customer a bit early on and find where I really stand in the deal. I don't like to waste my time answering questions, responding to lengthy RFPs or making presentations if I'm really only being included in the deal so the prospect can negotiate better with the vendor he's already chosen. The way I see it, if you ask for some things and he says no enough times, that's a pretty good indicator that he'll say no when you ask for the order, if you even get that far.

- **Say "No."** Sometimes, there comes a point where it pays off not to accommodate every request of the prospect. A client of mine who had totally cooperated with an extremely demanding prospect was dead in the water. He had earned credibility in the account and had proven himself to be a qualified potential supplier. But there was no feedback coming from the prospect relating to where my client stood versus the competition or what the prospect perceived as his strengths or weaknesses.

  After a lengthy strategy session, we decided that we were not going to provide any more information until the prospect began to share his perceptions, observations and concerns. We figured that if we were truly still in the running, the prospect would yield just a bit. If he held fast, we would lose either way— by not getting the information we needed to continue our selling effort or, by getting eliminated.

  We said, "No." The prospect was upset, but ultimately gave in. We were provided with the information we needed and began to knock off objections, one at a time.

  My client won the deal, but at times he's sorry he did. The customer turned out to be extremely difficult to work with and is never satisfied with anything my client does.

- **Create and maintain momentum.** Your strength or force is in your information, resources, customer references, specifications, conference room pilots, proof of concept projects, subject matter experts, future product plans, executives, insights, best practices, investors, board members and all manner of capital that should not be given away for free. The value of that capital to the customer during his evaluation should be carefully measured, and then dispensed so that you're developing interest first, then attention, then excitement and ultimately mindshare.

- **Demonstrate leadership and integrity.** As determined and educated a prospect may want to appear, the risks associated with decision-making are greater for him now than ever before. That scares him. If he believes you have integrity, you can often get in a position, over a period of time, to earn some control of the deal by leading him through his own buying cycle—by coaching, educating and guiding.

  If your prospect believes his success is foremost on your mind (his success is your success), he will most likely relent and allow you to gradually influence his thinking and behavior. One of the ways you can accomplish this is to introduce him to customers of yours who have gone through a similar set of challenges. Another is to have a strategic plan to win his business and to actually share (parts of) that plan with the prospect.

- **Sell higher, sooner.** You've heard this advice before. I can't tell you how many salespeople don't have a plan for getting executive access or miss an opportunity that presents itself because they aren't prepared. You want to gain control in an evaluation? Do everything you can to get access to the executive who is the real buyer and tell him exactly how you can get what he needs done sooner, with less risk, and with the highest return on investment. Then ask if he'll help you. He often will.

- **Recruit and train an ally.** Most selling takes place when you aren't there. If you haven't taken the time to recruit and train an ally within your prospect's company who will work on your behalf behind the scenes, you're taking a real chance. Once an ally trusts you, he becomes your sleeper agent, who can provide you with information about your competition, changing decision criteria, objections to your offering, insights into the real decision-making process, and most importantly, will sell in your place when you aren't there.

- **Get in early.** Now is the time to target the business you're going to be closing next quarter or next year. You want control? Get into that account before he knows he needs your solution or service. Understand his world, educate his, build demand and you'll get control.

If you find yourself saluting and responding to every unreasonable demand your prospects makes, try one or more of the proven strategies I've listed above and get control of the sale. ∎

Dave Stein is CEO of ES Research Group. For biographical and business information, see page 273.

Editor's Note: During his 30-year career as a salesperson, manager, executive and business owner in the construction, publishing, and financial services industries, Paul McCord has seen his share of economic changes. In this important lesson, he explains how you can survive and thrive during difficult times.

Selling In a Weak Economy
by Paul McCord

Pick up any newspaper and you'll find stories about how bad the economy is. Foreclosures are snowballing, the unemployment rate is inching up, gas prices are soaring, there are fears of runaway inflation, food prices are way up, layoffs are increasing, the stock market is down; why some days it seems the world, as we know it, is coming to an end.

For salespeople, this onslaught of bad economic news can have devastating psychological consequences. It erodes our confidence, heightens our anxiety, and may even convince us that our efforts are hopeless. The normal "no" we receive is no longer simply no, instead it's a sign of how bad the economy is. Rejection becomes magnified, lost sales are indications of how business has changed and our successes or failures are no longer within our control. As the negative economic news increases, we become more convinced that it isn't us, but rather the economy that's causing our sales to decline, our incomes to shrivel, and our futures to be in question.

Negative News Breeds Negative Outcomes

Having been through several economic ups and downs in my career, I've had the opportunity to experience first hand the insidious nature of paying too close attention to the news. When we're bombarded by negative reports, we tend to absorb those reports into our selling activities. The negative news we read becomes the negative outcome we expect, and the negative outcome we experience. We view our successes as the rare exceptions and our failures as the new norms.

This creeping negativism worms its way into all of our sales business. Our prospecting decreases—what's the use anyway? Our presentations and proposals become defensive, pricing becomes our centerpiece, and we no longer ask for the prospect's business but instead beg for it.

Yet, there are companies and salespeople who thrive in weak economies. There are those who view a weak economy as an opportunity to grow their businesses while their competitors are hunkering down with a bunker mentality, hoping merely to survive.

How can you turn a weak economy to your advantage? Here are five "musts" to maintain momentum during a weak economy:

- **Maintain perspective.** Don't allow yourself to be sucked in by the negative hype about the economy. Even during the worst of the Great Depression, there were people and companies buying all types of products and services. There are always quality prospects that want and need your products and services. Your job is to find them and connect with them in a manner in which they will respond.

- **Maintain prospecting.** Most salespeople will decrease their prospecting as the economy weakens. Their general feeling of malaise and helplessness can work to your advantage if you can maintain, or even increase, your own level of activity. Further, since most salespeople will be using the most ineffective prospecting methods such as cold calling and networking, employing prospecting methods that are more acceptable to prospects (such as referrals) will give you the opportunity to set yourself apart from the crowd.

- **Focus on solving issues, not price.** Most of your competition will be focusing on price, not solving real issues and problems. Although price may be a consideration, quality prospects are more concerned about resolving their issues and problems and value, not getting the lowest possible price. Focus on the prospect's needs, not your competitor's price. While your competitor is busy turning his products and services into commodities to be sold at the lowest possible price, concentrate on understanding the root issues your prospect has and develop solutions that create value for your prospect.

- **Relationships are key.** Human nature doesn't change just because the economy changes. Both businesses and individual consumers buy from people they trust and respect. Certainly, we all, on occasion, make purchases from people we don't have a relationship with, we may even make an occasional purchase from someone we don't respect or trust, but most sales are created through relationships, not price, hype, or fast talking. That doesn't change during a slow economy. People still purchase from people they trust and respect. While your competitors are looking for the quick sale, continue developing long-term relationships. Not only will it pay off in the long run, it will also create immediate selling opportunities.

- **Take advantage.** As your competitors become more concerned about the economy, they will begin to batten down the hatches, cutting costs, including their marketing and prospecting expenses. They may cut other corners, even sacrificing customer service to save a couple of dollars here and there. Take advantage of the opportunities your competitors open up for you. Cut out the fat in your business while increasing your marketing and prospecting. Make a conscious effort to target your competitor's best customers. While your competitors retreat to their bunker, become more aggressive in pursuing new business opportunities.

An economic downturn can be a time for you to expand and grow your sales by doing the opposite of your competition. While they are cutting marketing and prospecting expenses, allowing themselves to become incapacitated by the bad economic news, and hunkering down hoping to just make it through the bad times, you can turn the economy in your favor. You can eliminate your unnecessary expenses while expanding your marketing and prospecting. You can recognize prospects still buy solutions and that they buy based on relationships, not just price. And, you can take advantage of your competitor's complacency, fear, and mistakes, to sell more. ■

Paul McCord is president of McCord Training. For biographical and business information, see page 269.

Editor's Note: Brent Patmos began his career as the youngest store director, then youngest vice president for one of the fastest growing discount retail chains in the world. He later became vice president of sales and marketing for a major manufacturer. Today he is a leading expert on sales process, training, and development. Here he explains how to simplify your communication to succeed with clients.

Simplify For Sales Success
by Brent Patmos

Today's sales landscape offers more products, more services, more options, more choices, and more providers than ever before. Researchers tell us that the average consumer processes over 1,500 commercial or advertising messages on a weekly basis. Your customers' decisions, interactions, and communications with their customers are continually becoming more complex.

Business is moving at a dizzying pace and people are trying to juggle more projects, more priorities, more responsibilities and more balance. All of this while trying not to go nuts! Salespeople and business owners are trying to manage more customers, more information, more technology and more distractions that have nothing to do with selling more products and services.

This description is not a picture of doom and gloom but rather a picture of opportunity. It is an opportunity to communicate more effectively, to follow through more thoroughly, and to revolutionize the way your customers view you and your company. This is your opportunity to make your customers' lives easier, more effective, more productive, and more profitable.

Now is your opportunity to simplify.

Simplicity Leads to Understanding

Children's books have few words and lots of big pictures. If you have ever tried to capture the attention of a child, you know exactly what I am talking about and why the books are simple. Remember that "big" words lose meaning and are used more often for the benefit of our ego. Without minimizing the importance of proper presentation and interaction, it stands to reason that people have a limited attention span no matter what their age. If you want to sell more and increase profits immediately then pay particular attention to simplifying the following areas:

- **Simplify communication and content.** Maybe you have heard someone tell a story, but he wasn't a storyteller, and about half way through you were screaming inside, "Get to the point!" That's exactly what customers say about many of the sales presentations and "stories" they receive. The important part is the substance of what you say rather than how long you take to say it. Simplify by cutting in half any written, verbal or e-mail communications with your customers. Instead of beginning a proposal or presentation with "happy language," begin by simply stating the three key ways your product or service affects your customers. Be clear and concise. When you get to the point, your customers notice because you are immediately focused on their needs and requirements.

- **Simplify preparation.** This doesn't mean eliminate preparation and start winging it through sales presentations. Preparation always takes more time in our minds than it does when we actually sit down and take action. Thinking about preparation often leads to procrastination. I suggest you break your planning into 15-minute segments and designate a topic for each block. If one topic requires more time, then assign the necessary number of 15-minute blocks to that topic. You will avoid feeling overwhelmed and be amazed at how effective your investment in planning and preparation becomes.

- **Simplify helping them buy.** Help your customers buy rather than just trying to sell them. Help your customers buy in both short and long cycles through the use of multiple resources, decision-making levels and relationships. This defines effective selling. You want to avoid the typical perspective when a customer is referring to you and your sales effort.

- **Simplify tone and pace.** *How* you say something is as important as *what* you say to your customer. The key is to use a tone and delivery that are uniquely your own. When making sales presentations or having sales conversations, it's not uncommon for the tone of your voice to go up as the pace of your speech gets faster. When tone and pace increase, the art of being conversational is lost. This is often connected to nerves or a lack of preparation. Repeatedly practice your delivery and presentation with an emphasis on being conversational. Emphasize the skill of talking *with* your customer rather than talking *to* your customer. Practice dialogue scenarios that let you interact in a way that is realistic and focused. Breathing is the key to both tone and pace so insure that you have plenty of air in your lungs.

• **Simplify follow-through.** When it comes to productive sales behavior, follow-through ranks as the highest priority. Why? Because it's the most talked about and least executed activity in the sales toolbox. You will service your customers at a higher level and sell more products when you execute on follow-through relentlessly. It's not enough to think about follow-through. You must take action if you want to create an impact! Remember that it's the one or two things you do differently that make you memorable in the mind of your customer. Additionally, never underestimate the power of urgency and immediacy. Stated simply, you must do what you say you will do consistently and with greater focus if you want to put significant distance between your level of follow-through and that of your competition.

• **Simplify the experience.** Here's the bottom line: Your customers want you to simplify their lives by simplifying their experiences. The distractions of complexity are everywhere. Your customers are looking for every way possible to increase their sales and improve the profitability and performance of their companies. You possess key strategies, services and products to make these goals a reality. Simplify the products and services experience for your customers and get ready to increase your sales, margin and effectiveness! ■

Brent Patmos is president and CEO of Perpetual Development Inc. For biographical and business information, see page 271.

Editor's Note: Lee Salz is the author of two books on sales and an expert on hiring, managing and compensating sales teams. He explains how to use testimonials in your sales process.

References: The Most Underutilized Strategic Advantage
by Lee B. Salz

See if this sounds familiar. You've been chasing this account for six months. You feel optimistic as the buying process is coming to a conclusion. The sale is between you and two other firms. The competition is fierce, but you feel you are ahead. At 11 a.m., the procurement agent asks for three references to be provided by the end of the day. In a panic, you send a company-wide e-mail in search of these clients. At 4:58 p.m., you've got all three and quickly send them to the procurement agent. Whew! Mission accomplished! They wanted three references and you got it done. Of course, so did your competitors.

This scenario plays out every day. It doesn't matter whether the company is large or small, or what industry it's in; the request for references is a standard part of the buying process. Surprisingly, few salespeople use this reference stage to their strategic advantage. They simply respond quickly with the requested information. In the mind of the salesperson, the speed of the response communicates his performance as a supplier. While somewhat true, the prospect's discussions with the references will carry far more weight in the selection process than the speed with which the salesperson furnishes a reference.

Why do prospects ask for references? When I talk to salespeople, I usually hear that references are just a standard part of due diligence. Some use the term "rubber stamp." However, when I talk to buyers, I hear a very different message. Many buyers look at references as their opportunities to validate the messages they've been hearing from the potential suppliers. In essence, prospects are trying to determine whether a supplier can deliver on his promises. Can the supplier really handle this size account? Is he really that fast? Or, that accurate? Is the service as good as he described?

If a new supplier does not perform to the expectations that have been represented, there's risk for the buyer who selected him. Sometimes, a prospect asks the same questions of the reference that he asked of the salesperson to see if there is a difference in response. Other times, the buyer asks specific questions relative to his needs that may not have been shared with the salesperson. For the prospect, this is his most critical evaluation step.

It's the little things that winning salespeople do that makes them winners. If all of the competing salespeople provide good references, how can you present the best references? First, realize that the best references will be different for each prospect.

What Does the Client Want to Know?

Start by talking with the procurement agent. For example, say, "I received your request for references and I'm happy to supply them. So that I can provide you with the references that best support your initiative, what are you hoping to learn from our clients?" If you can gather that information from the procurement agent, you have the roadmap to identifying the best references. Even if he can't, or won't, provide you with this information, you have at least shown that you care. This effort alone can be the differentiator that pushes you across the finish line. All is not lost if you can't get the information.

Match Them Up

Now, think about the account and what's important to him. Reflect on what was learned during the needs analysis discussions. If the customer was concerned about implementation, provide a reference from an account that your company recently implemented. Perhaps, the decision is being made by a CFO, then provide a reference of a CFO who can speak about your performance. For the third reference, provide a client who's purchasing an equal amount of the same product. From the prospect's perspective, how great is the opportunity to speak to three clients who can relate to his needs? He will be able to gather the information he desires from someone with whom he shares something in common. He will feel confident in his ability to perform due diligence on you, the potential supplier. He will be able to make an informed decision.

Rather than simply sending the contact names and phone numbers to the procurement agent, instead provide a brief narrative of how each client serves as a reference. How many salespeople are doing that?

Sound the Alarm

Finally, contact the three references to alert them that a call is coming their way to discuss your performance as a supplier. Tell them that the prospect is calling to discuss particular areas of the business. Thus, when the prospect calls the reference, the reference is expecting the call and is prepared for the conversation. What a great experience for your prospect and your client. Keep in mind, one easy way to ruin a relationship with a happy client is to surprise him with a reference phone call. No one likes to be blindsided or unprepared. I've seen more than a few opportunities lost where the prospect cited the reference experience as the deciding factor. An unprepared reference reflects negatively on the supplier.

In a competitive marketplace, every opportunity that you have to demonstrate value to a prospect is critical. Leveraging the reference step of the process can give you that little edge that pushes you over the top. ∎

Lee B. Salz is president of Sales Architects. For biographical and business information, see page 272.

Editor's Note: Keith Rosen is an author, speaker and sales trainer who helps thousands of sales professionals each year. He is one of my favorite business growth authors. Use his advice to advance your sales process with every client contact.

While You Have Their Attention
by Keith Rosen

It would be great if every prospect became a new customer based on your timeline. Now step back to reality. It's a safe bet that some of the prospects you call will not be ready to take that next step with you, or at least, not yet.

The end result is that you place many prospects on your "call back" list to contact in the future. A typical conversation may sound something like this:

> You: "OK, Mr. Prospect. Based on what you're telling me, it sounds like this isn't the best time to explore what we can do for you in more detail. When might be a better time to reconnect with you?"

> Prospect: "Give me a couple of months to clear off what I already have on my plate. Then I'll be in a better position to discuss this with you."

> You: "That sounds fair. So, if I quickly check my calendar, you are suggesting I touch base with you again in early September, is that correct?"

> Prospect: "Yes, that sounds fine."

At this point, you thank the prospect and create a reminder to call Mr. Prospect in September. In September, you reconnect with Mr. Prospect to discover that, not only is he no longer with the company, but the company bought a similar product that you sell from another vendor!

While there is no foolproof method to prevent this situation, there is something that you can do to lower the odds. Let's continue the conversation between you and the prospect where we left off:

> You: "Mr. Prospect thanks again for your time today. Before we wrap up this conversation, I've noticed that in the past, when I have attempted to reconnect with someone months after our first contact, many things have transpired. Changes in his position, in his company, or in his life often tend to divert even the best-laid plans. Since there are so many things that can happen in two months, I was hoping that I could stay in contact with you without stepping over the line and being annoying about it. With your permission, can I contact you from time to time with updates about our product or valuable information that you may find of interest as it relates to your business?"

By asking this question, and gaining confirmation that it's OK to stay in touch, you now have a prospect that has given you permission to continue to contact him. You won't be sending unsolicited information that will aggravate and turn him off.

Sure, it may sound like the prospect may not be in a position to immediately explore your offering in more detail. However, that doesn't mean he will be in the same position in the future.

A monthly newsletter, a free trial, an article of interest, collateral material, or a great new product feature are just a few ways to deliver value during this "down time" and keep your finger on the pulse of every prospect.

Using this technique, you'll find that if things change on the prospect's side, you won't be the last person to know. ■

Keith Rosen is president of Profit Builders, LLC. For biographical and business information, see page 272.

Editor's Note: A noted author and speaker, Julie Thomas is president and CEO of ValueSelling Associates. Julie consults and trains in a wide variety of industries. Her corporate clients include Marquis Jet Partners, Exclusive Resorts, The Ken Blanchard Companies, NetJets and input. Use this advice to jumpstart a stalled deal.

Diagnosing the Stalled Decision
by Julie Thomas

Think about your forecast. How much of your pipeline suffers from stalled opportunities?

If you are like most, it's easily between 30% and 50%. In a tough market, one of the biggest returns you can reap is to reduce the impact of stalled decisions; however, to jumpstart a stalled sale, you must understand the cause of the stall.

After reviewing over 5,000 stalled opportunities, we have identified the five most common explanations for a sale that is stuck in limbo.

- **Lack of connection to a critical business issue.** Unless your solution has increased revenue, time to market, cost management, improved quality, competitive differentiation, or some other looming business issue tied to it, you can expect a stall. As purse strings tighten, senior executives will only spend on matters that directly impact their businesses.

  A sales rep only has to ask three questions to uncover business issues:

  1. Why do you want this solution?

  2. Why are those problems important to solve?

  3. Why would that matter to you or any other executive?

- **Lack of perceived value.** Most people can really only juggle five or six critical issues at a time. We all live with problems that we don't need to solve today. However, business issues are constant. Can your prospect articulate the value or impact of addressing the business issue? If your solution, from your prospect's perspective, doesn't have enough value to get in his top five or six, you get stalled or put on the back burner. Ask the prospect to quantify the impact of resolving the business issue. Better yet, ask him how the solution will impact him personally.

- **Lack of differentiation.** Lack of differentiation will cause the prospect to spend more time evaluating, which translates to a stall. If you are unable to differentiate on capabilities and solving problems, you will be forced to differentiate on price.

- **Decision authority.** Decision authority is one of the most common causes of stalled decisions. The buying frenzy of the late '90s all but eliminated the need to call on the real decision makers for everyday purchases. As purse strings have tightened, decision makers are becoming more involved in the buying process. It's important to ask, "Has the person you're in contact with made this type of decision before? When and how?" Triangulate your information by asking the same questions to multiple people in the organization to find out who really has the decision-making power in the organization.

- **Risk.** Selecting a new vendor or a new solution involves risk. The prospect's perception of risk can span business impacts like lost time or money or it can have personal ramifications including to his career or reputation. As a prospect gets closer to making a decision, the risk becomes greater in his mind. Common tools for alleviating risk include supplying references, trial usage, demonstrating credibility with iron-clad implementation plans, guarantees, and your executive backing. ∎

Julie Thomas is president and CEO of ValueSelling Associates. For biographical and business information, see page 273.

Editor's Note: Before founding the sales training and consulting firm, KLA Group, Kendra Lee sold hardware, software, and services for Fortune 500 companies in the high-tech computer industry. She consistently ranked in the top 1-2 percent of their worldwide sales forces and closed more than 95 percent of all qualified prospects. She shows you clever ways to get gatekeepers on your side.

Getting Past the Gatekeeper
by Kendra Lee

Many sales professionals fail miserably when trying to gain access to company executives. Unfortunately, rather than taking time to develop a strategy, they pick up the phone, smile and dial, hoping their canned pitch will be enough to get an appointment. This strategy doesn't get many reps past today's sophisticated gatekeepers, many of whom aren't willing to give a salesperson a second chance. So, it's imperative that you do your homework and are prepared to take full advantage of what could be a golden opportunity to gain access to a key contact.

Do Your Research

Before you even think about contacting a new prospect, do your research. You know your goal is to create an opening statement that will grab an executive's attention. However, don't overlook doing the same for the gatekeeper who is more likely to answer the telephone.

One of the key things to look for in your research is something that will cause the gatekeeper to think, "Mr. Executive needs to speak with this person." To do this, learn more about the company as a whole and the executive's area of responsibility. Use this information to create a powerful opening statement that will differentiate your message to both the executive and the gatekeeper.

Here are some things to keep in mind when conducting your company research:

- Read the latest press releases to see what the company is focusing on. Can your company help in these areas? How have you helped other clients focused in these same areas?

- Look at the job openings as clues to where the company is investing. Perhaps there are job openings for areas where you have offerings.
- Review the company's mission statement to identify a cultural fit with your company. Why try to prospect to a company whose values and culture won't be a fit with your own?

Consider these tips when researching the company's executive:

- Identify issues the executive may be facing that you have solved for other clients. How can you state those issues in compelling business terms?
- Determine priorities the executive may have in common with your other clients.
- Uncover business opinions the executive has expressed that are in line with your company's opinions.
- Find people you both might know. Find someone you can reference or who might offer you a referral to the executive.
- Identify companies the executive has worked for that you have in-depth knowledge of.

How do you find information about the executive after researching the company's website? Search Google for the executive's name or search a business information site like Hoovers.com.

Respect Company Gatekeepers

Once your research is complete and you begin to establish contact with a company, you will likely encounter one of two types of gatekeepers: a live person, or voice mail intended to screen calls. The first type of gatekeeper will likely be an executive assistant or receptionist, who is responsible for keeping people from wasting the executive's time. When confronting a live gatekeeper, make it apparent that you've done your research with a well-devised and differentiating opening statement. This will show the gatekeeper that you respect her position, and can help her bring something of value to her boss.

Once this is accomplished, ask the gatekeeper for help in identifying the right person to speak with. If the executive is the right person, ask for help in setting an appointment. The assistant will grant you an appointment if she feels it will be of value to the executive based on the executive's priorities. Or, the assistant may refer you to another contact in the organization with those priorities. Either way, you're in the door!

After hearing your opening statement, the receptionist may also be able to refer you to the appropriate contacts, provide the executive's email address, or give you insights into the best times to reach the executive. You may choose to seek out the receptionist to gather this information while also gaining access to other contacts.

Remember to follow up and thank gatekeepers for their assistance. Provide the executive assistant with updates on your progress and ask to leave a similar voicemail for the executive. Treat both types of gatekeepers with respect and professionalism and the assistant or receptionist will facilitate, rather than block, your entrance to the executive.

Be Persistent With Voice Mail Gatekeepers

The second type of gatekeeper you may encounter is voice mail. Unless you have brand recognition backing you, it can take as many as nine attempts to get through the voice mail gatekeeper and reach your target executive. Over these nine calls you have the opportunity to demonstrate to the executive your professionalism, confidence and knowledge. Don't give up. For those executives you simply must reach, try these techniques.

- Leave a voice mail every other day. Limit your voicemail message to four or five sentences and use your opening statement.
- Attempt to call multiple times a day throughout the day if there is no assistant to guide you. Call early and late when the executive may be available at his desk.
- If you reach an assistant, ask the best times to call. Better yet, ask for 15 minutes on the executive's calendar.
- Follow your voice mail message with an email recapping your opening statement and demonstrating your attention to detail. Include your contact information and website, while suggesting some times to talk.
- Book the times you suggested in your e-mail on your calendar and unless you hear from the executive, consider it an appointment. Follow up at the exact time you mentioned to demonstrate reliability. Use your message again and let the executive hear your interest

in speaking with him. Suggest another time to talk, and continue following up.

- Use Microsoft Outlook's calendar to schedule a tentative appointment on the executive's calendar. Many larger companies use Microsoft Outlook to maintain their calendars, and if you use it as well, turn it into an opportunity to schedule an appointment. If the executive felt value through your voicemail and email messages, he may accept your calendar invitation and meet with you.

For any sales rep, being able to successfully gain support from the gatekeeper to access an executive is a mandatory step in the sales process. It will take some research, patience and persistence, but the time you take to learn how to get the gatekeeper's respect and the executive's attention will put you light years ahead of making a blind cold call and losing any chance of setting up a meeting. Once you get the gatekeeper's support, an introductory meeting won't be far behind. ■

Kendra Lee is founder and president of KLA Group. For biographical and business information, see page 268.

Editor's Note: Art Sobczak held corporate telesales and management positions with American Express and AT&T before he launched his own telesales training business. Since 1984, he has written and published a popular newsletter, the "Telephone Prospecting and Selling Report." Art shares with us some of his real-world tips for making effective follow-up calls.

What to Say on Repeated Follow-up Calls
by Art Sobczak

As you scrolled through your follow-up files today, perhaps you ran across one or two prospects that you've called repeatedly and who continue putting you off. You feel there's some real potential there and you don't want to give up. Yet, it's grueling to come up with something more creative to say than, "Well, here I am again."

Or perhaps you have customers who currently buy from you, and your job description says you need to call them regularly, perhaps monthly, weekly, or more often. (I did a couple of training sessions at a national sales meeting for the Wholesale Florists & Florist Suppliers Association where I learned some wholesalers call retail florists every day!)

What you *never* want to say on these regular calls is:

- Well, I was just checking in with you to see how it's going.
- Wanted to touch base with you today.
- Thought I'd give you a courtesy call.
- Wondering if you needed anything?

So what's wrong with these statements? These approaches are reactive, provide nothing of value, can be viewed as nuisance calls, and leave you open to being treated as a simple vendor who can be manipulated into a price war. I've always said that these are some of the toughest calls to place because, they require creative thinking and lots of sales pros don't want to think that hard. Except the best sales pros. I bet you're in that group.

Lazy sales reps, or those who don't know any better are content calling to "just touch base," or to "see if there's anything on your desk I can bid on."

Calls to regular customers, and to prospects you're clinging to should always contain something of value. Include something that lets the customer feel you're contributing something useful by calling. Keep in mind that your regular customers are someone else's prospects. If they feel they are being taken for granted by a sales rep who simply calls and says, "Do you have an order for me?" they might eventually fall for the wooing of a competitor who is creative enough to dangle something attractive in front of them.

Also keep in mind your prospects are likely buying from someone else, and won't budge unless they see some value in what you have.

So, what to do?

Here are just a few ideas to spice up these calls to position you as a value-added resource, and not just a salesperson.

- **Begin with "you."** A good way to begin these calls is by saying something like: "I was thinking of you." Or, "I heard some interesting information, and you immediately came to mind." Or, "When this news came out, I thought about you."

- **Industry news.** Perhaps you have some news your clients or prospects might not be aware of. Or, maybe they are aware of it, and you have something to help them take advantage of it. For example: "Ms. Prospect, you're probably familiar with the new regulations regarding the reporting of waste disposal. We've developed a way to make that less of a headache for companies in your situation, and I'd like to ask you a few questions to see how much of a problem this will be for you."

- **New policies at your company.** If you change restrictive policies that would enable you to do business with people who didn't qualify in the past, call them again. For example, if your minimum order size has been dropped or you're now carrying a line that they previously asked but you didn't have or you've loosened credit requirements. With regular customers, calling with changes that benefit them is always welcome.

- **New regime at your company.** This approach can be effective for those accounts you haven't been able to break because of legitimate objections they've had. If, for example, new management has cleaned house and improved quality, decreased errors, etc., call again, since you're now selling a new company. Also, these can be spun into reasons for calling existing accounts.

- **New capability.** If you have products or services that deliver results you weren't able to previously deliver, that's always a good reason to call. Just be sure you're positioning them in terms of results to the listener. Don't say: "Hey, we have a new product and we think it's great."
- **New you.** Maybe you fell to pieces and self-destructed on a previous call. Since then you've acquired more skills and confidence. Maybe you've come up with new ideas, or a new strategy.

And here's the best way I know for you to come up with great value-added reasons for calling:

Your Action Step

Have a brainstorming session with your colleagues. Invite customer service, production, advertising, marketing, operations—anyone who knows your products and services. Make it a game or competition. The goal is to fill in the blank:

"The reason I'm calling is ____."

The main rule is that the listener must perceive what goes in the blank as something valuable and interesting to him. Believe me, I've done this many times with clients in training sessions and we've come up with 20, 30 or more great ideas to use.

So get creative, get working, and you'll find yourself converting more of those prospects collecting dust in your follow-up file, and you'll also provide more value and sell more to existing customers. ∎

Art Sobczak is president of Business By Phone, Inc. For biographical and business information, see page 273.

Editor's Note: Wendy Weiss is a former ballet dancer who set appointments for clients as her day job. She was so effective one of her clients dubbed her the "Queen of Cold Calling." The title stuck. When injuries sidelined her dance career, Wendy transformed her day job into a full-time career as a sales trainer, coach and author. Her clients include ADP, Avon, and Sprint.

A Confused Prospect Does Not Buy
by Wendy Weiss

Once, I received this voice mail from a sales representative:

> "The purpose of my call today is to introduce myself and take a moment to briefly describe for you two core-based technologies; laser Internet online office and an Internet broadcasting technology. I don't know whether or not any of these applications may be of interest to you, I would appreciate a brief moment of your time to review that."

They weren't of interest. I didn't call back. Well, actually, to be more exact, I didn't know if they'd be of interest. I am a techno-moron. While I use technology for my business, I only use technology when I understand the value of what that technology enables me to do. I have frequent conversations with my IT consultant and I tell him what I'd like to be able to accomplish and he makes recommendations in very plain English.

Getting back to the message above, I have no idea what "core-based technologies" and "laser Internet online office," mean. While I have a sense of what "an Internet broadcasting technology" might be, I don't know or understand its value to me. And that's the heart of the matter: What is the value? There was nothing in his message that enabled me to understand the value he had to offer. There was, therefore, no reason for me to call him back.

This same representative called me a few days later. Because I generally talk to salespeople who call me, we did talk for approximately five minutes. I still didn't understand what his product was, what it did or what its value to me might possibly be. I told him so. He still couldn't make himself clear.

Instead, he said he'd send an e-mail, which would miraculously explain everything. I never received it.

Instead, a few days later there was another voice mail. It was the exact same message that he'd left the first time. No acknowledgement that we'd talked (clearly he'd forgotten or simply didn't check me off in his database) and no mention of the promised e-mail. I didn't return his call.

Later I received yet another voice mail from this representative. This one went: "Just wanted to follow-up on our conversation and the information I sent to you." Again, this message contained nothing about the value he had to offer. He gave me no compelling reason to respond and I did not.

So what are the lessons here?

- **Lesson 1:** Keep good records. This way you will know whether or not you have spoken with a prospect, what you talked about and what your next step is.
- **Lesson 2:** If you promise to send something to a prospect, send it.
- **Lesson 3:** Always lead with value. "What is the value to me?" That's the question that all prospects are asking when they hear your message and/or when you get them on the telephone. It's really your job to tell them. They will not guess, read your mind or figure it out on their own.
- **Lesson 4:** Be crystal clear. You are the expert in what you do. You are the expert on your product, your service and/or your offering, your prospect is not. It's a huge mistake to assume that your prospect knows or understands the value of what you have to offer. You must make your message so clear that even a child would understand the value.

A confused prospect does not buy. ■

Wendy Weiss is known as The Queen of Cold Calling. For biographical and business information, see page 274.

Editor's Note: Craig James spent more than 15 years in sales and sales management for technology and software companies. He holds an MBA from the University of Chicago's Graduate School of Business. In addition to training, coaching, and consulting, he teaches at New York University's School of Continuing and Professional studies. Craig has been widely published and quoted in business publications, including Business Week, Sales and Marketing Management, *and* Selling Power.

Building the Case for a Meeting
by Craig James

How many times have you gotten prospects interested by grabbing their attention on your initial phone call, but then you spend the next two weeks chasing after them? Where did that interest go? It waned because you didn't take it to the next step: transforming that interest into desire. You must transform your prospect's interest into a desire so strong that the tables turn, and the prospect is asking you when you're available for a meeting.

How do you do this? Simply by asking questions, questions that help you understand the prospect's current situation, his desired situation, and how big the gap is between the two. Ask questions that get the prospect thinking about the consequences of doing nothing, and how wonderful things will be once he's using your product or service.

As your prospect is answering your questions, listen with one thought in mind: Is the gap between his current situation and his desired situation big enough that he will want to invest time and money to bridge it? If not, what questions can you ask to draw attention to that gap so you can emphasize that doing nothing is more painful for him than deciding to do something? When you get your prospect to that point, he'll be eager to learn what you can do for him and how. Then simply recommend a meeting date and time, and gain agreement.

The Uncooperative Prospect

If your prospect isn't willing to answer all your questions, then you need a fall-back position. When your prospect is stalling, the best tactic you can fall back on is to simply and directly ask for a brief meeting. Ask for a 15-

20 minute meeting. What could you possibly accomplish in such a short time? The purpose of this meeting is to do what you didn't get the chance to do on your initial phone call—to get your prospect excited about moving forward. From there, you can easily schedule a longer meeting, only this time it will be with additional members of the decision-making process.

Why specify a 15-20 minute meeting, and not just a meeting? Think about it: Why are most prospects reluctant to meet with you? It's not necessarily because they don't believe what you're offering can help them. It's because granting a meeting will force them to give up one of their most precious, limited resources—time. The customer's expectation, based on experience, is that you're going to take up at least an hour of his time, probably more. Who wants to commit that kind of time to meet with someone whose product they're not even sure they need? I wouldn't.

But, if all you ask for is 15 minutes, few people will argue with you. Especially, if you emphasize that you'll stick to those 15 minutes. Your expectation is that, as you pack up your bags at the 15-minute mark, you'll have created such desire for your product or service that the prospect won't let you go, and you'll get the time needed to conduct a proper meeting.

Your Action Step

Make a list of a half dozen or so questions you could ask prospects to stimulate their thinking about their dissatisfaction with their current situations, and where they'd ideally like to be. Practice asking these questions in role plays with your manager or with your peers. Work on transitioning to your fallback position in case a prospect doesn't "bite." Do this several times, then put it to work with a real prospect. I assure you that your appointment-to-call ratio will head north in a hurry and you'll find yourself closing more business, faster. ■

Craig James is the founder and president of Sales Solutions. For biographical and business information, see page 266.

Editor's Note: George Ludwig is a noted sales speaker, trainer and consultant for clients like CIGNA, Abbott Laboratories, Johnson & Johnson, and Northwestern Mutual. He is also an authority on peak performance psychology. He shows you how to get the edge in your sales presentations by getting physical.

Get Physical: Involve Your Prospect for a More Effective Presentation
by George Ludwig

"Lena, just press that green button to open the chamber door," was all I said. The group from Chicago stepped in closer and watched with amazement as the door opened. Then I handed a new high-tech cassette for dispensing sterilant to another prospect and said, "Woody, just insert it here, and the machine will pull it in the rest of the way." Again the group let out some "oohs" and "aahs" after Woody had inserted the cassette. Next I said, "Diana, please put those trays in the chamber." Diana slid two bright blue trays into the deep chamber and commented, "This chamber holds much more than I thought it could." The group nodded in agreement, and I continued my sales presentation.

The presentation described above took place in 1994 in the sterilization area at Long Beach Memorial Hospital in Long Beach, California. I was with a group of prospects from Chicago who had flown in to see a brand new low-temperature sterilization technology called Plasma Sterilization. That day, quite by accident, I discovered a very powerful selling technique that led to many more sales in the years that followed.

What I discovered was the more prospects were involved in the presentation, the more I was able to lead them toward a feeling of ownership. I realized that tactile involvement, when used early and often during the entire sales process, engages more of your prospects' senses, which in turn creates greater emotional involvement.

Emotional involvement can generate greater sales. Customer motion leads straight to customer emotion and vice versa. Physical involvement also helps you find out how receptive your prospects are by watching their nonverbal actions. Most prospects are not skilled actors, so when you involve them physically, you can often gauge where they are in terms of moving from resistance toward acceptance.

Usually it's easier to get a prospect involved in a product sale than in a service sale. But if you use your creativity, you will be amazed at the ways in which you can involve a prospect. Below are some ideas to consider.

Involvement in the presentation setup:
- Ask for help with an easel, projector, or video machine.
- Ask for something—a pencil, paper, Magic Marker.
- Ask the prospect to plug something in or move something.
- Accept the offer of coffee or soda.
- Use the setup time for humor and small talk, too.

Involvement in the product demonstration
- Get the prospect to run the demo.
- Get him to push the buttons.
- Get him to work the copier, drive the car, walk the property.
- Get him to hold something.
- Get him to help you assemble something.
- Get him to actually use the product and experience the benefits.

Even though you know how to do it, you're not going to impress the prospect much with a whiz-bang demonstration. All you're going to do is bore him if you don't get him physically involved. Try to get your prospect to lead the entire presentation, if possible. The more involved the prospect is, the more ownership he experiences, and the closer you move to an affirmative decision.

The group members all loaded the Plasma Sterilizer with wrapped surgical instruments, and we left for lunch. We returned an hour later, and the prospects were shocked to find the sterilization cycle completed. The process they all had been using back in their Chicago hospitals often took as long as 18 hours to sterilize the instruments. "Go ahead, open the door, unload her, and examine your load," I said to the group.

Those eight sterilization professionals excitedly pushed the buttons, opened the door, unwrapped the load, and then acted almost like kids at Christmas trying out a new toy. They had all moved a giant step closer to purchasing the new technology. In fact, seven of the eight prospects did eventually purchase Low-Temperature Plasma Sterilizers, which represented more than half a million dollars in sales revenue.

What I learned that day was to get more of the sales prospects' senses involved. If you want to generate more sales you have to get physical. ∎

George Ludwig is president of GLU Consulting. For biographical and business information, see page 268.

Editor's Note: Steve McCreedy was a successful general manager for a group of major radio and television properties when he attended a sales management symposium at The Brooks Group. He was so impressed, he joined the renowned sales training company. Today he's their resident expert on selling at higher margins. Take his advice and sell the right solution at full price.

Getting Full Price Even in a Difficult Economy
by Steve McCreedy

The key to earning serious income as a salesperson is understanding how to emphasize the overall quality of the product and services you sell effectively. Learning to position the viable quality of your product or service offers a distinct competitive advantage. People are far more likely to buy when they know they are getting an appropriate level of 'bang' for their buck.

But I can't sell on quality! Ours doesn't feature the best…most…latest….

Surprisingly, many salespeople erroneously believe that quality is somehow defined by having the best ratings, highest price, or latest bells and whistles. True quality actually has very little to do with any of that. Simply put, quality is defined as the ability of a product or service to conform to set standards and expectations. Those standards and requirements are typically highly subjective, depending solely on each individual prospect's requirements and needs.

Having "the best product that money can buy" isn't always ideal. Take for example your average, middle-class mother of two. If she were in the market for a new vehicle, you probably wouldn't suggest she stop by her local Maserati dealership. The vehicles she'd find there would likely offer the very best and brightest features, equipment and luxury that a vehicle can carry. However, she is equally (if not more) likely to find a vehicle that suits her unique needs and requirements in models that don't cost as much as a Maserati. To her, a Ford, Honda, or Toyota might represent the perfect balance of "quality" features and affordability she needs in order to shuttle her kids safely and successfully.

The only way to determine whether your products or services genuinely represent a good fit for a particular prospect is to employ three deep, open-ended questions like: What are you going to use it for? What are you currently using? What, if any, features are absolutely essential to you?

Avoiding the "Your price is too high" Objection

If you want to avoid the "your price is too high" conversation with prospects, you'd better have "the right stuff." Selling certainly includes telling your prospects that your offering is the correct product (and why it's the right stuff) for them. But if your offering is not the right stuff—if you're selling high quality walnut wood and your customer only needs cheap plywood, for example—the only way you'll get your customer to buy the wrong stuff is to cut your price. If he's building fine furniture, he might buy your walnut. But if he's putting in sub-flooring, he won't. He doesn't need it, doesn't want it, and can't afford it. The only way you'll sell him high-quality walnut for sub-flooring is to cut your price.

If you don't have the right stuff for your customer—the quality of products or services that conform to his standards and expectations—you have a problem. You'll never get full price, rate or fee for products or services if you try to sell your prospect the wrong stuff for his specific application … you'll be selling high-quality walnut at the price of plywood!

But I sell a commodity—commodities are always sold based on price alone.

Many salespeople feel that they're in the commodity business, and as a result must sell exclusively on price. Fortunately, nothing is further from the truth. A commodity, by definition, is any item that cannot be easily distinguished from others in the marketplace—something that is in direct competition with a large number of extremely similar products or services. For example, suppose we have two water glasses for sale that are identical in terms of size, shape and appearance. If we tell you one sells for two pennies and the other sells for one penny, which are you going to buy? The "obvious" answer is that you'd buy the one-penny glass because—all other things being equal—people always buy on price, right?

Wrong. For one thing, all factors are rarely ever completely equal beyond the surface. For example, what if the company making the less expensive glass doesn't have a good reputation in the marketplace? What if you don't trust the salesperson who is selling you the glass? What if the vendor couldn't ship the glasses until next month? What if the manufacturers of the more expensive glasses had a website, making it simpler for you to order a replacement if one were to break?

It's your responsibility as a salesperson to make sure the customer knows that there are additional benefits inherent to purchasing your product or service. Know how to use options such as better service, better delivery, more reliable vendor history, etc., to distinguish your offering as the "better quality" deal.

The Final Word

As a salesperson, you *must* differentiate your company's product and services from your competitor's somehow, some way. Potential customers *want* you to show them how your product represents a unique, quality solution to their challenges and needs. That's what selling is all about. Otherwise, we'd simply rely on computers to answer the phone, direct the customer to price quotes on the web, and digitally fill orders. What truly matters in closing a sale is your ability to provide quality and tailored solutions. ∎

Steve McCreedy is a National Accounts Manager with The Brooks Group. For biographical and business information, see page 270.

Editor's Note: While working for Sony of Canada, Kelley Robertson helped make Sony Stores one of Canada's top retailers of consumer electronics. Today he helps sales teams improve their sales and develop better negotiating and customer service skills. Learn some of his strategies for negotiating better deals even in an economic downturn.

Five Ways to Negotiate More Effectively
by Kelley Robertson

Most salespeople and business owners hear statements like these everyday: "What's your best price?" or "That's too expensive." or "Your competitor is selling the same thing for... ." These statements are clues from buyers and prospects that you need to learn how to negotiate more effectively. Here are five strategies that will help you drive more dollars to your bottom line:

- **Learn to flinch.** The flinch is one of the oldest negotiating tactics but one of the least used. A flinch is a visible reaction to an offer or price. The objective of this tactic is to make the other person feel uncomfortable about the offer presented. Here is an example of how it works.

  A supplier quotes a price for a specific service. Flinching means you respond by exclaiming, "You want *how* much?" You must appear shocked and surprised that he could be bold enough to request that amount. Unless the other person is a well-seasoned negotiator, he will respond in one of two ways: He will become very uncomfortable and begin to try to rationalize his price; or he will offer an immediate concession.

- **Recognize that people often ask for more than they expect to get.** This means you need to resist the temptation to automatically reduce your price or offer a discount. I once asked for a hefty discount on a pair of shoes hoping to get half of what I asked for. I was pleasantly surprised when the shop owner agreed to my request.

- **The person with the most information usually does better.** You need to learn as much as possible about your customer's situation. Ask your prospect more questions about his purchase. Learn what's important to him as well as his needs and wants.

  Develop the habit of asking questions such as:
  - "What prompted you to consider a purchase of this nature?"
  - "Who else have you been speaking to?"
  - "What was your experience with... ?"
  - "What timeframes are you working with?"
  - "What is most important to you about this?"

  It's also important to learn as much about your competitors as possible. This will help you defeat possible price objections and prevent someone from using your competitor as leverage.

- **Practice at every opportunity.** Most people hesitate to negotiate because they lack the confidence. Develop this confidence by negotiating more frequently. Ask for discounts from your suppliers. As a consumer, develop the habit of asking for a price break when you buy from a retail store. Here are a few questions or statements you can use:
  - "You'll have to do better than that."
  - "What kind of discount are you offering today?"
  - "That's too expensive."

  Wait for a response afterward. Learn to flinch. Be pleasant and persistent but not demanding. Conditioning yourself to negotiate at every opportunity will help you become more comfortable, confident and successful.

- **Maintain your walk-away power.** It's better to walk away from a sale rather than make too large a concession or give a deep discount on your product or service. It's particularly challenging to walk away when you are in the midst of a sales slump or slow sales period. But, remember that there will always be someone to sell to.

Negotiating is a way of life in some cultures, and most people negotiate in some way almost everyday. Apply these strategies and you will notice a difference almost immediately. ■

Kelley Robertson is a president of The Robertson Training Group. For biographical and business information, see page 272.

Editor's Note: Frank Rumbauskas is a New York Times *bestselling author, speaker and career salesman who has taught tens of thousands of salespeople how to generate leads without cold calling. He never cold calls, and recommends you don't either if you want to close more sales. He advises to gain the power in your relationship with prospects and give up cold calling.*

Prospecting from a Position of Power
by Frank Rumbauskas

Look at any steps of a sale chart. Ask anyone what the first step toward getting a sale is. Or ask someone to identify the most basic and fundamental part of selling.

What does that person invariably say?

Prospecting. Getting leads. Cold calling.

Now, if you know anything about me, you know that I hate cold calling. In fact, most of my career as a sales expert has been devoted to getting salespeople to stop cold calling and to start using more effective, efficient, and respectful techniques instead.

Another big focus for me has been teaching salespeople how to control every sales interaction from a position of power, and how to keep that power through to the end to benefit yourself and your prospect (or, hopefully, new customer).

What is power, and how do you get it?

Power, quite simply, lies with the person who has the authority to say "yes" or "no." And that's where nearly all salespeople screw up. They allow prospects to have that powerful position, rather than getting and keeping it for themselves.

The correlation between the position of power and the authority to say "yes" or "no" is a basic fundamental of negotiating. Every sales interaction is a negotiation, whether you're face-to-face with a prospect, on the phone, communicating via email, or even sending an old-fashioned letter via snail mail.

Why?

Because, in every salesperson-to-prospect communication, you are trying to get the prospect to take some sort of action. Whether it's calling you, expressing an interest in your product, buying from you, or referring others to you, you're always trying to get the prospect to do *something*. No one in sales communicates with prospects just for fun, or to waste time. It's all about action, and that is why every sales interaction is defined as a negotiation.

Now that we've established that all sales communications are negotiations in one form or another, let's look at a basic rule of negotiating:

The person who has a need does not have the power. It is the person who can *fulfill* a need (the one who can say "yes" or "no") who has the power, and who will ultimately win.

Let's look at that from a sales perspective. Most salespeople initiate a sales process through some sort of outward prospecting, usually a cold call. What happens when you make a cold call? You got it—you are communicating to the prospect, either directly or indirectly, that you are in *need* of a sale.

In other words, you have just identified yourself as the one who needs something. That means you don't have the power. You just handed it off to the prospect who can now say "yes" or "no."

That means the prospect will ultimately win. What do prospects want in a sales interaction? That's easy—it's always one of two things, without exception:

- They want to get rid of you without buying. In other words, they want to say "no."
- They want to buy, but they want to do so at a deep discount, thereby destroying the profit margin in the sale, and probably your commission along with it.

By identifying yourself as the one in need, you have set yourself up to endure one of these two eventual outcomes. And neither is the one you want.

Now let's turn things around. Let's say you are using some lead-generation technique other than cold calling to get people to call you: referral selling, speaking at free events, direct mail, Internet marketing, you name it.

A prospect then picks up the phone or types an email to contact you.

What is the purpose of this communication?

To say, "I think you may have something we need."

In other words, the prospect is now identifying *himself* as the one in need, giving you the position of power! You can now say, "Yes, I can fulfill your need," or, "No, I cannot."

Do you see how that works? The person expressing a need does not have the power. The person who can say "yes" or "no" to that need has the power.

The person with the power wins. To you, that means not just making a sale, but doing so at a price and a profit margin that's fair to you and your company.

This is why it's so important that you prospect intelligently, in ways that get a prospect to tell you what he needs, rather than appearing like you need a sale!

This is one of the concepts that I explain to people when they object to my statements that cold calling is bad and should be done away with. When someone says, "Frank, I do just fine cold calling and I meet my quota every month," I explain that by handing his power away at the start, he's losing sales and losing profits. If that same salesperson, with the same selling abilities, were to contact the same number of people every month but from a position of power, sales would probably double or even triple!

The problem with approaching prospects from a position of need is that you not only give away your power at the start, you also put yourself in a negative light. There's a story about a couple of cars that I like to use to explain this principle.

Let's say you've just won the lottery, or sold your business, or you've done something that has suddenly put millions of dollars in your pocket. If you're like most people, you'll probably get yourself a high-end luxury car almost immediately, something along the lines of a Bentley or a Ferrari, or whatever your dream car may be.

I'm guessing you won't need to go out and test drive your dream car. I know I didn't when I bought mine. I called the dealer to place my order and that was that.

Why?

Because, when it comes to your dream car, or any other high-end automobile, you don't need a test drive because *you already know it's good*. You know it's the best. You know the quality, luxury, materials, performance, are all unmatched.

Let's consider the opposite extreme.

Someone who has a financial hardship and who has little money must spend that money very wisely, and obviously cannot afford luxury goods. Let's say that person needs a car, and sees a classified ad for a used Ford Escort that's a bit beat up. That's the most car he can afford, so he goes out to look at it.

Will he test drive it? Of course he will. Why? Because the quality is not obvious, it must be tested and must be proven before he plunks down his hard-earned dollars.

This is how prospects view *you* when you approach them from a position of need!

When you contact a prospect and do it without power, the prospect has immediate doubts—conscious, subconscious, or both. He will need a test drive to make sure you are the real deal.

What does that mean to you?

Yep, you guessed it—a long, drawn-out, stressful sales cycle.

On the other hand, when you get a prospect to approach *you* and give *you* the power, all that nonsense becomes unnecessary. When you have the power, quality and integrity are assumed. You are now the Bentley or the Ferrari in the eyes of the prospect. You can be trusted with his business, and you will be.

Oh, and how will your competition fare compared to you when you're seen as the Bentley and they're seen as a bunch of used, beat-up Ford Escorts?

That's right. They won't be taken seriously, if they get appointments at all. You are the consummate professional the prospect wants to work with. They are seen as pests who seem to need sales to save their own skins.

Power isn't just about sales prospecting. Yes, it's very important to avoid prospecting activities like cold calling that make you look needy and give all your power away. But it's just as important to *keep* your power throughout the entire sales cycle, because once you give it away, it's nearly impossible to regain.

In my sales career I was constantly taught to view and treat prospects as superiors. This didn't work. All it did was give my power away, and put me in the position of weakness. This didn't result in many sales.

When I turned that around and worked on seeing myself as a powerful adviser prospects sought out for advice, everything changed. I not only had the power, but I had also internalized it. I soon walked, talked, and looked the part, like a young Donald Trump. This not only made my sales career take off, but it had positive outcomes in all areas of my life. Wherever I went, I commanded respect and trust from people, and you can't put a price on that.

Get the power at the start, and keep it through to the end. Your bank balance will thank you for it! ■

Frank Rumbauskas is founder of FJR Advisors, LLC. For biographical and business information, see page 272.

Editor's Note: John Boe has an uncanny ability to analyze an individual based on a picture, phone conversation, or face-to-face meeting. He teaches his techniques to trial lawyers, poker players and salespeople. Our editor at SalesDog.com was impressed with John's skill when he accurately analyzed her after just a brief phone conversation. Here, he shows you how to determine your prospect's temperament style so you can quickly develop trust and rapport. These are critical skills in difficult times.

Different Strokes for Different Folks
by John Boe

Have you ever wondered why you seem to hit it off right away with some customers, while with others it's more like oil and water? That's because we respond intuitively to the natural chemistry, or lack thereof, between temperament styles. Our temperament style not only determines our behavioral traits, body language patterns, and "buying styles" but it also influences our compatibility with others.

Today we have access to innovative tools such as the Internet, cell phones, faxes, and voice mail. All are designed to enhance our communications and support us in selling more effectively. Nevertheless, even with all of these technological tools at our disposal, the alarming number of failed relationships, dissatisfied employees, and lost sales reflect the fact that none of us are as effective at understanding others as we would like to believe.

For example, what about that sale you thought you had made but at the last minute your prospect changed his mind and didn't buy … or at least he didn't buy from you? Chances are you lost that sale because of your inability to recognize your prospect's buying style.

Research in the field of psychology tells us that we are born into one of four primary temperament styles (Aggressive, Expressive, Passive, or Analytical) that is unrelated to race or gender. Each of these four behavioral styles requires a different approach and selling strategy. As a professional salesperson your income depends on your ability to identify your prospect's buying style and adjust your presentation accordingly.

Ancient Wisdom

Hippocrates, the father of medicine, is credited with originating the basic theory of the four temperament styles 2400 years ago. Since the days of ancient Greece, there have been many temperament theories and a wide variety of evaluation instruments, but essentially, they utilize the four temperament styles that Hippocrates identified. Hippocrates observed that these four styles have a direct influence on our physiology, character traits, and outlook on life.

- **The Aggressive or Worker style is:** Extroverted - Determined - Demanding - Domineering - Controlling - Practical - Self-reliant - Decisive – Insensitive. The impatient and goal-oriented Workers prefer fast, bottom line presentation styles. Be on time and well prepared. Avoid small talk and get right to business. They are generally quick to make decisions. Workers are focused on results and ask "what" questions. Keywords to use are: results, speed, and control. Give them options so that you don't threaten their need for control.

- **The Expressive or Talker style is:** Extroverted - Enthusiastic - Emotional - Sociable - Impulsive - Optimistic - Persuasive - Egotistical - Disorganized. The playful and friendly Talkers prefer fast and entertaining presentation styles. Talkers are quick to make decisions and tend to be impulsive shoppers. Keep them focused on the subject and give them time to express their opinions. Talkers seek social acceptance and ask "who" questions. Keywords to use are: exciting, fun, and enthusiastic. Keep your presentation big picture—avoid details and numbers. Use colorful pie charts or graphs. Use testimonials with the status conscious Talker.

- **The Passive or Watcher style is:** Introverted - Accommodating - Harmonious - Indecisive - Patient - Uninvolved - Sympathetic - Supportive - Stable. The peaceful and stoic Watchers prefer slow, deliberate presentations and require time to warm up. They are very sensitive to conflict or perceived "sales pressure." Watchers have a need to accommodate others and ask "how" questions. Keywords to use are: family, service, and harmony. Condition Watchers for change; they are natural born procrastinators who love the status quo. Help the Watcher make a decision by giving him assurance.

- **The Analytical or Thinker style is:** Introverted - Thoughtful - Organized - Critical - Shy - Detailed - Pessimistic - Introspective – Private. The cautious and frugal Thinkers prefer slow, detailed presentations and require time to warm up. They are skeptical and typically research before they purchase. Thinkers want detailed information and ask "why" questions. Keywords to use are: logical, safety, and quality. Expect them to take their time "thinking it over." They will "shop your numbers" to make certain they are getting the best deals possible. Help the Thinker reduce his fear of making a mistake by giving him evidence and guarantees.

While there are certainly many factors that influence the selling process, by far the most important is learning how to identify your prospect's buying style. In fact, the majority of lost sales can be directly attributed to poor communication and failure to establish trust and rapport. Once you learn how to quickly and accurately determine your prospect's buying style, you will be able to develop trust and rapport quickly and thereby dramatically increase your sales effectiveness! ■

John Boe is president of John Boe International. For biographical and business information, see page 262.

Editor's Note: Our lives are often swept along by the duties and responsibilities we have assumed. We don't have time to reflect on the course of our lives. In difficult economic times, it's particularly important to remember that you are greater than your problems. If your obligations and commitments seem to control your life take a moment to reflect on these points.

Reflections on Your Greatness

by Michael Dalton Johnson

You are great. You are far greater than you imagine. You are a unique entity given the power to create your own life. When you look outside yourself for self-definition you are giving your power away. However, when you understand and accept that you alone possess the power to define yourself and your life, there are dramatic changes. You will find new clarity, focus and confidence. You'll also find that using this incredible gift is both exhilarating and challenging.

You are in charge. Think of your life as a movie. You are the writer, director, producer and star. You choose your co-stars and extras. Whether the movie is a smash or a flop is in your hands.

Your thoughts determine your outcomes. This is one of the great mysteries. There are a lot of theories about this phenomenon but no one really knows how it works. However, it does work and reveals the astonishing power of your thoughts. If you think you are average, you are. If you think you can't win, you won't. Conversely, if you see yourself succeeding, you will. If you expect great things to come to your life, they're on their way.

You bring others with you. Your courage and confidence to examine your life and make changes will have a profound effect on those around you. When you lift yourself up, others are lifted up too.

Your life. Your responsibility. The first and most important rule is to take responsibility for everything that happens in your life. Following this rule puts you in command. Winston Churchill said, "The price of greatness is responsibility." While I'm certain he was talking about fighting wars and leading nations, his statement applies to your life as well.

You have the power. Life will inevitably send you your share of setbacks, problems, disappointments and losses. These things are beyond your control. How you react to them is not. Listen to the voice within you and realize you have a choice. You have the greatness to persevere, to forgive, to smile, to lift yourself and others up and to move on.

Michael Dalton Johnson is founder and president of SalesDog.com. For biographical and business information, see page 267.

ABOUT THE AUTHORS

Dr. Tony Alessandra

Dr. Tony Alessandra is president of www.Assessment Business Center.com, a company that offers online 360-degree assessments; chairman of www.BrainX.com, a company that created the first Online Learning Mastery System™; and founding partner in www.TheCyranoGroup.com, a company that has successfully combined simple, cutting-edge technology and proven psychology to give salespeople the ability to build and maintain positive relationships with hundreds of clients and prospects. He is a widely published author of numerous products at www.alessandra.com/products/index.asp.

D. M. Arenzon

Known as Mr. Cold Call he is the author of *How to Have Fun Cold Calling and Get Your Telephone Ringing Off the HOOK*. He says, "Your cold call success is dependent on 11 winning personality traits. Collectively, these traits allow you to uniquely market yourself over the telephone so you can inspire your prospect's curiosity, reduce their resistance and close even more sales!" To learn more, sign-up for his free weekly cold calling tips at www.mrcoldcall.com.

Joanne S. Black

America's leading authority on referral selling, captivating speaker, and innovative seminar leader, Joanne Black helps salespeople, sales teams, and business owners get more referrals and attract more business fast without increasing costs. She is the author of *No More Cold Calling*™: *The Breakthrough System That Will Leave Your Competition in the Dust.* (Warner Business Books) Contact Joanne at 415-461-8763 or joanne@nomorecoldcalling.com. Enjoy Joanne's articles and newsletters at www.NoMoreColdCalling.com.

Jeb Blount

Jeb Blount is a bestselling author and the founder and CEO of SalesGravy.com, one of the largest online sales portals in the world. He is the author of *Power Principles*, host of The Sales Guy's Quick and Dirty Tips podcast and the Sales Gravy podcast. In 2008 he set the record with the highest ranked sales content podcast in iTunes history. Jeb is a regular speaker on the motivational and sales training circuit. Visit his site at www.SalesGravy.com.

John Boe

John Boe presents a wide variety of motivational and sales-oriented keynotes, breakout sessions and seminar programs for sales meetings and conventions. An entertaining speaker who can keep an audience riveted and motivated, John is a nationally recognized author, sales trainer and business motivational speaker with an impeccable track record in the meeting industry. For more information, visit www.johnboe.com.

Jon Brooks

Jon Brooks has more than 12 years of sales and marketing management and consulting experience. After managing large sales teams in the technology industry, in 2001 he founded Brooks Dreyfus Consulting, a sales and marketing consulting firm specializing in business-to-business telesales. Jon has helped many clients across a diverse range of industries build or improve telesales departments. As an author, Jon's work appears in various sales and marketing-related publications. Visit www.brooksdreyfus.com or contact jbrooks@brooksdreyfus.com.

Mike Brooks

With over 20 years' inside sales closing experience, Mike Brooks is known as Mr. Inside Sales. Once a bottom 80% producer, Mike learned and perfected the skills of top 20% producers to become the number one rep out of five Southern California financial securities branch offices. His best-selling book, *The Real Secrets of the Top 20%* is packed with proven techniques, which are used successfully in a wide range of industries. Visit www.MrInsideSales.com for more information.

Leslie Buterin

Everyone wants to start at the top. No one knows how. Leslie figured it out. With a paralyzing fear of cold calling and a $140,000 investment of her services, Buterin developed a system to reach high-level decision-makers as a regular course of doing business, not a matter of chance. You can have sustainable, predictable, cold-calling success and double, triple, even quadruple your results. Find "Secrets to Scheduling the Executive Level Sales Call" and more at www.ColdCallingNetNews.com.

John Carroll

John Carroll is president of Unlimited Performance, Inc. in Mount Pleasant, SC. John has helped hundreds of sales professionals in organizations large and small. An accomplished and engaging speaker, John has earned recognition for sales and consulting excellence. His approaches have attracted attention around the globe, including his book *Sales Illustrated: 68 Sales Lessons from Everyday Life* (available in three languages) and sales articles appearing in *Chief Executive China* magazine. Call 877-755-8844 or visit www.johncarroll.com.

John Costigan

John Costigan, president and founder of John Costigan Companies, conducts sales training classes around the world for a list of clients that reads like a *Who's Who* in the corporate world: Hewlett Packard, SAS Software, Experian, Exxon-Mobile, Tommy Hilfiger, IBM, Oracle, and the NHL. John has produced several CDs and DVDs that are sold worldwide offering every sales professional the opportunity to learn new techniques and break old habits. For more information, visit: www.JohnCostigan.com.

Susan C. Daffron

Susan C. Daffron is the president of Logical Expressions, Inc., a book and software publishing company that helps aspiring authors publish books. Susan is the author of 11 books, including *Publishize: How to Quickly and Affordably Self-Publish a Book that Promotes Your Expertise*. She has worked in the publishing industry since 1986 and is also the President of the non-profit Small Publishers, Artists and Writers Network (SPAWN). Susan is the founder of the National Association of Pet Rescue Professionals and does a weekly radio show that features pets available for adoption. For more information and to receive her free report "Seven Steps to Publishing Success" and her Publishize newsletter, visit www.LogicalExpressions.com

Jim Domanski

President of Teleconcepts Consulting, Jim Domanski works with businesses and individuals who are frustrated with the results they are getting when using the telephone to generate leads and sell products. For more information, visit www.teleconceptsconsulting.com or call 613-591-1998 or e-mail jim@teleconceptsconsulting.com.

Kim Duke

Kim Duke is CEO of The Sales Divas, a company providing savvy, sassy sales training with a twist (and NO cold-calling!) Her history: 15 years with Canada's largest national television networks in sales and management. Kim is a national award winner, speaker, and author. Now a successful entrepreneur, Kim provides international training for solopreneurs as well companies like the WNBA. Visit www.salesdivas.com to receive her fabulous tips and free report: *The 5 Biggest Sales Mistakes Women Make.*

Craig Elias

Craig Elias is the creator of Trigger Event Selling™ and author of the upcoming book *SHiFT!* For almost 20 years Craig used Trigger Event strategies to be a top sales performer at every company he worked. Craig's knowledge of Trigger Events has resulted in coverage on NBC news, in the New York *Times, The Wall Street Journal,* and winning a $1,000,000 prize in a billion dollar idea competition. Contact Craig by phone (403-874-2998), Skype (Craig.Elias) or at www.shiftselling.com.

Colleen Francis

Sales and Marketing Magazine has ranked Colleen Francis, president of Engage Selling Solutions, one of the "five most effective sales trainers in the market today." Ask Colleen's clients why they call on her services—again and again—and you'll hear a common refrain: she gets results! Her refreshing candor, genuine, sincere message, and personal experiences she relates as a top-ranked sales executive motivate sales professionals to get to the top and stay there. colleen@engageselling.com, www.engageselling.com, 877-364-2438.

Charles H. Green

Charles H. Green is the author of *Trust-Based Selling* and co-author of *The Trusted Advisor*. Charlie helps make salespeople, sales organizations and sales processes more trustworthy. Clients come from professional services, financial services, commercial real estate, technology, construction and other businesses selling complex products and services. He has taught in executive education programs for Kellogg and Columbia business schools, and published in *Harvard Business Review, Directorship Magazine,* and *Management Horizons.*

Gerhard Gschwandtner

Gerhard Gschwandtner is founder and publisher of *Selling Power*, the leading magazine for sales professionals worldwide. *Selling Power* is the most trusted site for professional selling skills, motivation and sales management know-how in the business-to-business environment. The company presents by-invitation-only leadership conferences for organizations with high sales volume and large sales forces. For more information, or to subscribe to their newsletters or daily report, visit www.sellingpower.com.

Joe Guertin

One of America's hottest sales trainers, Joe Guertin specializes in new business and selling value versus price. As a sought-after speaker and consultant, Joe has worked with thousands of salespeople, managers and business principals to measurably boost internal sales systems, customer development and team skill-building. His firm also features a state-of-the-art online training system. Visit The Guertin Group at www.guertin group.com to receive his monthly e-zine newsletter. Joe can be reached at 414-762-2450, or joe@guertingroup.com.

Tom Hopkins
Author of the million-plus selling book, *How to Master the Art of Selling*, Tom Hopkins is known as The Builder of Sales Champions. Over 4 millions students worldwide have benefited from his simple, yet proven-effective selling skills training. Other books by Tom Hopkins include three for the popular *...for Dummies*™ series. Tom teaches from his own years of personal experience. His training materials are available via seminars, books, videos and audio CDs at www.tomhopkins.com.

Mark Hunter
Mark Hunter, "The Sales Hunter," helps individuals and companies identify better prospects, close more sales, and profitably build more long-term customer relationships. He is a consultative selling expert, specializing in custom-tailored sales programs that allow businesses to gain the edge they need to compete and win in today's marketplace. To find out more about Mark's selling philosophy, you can visit his website at www.TheSalesHunter.com or his Sales Motivation Blog at www.TheSales Hunter.com/blog.

Craig James
Craig James combines proven sales training methods with real world experience in-the-trenches, to help salespeople take their performance to the next level. Craig has been published and quoted in *Business Week, Sales and Marketing Management*, and *Selling Power*, and been interviewed by Sales Rep Radio. www.sales-solutions.biz.

Brian Jeffrey
Brian Jeffrey, CSP (Certified Sales Professional) and president of Salesforce Assessments Ltd, is a sales management consultant and former sales trainer with over 40 years' experience. His company helps sales managers take the guesswork out of hiring salespeople by providing an easy-to-use online assessment tool. Visit his website at www.SalesforceAssessments.com and get a free copy of *The 8 Biggest Hiring Mistakes Sales Managers Make* by subscribing to his free monthly newsletter.

Michael Dalton Johnson
Michael is a successful entrepreneur with decades of business leadership. Among his many business activities, he is publisher of SalesDog.com, a website for sales professionals. Among his accomplishments, he has taken a small publishing company from three employees and two products to a multinational corporation with hundreds of employees and over 100 products. He has founded several successful businesses and published hundreds of magazine and newspaper articles. You may email him at Michael@SalesDog.com.

Paul Johnson
Consultative Selling is the Gold Standard in sales education. Founder Paul Johnson describes Consultative Selling as the sales method that supports complex buying decisions by providing expert guidance from trusted advisers. To help you decide if Consultative Selling is the right "system" to be using, explore the brief articles at http://www.ConsultativeSelling.com. Then you can decide for yourself. They're not for everybody. Email them at hello@consultativeselling.com, or call Paul direct at 770-271-7719 in Atlanta, Georgia.

Dave Kahle
Dave Kahle is a consultant and trainer who helps his clients increase sales and improve productivity. Dave has trained thousands of salespeople to be more successful in the Information Age economy. He is the author of over 500 articles and seven books. *Question Your Way To Sales Success* was recently released by Career Press. Join Dave's weekly *Thinking About Sales* ezine at www.davekahle.com/mailinglist.html. Contact him by e-mail at cheryl@davekahle.com, visit www.davekahle.com, or call 800-331-1287.

Jim Kasper
Jim Kasper is CEO and founder of Interactive Resource Group, an 18-year old customized sales training firm and PrecallPro.com. Jim also holds a MBA, has been an assistant professor at Regis University, and is the recipient of the Regis University Faculty Excellence Award. Jim is the author of *Short Cycle Selling: Beating Your Competitors in the Sales Race* and *Creating*

the #1 Sales Force: What it Takes to Transform Your Sales Culture.
Jkasper@salestrainers.com.

Jill Konrath

Jill Konrath, author of *Selling to Big Companies*, helps sellers crack into corporate accounts, shorten their sales cycle and win big contracts. She's a frequent speaker at sales meetings and industry events. Her Selling ToBigCompanies.com website is full of articles, resources and tools for salespeople. Get a *Sales Call Planning Guide* ($19.95 value) when you sign up for her free e-newsletter. Contact info: 651-429-1922 or jill@sellingto-bigcompanies.com.

Kendra Lee

Kendra Lee is a top IT seller, sales advisor and business owner who knows how to shorten time to revenue in small-medium size companies. A master at delivering leads without cold calling and getting SMB executives to buy, she is the author of the bestselling book *Selling Against the Goal*. Visit www.klagroup.com for SMB selling resources, subscribe to Kendra's free sales newsletter, and get a Quota Gap Calculator ($18.95 value). Reach her at 303-773-1285 or klee@klagroup.com.

George Ludwig

George Ludwig, President of GLU Consulting, specializes in helping clients like Johnson & Johnson, Abbott Laboratories, and Northwestern Mutual improve their sales force effectiveness and performance. George is the bestselling author of *Power Selling: Seven Strategies for Cracking the Sales Code* and is a widely recognized authority on sales success and peak performance psychology. He can be reached for consulting, training, or speaking at george@georgeludwig.com or by calling 888-999-4811. www.georgeludwig.com.

Chris Lytle

Chris Lytle wrote *The Accidental Salesperson* published by the American Management Association's AMACOM division. The book was named a top ten career book by Tribune Media Services and has a consistent 5-star rating on Amazon.com. His current passion is partnering with sales managers to conduct sales meetings their people would attend even if they were optional. Contact him directly at Sparque, Inc. His direct line is 312-226-9920 x202. Or e-mail him at chris.lytle@sparque.com.

Steve Marx

Steve Marx has been selling, helping salespeople, and consulting on the development of consistently high-performing sales organizations for nearly his entire career. In 1983, he founded The Center for Sales Strategy, a sales and management consulting firm whose growth he led for 25 years. In 2007, Steve published the bestselling *Close Like the Pros: Replace Worn-Out Tactics with the Powerful Strategy of Interactive Selling*. Visit www.CSScenter.com or www.InteractiveSelling.com, or email Steve at SteveMarx@CSScenter.com.

Paul McCord

Paul McCord (www.mccordandassociates.com) is president of McCord Training, a sales training and consulting firm headquartered in Texas. The author of two bestselling books on sales, Paul is recognized worldwide as a leading authority on referrals, prospecting and personal marketing, and works with salespeople and companies to help them grow their business through teaching strategies to connect with prospects in ways prospects respect and respond to. Contact Paul at 432-853-8685 or email him at pmccord@mccordandassociates.com.

Jim McCormick

Jim McCormick is a sales motivator who draws on his experience as a World Record and North Pole skydiver, MBA and former corporate Chief Operating Officer to help sales professionals move past self-imposed limitations through presentations, seminars and performance coaching. Jim is the author of the award-winning book *The Power of Risk*. More information on Jim is available at www.TakeRisks.com.

Steve McCreedy
Steve McCreedy is a National Accounts Manager with The Brooks Group, who specializes in training companies to sell effectively at higher margins against lower-priced competition. The Brooks Group is an international sales training and management development firm based in Greensboro, North Carolina. For more information on The Brooks Group's numerous training events and services, visit www.brooksgroup.com or call 800-633-7762.

Adrian Miller
Adrian Miller is president of Adrian Miller Sale Training, a company that provides highly customized sales skills training programs and sales strategy solutions based on real-world selling situations. Author of *The Blatant Truth: 50 Ways to Sales Success*, Adrian is well known for her no-BS approach to training as well as her highly entertaining and energetic style. She can be reached at 516-767-9288 or amiller@adrianmiller.com.

Anne Miller
Anne Miller is a popular sales and presentations expert and author of the book, *Metaphorically Selling: How to Use the Magic of Metaphors to Sell, Persuade, & Explain Anything to Anyone*. She works with people in high stakes situations and clients like Yahoo!, Citigroup, and Time, Inc. to sell millions of dollars of business every year. Her free newsletter is available at www.annemiller.com. Reach her at 212-876-1875 for creative ideas for your next sales meeting.

Andrea Nierenberg
Andrea Nierenberg is an internationally known speaker, author, trainer and consultant. The Nierenberg Group specializes in sales training, presentation skills and networking to grow business. She is the author of 3 books: *NonStop Networking, Million Dollar Networking-The Sure Guide to Find, Grow and Keep Your Business* and *Savvy Networking-118 Tips for Business Success*. Visit her interactive website www.nierenberggroup.com and her blog http://thenierenblog.typepad.com.

Brent Patmos
Brent Patmos, CPTA, CPDA serves as the Chief Sales Consultant for select, high potential companies across a variety of markets. Perpetual Development, Inc. works with clients to create a performance driven culture that allows them to establish a distinct sales advantage. Brent and his company specialize in assessing and aligning competencies throughout client organizations so that each member of the team understands how they directly contribute to sales results, performance and profitability. www.perpetualdevelopment.com, e-mail: bpatmos@perpetualdevelopment.com.

Tom Richard
Tom Richard, a Toledo-based sales trainer, gives seminars, runs sales meetings, and provides coaching for salespeople nationwide. Tom is also the author of *Smart Salespeople Don't Advertise: 10 Ways to Outsmart Your Competition With Guerilla Marketing*, and publishes a free weekly e-zine on selling skills titled *Sales Muscle*. For more information, visit www.TomRichard.com, or email info@tomrichard.com.

Linda Richardson
Linda Richardson is president and founder of Richardson (www.richardson.com), a leading sales training and consulting firm. A recognized leader in the sales training industry, she is credited with the movement to consultative selling. She has written nine books on selling including *The Sales Success Handbook*. She has been published in industry and training journals and featured in numerous publications including *Forbes, Nation's Business, Selling, Selling Power, Success, The Conference Board Magazine*, and *The Philadelphia Inquirer*.

Alan Rigg
Sales performance expert Alan Rigg is the author of *How to Beat the 80/20 Rule in Sales Team Performance* and the companion book, *How to Beat the 80/20 Rule in Selling*. His 80/20 Selling System™ helps business owners, executives, and managers end the frustration of 80/20 sales team performance, where 20 percent of salespeople produce 80 percent of sales. For

more information and free sales and sales management tips, call 866-531-3917 or visit http://www.8020sales.com.

Kelley Robertson
As president of the Robertson Training Group and author of two books, including *The Secrets of Power Selling*, Kelley helps sales professionals and businesses discover easy-to-implement strategies to improve their sales and profits. Receive a free copy of *100 Ways to Increase Your Sales* by subscribing to his free newsletter available at www.RobertsonTrainingGroup.com. Kelley conducts workshops and keynote speeches at sales meetings and conferences. For information on his programs contact him at 905-633-7750 or Kelley@RobertsonTrainingGroup.com.

Keith Rosen
An engaging speaker and coach, award winning columnist and bestselling author, Keith Rosen is one of the foremost, respected authorities on coaching top executives and sales professionals to achieve positive change. The author of *Time Management for Sales Professionals* and *Coaching Salespeople into Sales Champions*; Keith also sits on several editorial boards as well as advisory boards. To contact Keith or receive his free resources, call 888-262-2450, email info@ProfitBuilders.com, visit www.ProfitBuilders.com or www.CoachingSalespeople.com.

Frank Rumbauskas
Frank Rumbauskas is *The New York Times* bestselling author who turned the sales world upside-down with his *Never Cold Call Again* series of books and products. To learn more and to download ten free chapters of Frank's home study course, visit www.nevercoldcall.com.

Lee B. Salz
Lee B. Salz is a sales management guru who helps companies hire the right salespeople, on-board them, and focus their sales activity using his Sales Architecture® methodology. He is president of Sales Architects, CEO of Business Expert Webinars and author of *Soar Despite Your Dodo Sales Manager*. Look for Lee's new book in 2010 titled, *The Sales Marriage*. Lee

can be reached at lsalz@SalesArchitecture.com or 763-416-4321. Visit his web site www.SalesArchitecture.com.

Dan Seidman

Dan Seidman of SalesAutopsy.com is a World Master's athlete with two gold medals playing on the U.S. basketball team and has been designated "One of the Top 12 Sales Coaches in America." His bestselling book *Sales Autopsy* is now an award-winning training experience as recognized by *Selling Power Magazine's Sales Excellence Awards*. For a great keynote or training program on the best practices of world-class sales pros, contact Dan at 847-359-7860 or dan@salesautopsy.com.

Art Sobczak

Art Sobczak helps sales pros use the phone to prospect, service and sell more effectively, while eliminating "rejection." He presents public seminars and customizes programs for companies. See free articles and back issues of his weekly emailed sales tips at www.BusinessByPhone.com. Also ask for a free copy of his monthly *Telephone Prospecting and Selling Report* newsletter, and the new *Telesales Success* tips and resources magazine by e-mailing ArtS@BusinessByPhone.com, or calling 402-895-9399.

Dave Stein

Following a career in sales and sales management, Dave focused his unique skills in competitive sales strategies training and coaching. In 2004 he authored the business bestseller *How Winners Sell* and is currently the featured monthly columnist for *Sales & Marketing Management* magazine. He is Visiting Professor of Selling Strategies to the Dublin Institute of Technology and CEO of ES Research Group, which advises companies on how to get the highest return on sales training. Website: www.ESResearch.com.

Julie Thomas

Julie Thomas is president and CEO of ValueSelling Associates, a world-wide leader in competency and process-based sales training offering proven strategies for seasoned and beginning sales executives through its proprietary ValueSelling Framework™ and ValueSelling Essentials™ online training. Julie is a leader in sales and sales management for 20 plus years, and a noted public speaker, consultant and author of *ValueSelling: Driving Up Sales One Conversation At A Time*. Contact her at 800-559-6419 or julie@valueselling.com.

Rochelle Togo Figa

Rochelle Togo-Figa is a sales coach, trainer, and motivational speaker with 23 years in the corporate world. Rochelle is the creator of the Sales Breakthrough System™ and the Inner Game of Sales™. She is the author of the sales home-study manual *Sell Without the Slick* and *The Surefire Design Sales Formula for Design Professionals*. To receive the free audio CD *The 9 Best-Kept Secrets to Exploding Your Sales*, go to www.Sales Breakthroughs.com.

Tim Wackel

Tim Wackel is a trusted resource for sales executives who want to create more success in business and in life. Tim's "no excuses" programs are insightful, engaging and focused on providing real world strategies that salespeople can (and will!) implement right away. Download your copy of a recent live training event and discover new ideas for creating your best year yet at www.timwackel.com. You can also contact Tim directly at 214-369-7722 or tim@timwackel.com.

Wendy Weiss

Wendy Weiss, *The Queen of Cold Calling*, is an author, speaker, sales trainer, and sales coach. She is recognized as one of the leading authorities on lead generation, cold calling and new business development. She helps clients speed up their sales cycle, reach more prospects directly and generate more sales revenue. To download the free report: *Getting in the Door: How to Write an Effective Cold Calling Script*, visit www.queenofcoldcalling.com. Email Wendy at wendy@wendyweiss.com.

NOTES

NOTES

NOTES

Presented by SalesDog.com

2701 Loker Avenue West, Suite 148
Carlsbad, California 92010
760-476-3700
www.salesdog.com

This book is available at quantity discounts.
For information, call 760-476-3700.